G000036982

Three Wise Monkeys
By
Terry Anton
ISBN: 978-1-8380929-9-3

Published By: -

i2i

PUBLISHING

i2i Publishing. Manchester.
www.i2ipublishing.co.uk

Acknowledgements

I would like to thank my wife just for being there for me and for helping me to get all this on paper. It's good to know that there are decent people around.

I once wrote to Marjorie Proops asking for her advice when I was in the depths of alcoholism and every man and his dog just wanted to abuse me. Her advice was: *True friends are like diamonds; they are very rare and hard to find.*

"My wife is that diamond."

Note: I have been advised not to name anyone or any organisation in this book for legal reasons. It seems some folk cannot handle the truth.

Introduction

First of all, I think I need to clarify I am in no way anyone special. I am not an actor or a footballer. In fact, I am not in any way God's gift to anything in particular. I have never, ever classed myself as better than anyone else or for that matter worse than anyone else. I like to think of myself as equal to most people, whether they are a millionaire or a rough sleeper. My reasoning is quite simple, we all s- the same, we are all born the same, mostly, and we are all in God's waiting room from birth.

In my past I have tried mainly to treat people as I would like to be treated, even when I was a suffering alcoholic (in case you are wondering I am 23 years sober at the time of writing) but to some people this has made me look weak and throughout my life, I have suffered abuse of all kinds. My favourite saying is *I am a good friend to all, but I am also a bastard of an enemy*. This book is not about revenge in any shape or form or a way of making money. It's simply my way of getting my story out.

It is written from the perspective of a victim of abuse as a child and as someone who has suffered press abuse and as a gang rape survivor. I have tried to tell my side of the story over the years since and in vain to find out what my low life friends and family have all said behind my back in a tabloid since 1985 to 1993.

For some reason I have always seemed to hit a brick wall. I now realise why the tabloid in question is hardly known as trustworthy when it comes to the truth, so I really never stood a chance of telling my side of the story where they were concerned. They have even threatened me with court action, but perhaps I think I must have hit a raw nerve..

I have never ever thought of myself as being sexy in any way, never in any way sexier than my shirt. Quite the opposite in fact. I am just an ordinary guy who worked nine to five for a living. In March of 1993 I found my face looking back up at me from one of the pages of a tabloid, thankfully not a reputable one. I only call it a newspaper because that is how it portrayed itself. In reality, it is a comic, in fact, *Viz* is more truthful and accurate. I didn't find myself on a page 3 type pic and my man boobs were nowhere in sight or hanging out. Not a pretty sight anyway.

I have to admit though, many people have seen my penis/backside in the past. In my defence, it was never purposely done. They had to peep through a small gap in my curtains and even at one point, through a vent in my bedroom. The peeping toms even turned round and said I was flashing, but tabloids never reveal how they get their pics and stories, but I will cover that later. Shame I did nothing between 1985 and late 1992.

From mid 1992 until early 1993 I had been writing to my ex from south east London some very smutty letters, but, being as we were ex-lovers and she was the mother of our daughter, it's not unheard of that two ex's should write such letters to each other. It's not a rarity of any kind, hardly something to put in a newspaper, but this tabloid seemed to deem anything as newsworthy or in the public interest and is quite well known for printing rubbish about people It's quite well known that they can dole it out, but not take it. I liken them to school bullies in the playground who, if they don't get their own way, stamp their feet in a tantrum or spit out their dummies. There is not much difference either way.

As I look back now, I knew that something was not quite right. For seven years, from late 1985 to early 1993, I had been suffering all kinds of abuse from total strangers in the street. I would often get attacked or slagged off nearly everywhere I went and even spat at. I couldn't go anywhere without some kind of hassle. I obviously asked different members of my family countless times and all my friends the same thing, but they were all adamant. They knew nothing about it and couldn't help me, but from what I know now, they didn't want to help me. It was as if I had the three wise monkeys as friends and family, but when some people have the pounds sign in their eyes, decency and loyalty doesn't enter into it.

When I saw my face looking back at me from the tabloid in March 1993 it felt like someone had ripped out my heart and stamped on it and then replaced it. My whole world fell apart and I knew then that the family I had unknowingly put on a pedestal for most of my life and would have done absolutely *anything* for, were in fact liars and backstabbers. Thieves, to say the least.

It has taken me as long as this to get to where I want to write about what happened, mainly because I didn't have any genuine people around me that I could open up to and share what I needed to share, to move on and process all that had happened throughout those seven years and even throughout my life. It's all relevant, plus in March 1993, something happened that left me suicidal and until recently I wasn't able to talk or even think about. I had no idea who I could trust, not until I met my now wife in 2008. Until then I had no one I could trust completely. I only had myself but I couldn't even do that.

It was a nightmare at first not knowing who I could confide in to get it sorted in my head and put it into some kind of perspective. I needed to talk about it with a trustworthy person to make sense of it all and I have learned the hard way that not everyone who smiles at you is your friend or even for that matter genuine, but I will do my best to explain all of this fully as I go through everything that has happened. Not just in the seven years from late 1985 until early 1993, but throughout my life. It is the only way I think I can fully explain everything for you, the reader, to understand although without you actually being in my shoes you will never fully understand.

It took me until 2008 when I met my wife that slowly she gained my trust and began to break down the invisible barriers I had put up over the years to stop getting hurt any further by people in general.

My wife helped me to talk about my abusive childhood and the abuse I'd received from a tabloid. It was without doubt my seven-year nightmare. But to be honest, most of my life has been a total nightmare. My eighteen years of alcohol problems effectively drowned out most of the bad feelings, thoughts, and memories. I am now 23-plus years sober and the fact that while drinking I thought I had banished all the badness in my life, they were still there waiting for me. You can never hide away from your past. No one is that lucky.

I would like to make it clear. I don't have any kind of scrapbooks full of newspaper cuttings. To be totally honest, I have one or two cuttings, so this book is being written without prior knowledge of what the tabloid has said, although I have done my best to find out. I have come to believe that this newspaper has conveniently buried it as best it could, like a non-genuine newspaper would do (I will explain that comment later on).

This book may answer some of what has been said by this tabloid. It may enlighten some people, it might even annoy some but I'm quite sure it will conflict more with what the tabloid in question has alleged over those seven years. I really hope it will inspire people who are going through abuse or addiction. Let me reassure you all there is light at the end of that very dark tunnel and it is not a train. Hopefully, when people read my book and compare it with the newspaper story, they will learn the truth. I have nothing to hide or gain by lying although in the past I have been asked to lie for people regarding what this book is about.

I wholeheartedly refused to lie for people who have stabbed me in the back for most of my life and I still refuse now, but if what I say here leaves questions I am willing to answer them in full, in every way. I am even willing to take a lie detector test if need be, as long as the people who have made the allegations against me in the past, do the same. It is only fair, don't you think?

In no way do I admit to anything this tabloid or the media have alleged against me without seeing it first, but that goes without saying. Looking back now, I realise if I had been willing to lie to cover up other people's wrongs I would have had lots of help, but I am a terrible liar, so I try to be as honest as much as I can be and to write about all that has happened in my life. It means that I've been reliving it all over again and what I went through in those seven years was absolute hell in every way, due to the tabloid's lies and also my friends and my families' lies.

Firstly, I am writing this in light of the Jimmy Savile saga. I am in no way saying he is innocent or for that matter guilty. I will sit on the fence there.

Secondly, health wise, I feel that I am either in God's waiting room or the Devil's, but whichever way, I am now a happily married guy to someone I love with every part of me and I would do anything for her. But I know that when

I'm dead and gone the low lives from my past will come out from under their stones and start making all kinds of allegations against me, which I will have no way of responding to. My wife makes me mega happy and I do my best to keep her happy, so by me writing this book, I hope there will be no scumbags coming out with rubbish about me when I can't answer back.

I have never been party to whatever is being said behind my back. I'm just like everyone else, in that respect, as in one pair of ears, eyes and one mouth and I have never been blessed with genuine people around me.

Thirdly, I have had no help from my family or my so-called friends, even to date. It has taken me till meeting my wife (in 2008) to be able to trust someone enough to talk freely and to put everything into some kind of perspective. I feel sure sometimes she must have wondered how the hell did she ever get involved with this guy (me) but she has never said anything like that to me, which to me means we love each other the same, unconditionally. That is until she knows how bad I really have been, but I've been open with her about my past and I have told her *everything* and I mean *everything* and she hasn't done a runner, *yet*.

For roughly eighteen months after seeing myself in the tabloid in 1993, I did everything I could to get them to print my side of the story and I have proof of this, but at the time I should have realised that in no way would they have printed the *real* truth (my side of the story) mainly because it would have shown them in a bad light) but I think the intelligent ones in our society are noticing just what the tabloids are all about now.

I simply want to try and sort it out and put closure to it all, so, when I go to my Maker or the Horned One, I can rest more easily knowing my wife will not be hassled by low lives from my past. Secondly, I have had all this rattling round in my head for far too long now. I need to get it down on paper and I believe this tabloid once came out with the expression 'ignorance is bliss'. Believe me, it isn't. As far as I know, it has never actually used my real name and was always using the word, allegedly, after saying something about me, which to me, says they knew it was all lies and shows how cowardly they really were. But they printed it regardless, so I think I might use, allegedly too, if at some point I am not certain or just to cover my back. After all, I am dealing with scum who will spin it to suit themselves or to suit their own agenda. But I'm the one with a criminal past and, as I know, there are more criminals who have never seen the inside of a cell, than the ones that have, so by not ever being nicked in your mind makes you a good person. To me it means you are living a lie, you're just lucky enough not to have been caught. That is the truth of it.

It has taken me as long as this mainly because I have had no support, not even to get sober, apart from AA and one-to-one counselling, but when I mean no help I mean, as in a sit-down conversation with any member of my family or any of my friends about what the tabloid may have written. Even now 30 years on they have all refused to help in any way and have even tried to deny it, even after I have seen myself in the tabloid My family and so-called friends have done their best to plant as many negative seeds to hinder me to get to this point, but the truth always comes out in the end and I firmly believe in karma.

I'm not sure who said it, but writing a book is like peeling an onion layer by layer and at times it has been very emotional, even traumatic. I have found it hard to comprehend just how vile the people were around me and how blatantly stupid I have been at times not to have seen through their lies. I wonder how the hell I got through it all. In my defence, from my early twenties I was a suffering alcoholic and alcohol has been a cushion to me. It was my crutch to get through all the abuse I had suffered.

I keep thinking how I endured all this for as long as I did. As for the tabloid, I'm not quite sure why I am using upper case letters for them. They are the lowest of the lower case. I have even had to see a counsellor while writing this book, for PTSD (Post Traumatic Stress Disorder) as in CBT (Cognitive Behavioural Therapy) because I am constantly reliving or revisiting my past, again and again. Most of it has been quite bad, but when I was living through it the first time round, some, if not all of it, was cushioned by my alcoholism and drug-taking. Now I'm sober but I still bear the mental and physical scars from all that has happened throughout my life. When I saw myself in the tabloid, I strived to be the one telling my story and by the grace of God I will.

My Abusive Childhood

I think I might as well start from the beginning, i.e. from birth. My mother fell pregnant with me because of a married guy having a fling. (I have recently heard stories about my blood father and all I can say is that the apple does not fall far from the tree. I am very much like him, in some respects). He was a quite well-known shopkeeper in the Chorley, Lancashire area.

I was born in July '57. My mother was seventeen at the time. My mother's parents had banished her to a mother and baby home run by nuns in Kendal, Westmoreland (now Cumbria). In those days it was in no way fashionable to be a one-parent family (not like it seems to be today). It turns out that I was born with a double hernia and quite a few other health problems, so as you can imagine I was constantly crying because of the pain I must have been in at the time. Apparently, the hernia took 12 to 18 months to spot. Not sure if that was due to my mother's inexperience or the doctors around that time being as bad as they seem to be now. Were they as clueless as they are now or more than likely they might have prescribed Calpol or whatever they gave you in those days? It's no wonder I have no faith in doctors now, but that is another story and something I will touch on later in this book.

One of my earliest memories was when I was in my pram. I know how some things stick in your mind, but anyway, it was a sunny day and I remember the plastic bears on an elasticated string in front of me, because I kept smacking them as you do. I can recall this woman taking me out of my pram then cuddling me. Then without warning I was sick all down her back, which turned out to be a good thing later on as I grew up, because the woman was one of my aunties. She was my first stepdad's sister and it seemed she hated everyone as I was later to find out. But until I was in my fifties, I just thought it was just me she hated. I had no idea why. I thought it might have been something to do with me being sick all over her, as some people can hold resentments for a lifetime over nothing as she seemed to have done with me. Either way I knew she hated me, because she used every opportunity to show how she felt.

One Saturday afternoon I was about seven or eight and I had to go to her son's birthday party, even though I didn't want to. Then for some reason she kicked me out in the rain, but as luck would have it, my mother came along to pick me up soon afterwards. She asked why I was there. After I told her what had happened she went inside and more than likely tore a strip off my auntie. That was just one of many times, but it seems the vileness ran through most of my first stepdad's family. Looking back, there was only one uncle on my first stepdad's side who treated me in any way properly and sadly that included my first stepdad. Even to this day I have no idea why.

(I recently accompanied my first stepdad to her funeral about five years ago (2015), because my first stepdad was concerned that her son would kick off with him at the funeral. I'm not sure why he thought this, but once her son saw me he behaved. The most amazing thing was there was hardly anybody at her funeral, so she must have angered quite a lot of people in her time to be so unpopular).

When I was first born and in the mother and baby home, my grandparents came to see us and they apparently loved me at first sight. But what was there not to love? Up to the age of ten my granddad took me everywhere, bought me stuff, built bikes for me. My grandparents were a hundred times better than my actual parents in the way they treated me and I obviously loved them more than my own parents, not because they gave me stuff, but because they showed me love and treated me as loving parents should do. I can hardly remember any loving things my parents ever did for me.

Now I know why. The dad I thought was my dad turned out to be my first stepdad. My mother was far too young to have had me, but neither was my fault, and throughout my childhood I never felt wanted or loved. But I knew my grandparents loved and respected me.

My granddad took me to see Chorley FC every Saturday, even to away matches. That all happened until once we went to a home match when I remember some opposing fans, maybe a bit older than me, beating up one of our fans. I had never seen such violence like it before, not even on telly. It was sickening to see. Three of them were repeatedly kicking the other guy. The ringleader wore steel toecaps and was kicking and stamping on his face. It made me sick to the stomach just witnessing it and after that, I preferred to watch it on the telly. I felt far safer. Violence sickens even now.

Although my parents were skint most of the time, we always had a fortnight away. Usually we would go to Blackpool or Morecambe. I have got to say I enjoyed those holidays. In those days not many people went abroad, that was for the rich snotty totty. The beaches were always jam-packed.

When I was about seven we had a day out in Blackpool. There was just my mum, my two sisters and me. It was a sea of faces on the beach, so much so, that after I'd gone on the prom to get an ice cream I got lost. I walked up and down for what seemed like ages, getting more and more stressed and confused and upset. This woman noticed me and took me to this trailer on the prom, where there were quite a few other lost children.

Eventually, my mother turned up and told me off for getting lost (like I wanted to be lost) and when we got outside the trailer she smacked me. She was a bully in many ways, always image-conscious and very selfish with it, not just with me, but with my first stepdad. I witnessed quite a few times how vile she was with him.

As a family we sometimes went on coach trips to Blackpool, because at that time everything shut down in Chorley for two weeks in the school holidays apart from corner shops. It was on one of these days out that I remember something happening.

We had parked up on the coach park and not long after leaving the coach, the driver started following us. He was coming on a bit too strong with my mother in front of my dad. (I didn't know at the time, but my mother was quite well known for giving it out). I was quite young, about six or seven and I could sense there was a problem. My first stepdad was never a fighter, so for some reason I turned towards the coach driver. I had a good height advantage for what I was about to do. I smacked him squarely in the nuts. Strangely, it seemed to put him off following and badgering us any further, mainly because he was doubled up in pain and was having a lot of trouble walking. I have always been handy with my fists even though I hate using violence. But sometimes there is no other option.

One thing that really sticks in my mind was when I was about nine or ten. I stole 50p from the savings box my parents had hidden. It was soon noticed it had gone, because I wore a tank top with a little pocket to keep me warm (we had no central heating). I had hidden the 50p in the pocket. One night my mother came into my bedroom when I was fast asleep went into the pocket and found the 50p. Within seconds I was pulled out of bed by my hair and dragged downstairs still by my hair. My dad was waiting for me. He grabbed my hand and held it down on the table. He moved a carving knife to the back of my fingers and was threatening to cut them off. As you can imagine I started to scream in terror and tried to struggle free, but my dad then elbowed me in the mouth which cut my lip and chipped a tooth. I still remember this vividly like it was yesterday. It was a truly traumatic experience.

My mother wore a black wig most of the time when she was out and about, probably because she was unhappy about her own hair. She was forever dyeing it I think to the point where she was losing her real hair, due to the chemicals in the dye. I think because of this her real hair was a bit of a mess. I can honestly say I have never really seen her real hair much, so I cannot really comment about it too much.

Quite often when she was getting ready to go out on the town, the day or night before, to style her wig she would put it on my head which I hated. To me she might as well have put a dress on me, so I complained many times only to get smacked and ignored. The thing I hated most apart from the actual wearing of the wig, was that my mother was quite a heavy smoker for as long as I can remember and she would be styling the wig with a fag hanging from her mouth, a bit like Andy Capp's Mrs. The other thing I hated was she would use about a can of hairspray on the wig. If a brick had landed on her head it would have bounced off it she put that much on. Even to this day I hate the smell of hair spray and even though I hated cigarettes I still ended up smoking when I was eighteen.

We were quite poor for most of my childhood. That's how I looked at it at the time and even now. I was quite a good swimmer, not fast, more a strong, long distance swimmer. I did all my bronze, silver and gold awards, even my life saving, but when it came to getting my badges we had to buy them. My parents told me that we couldn't afford them, so I had to let it go and do without them. I was fine with it until a few years later when my sister did the same awards and they were all bought for her. It was the same thing with clothing. I always seemed to be the last one to get things bought for me. I suppose I should be thankful that I was the eldest and the only lad in our family at the time, so there were no hand-me downs and I grew up at the time with two sisters, otherwise I might have turned out to be a cross-dresser. Not a pretty sight and extremely unconvincing. Dame Edna would have been more convincing than me.

This also meant I was always mending my own clothes, at times sewing patches on patches. My mother was more interested in preening herself ready to go out on Thursday nights than looking after her kids like she should have been.

When I was about seven or eight my grandparents pulled me up because I kept itching quite a lot around my testicles. It turned out I hadn't been washing myself or drying myself properly. Mind you, we had to share our bathwater and of course, I was always the last one to bathe. My grandparents made a point that every time I went to their home, I would have to wash myself down below. Looking back, it seemed at times that my mother thought she had given birth to me and that was all I was getting from her.

I was not aware until I was 11 or 12 that my dad was not my real dad, but before I found out, I could never understand why he was always so vile and bullying towards me. He treated me as though he had stood in something most of the time and I could sense not having love from him all through my childhood. If I had known he was not my real dad I might have understood a bit better why he was treating me like he did, but to grow up with all that confusion, was a total nightmare at times and I am quite sure it has affected me while growing up and even now.

From a fairly young age I would be stitching my own clothes and even washing all the family's clothes in the twin tub, often nearly catching my fingers in the mangle. Mainly because of health and safety reasons kids nowadays are not meant to use these kinds of machines. It seemed that I was the male version of Cinders, albeit an uglier version of her, but I can strongly relate to her, and I am not trying to steal her limelight.

So most of the time in primary school and even in my secondary school, I would be putting patches on patches on the seat of my pants, so, I learned all about sewing at a very early age. I didn't think it was any hardship at the time. I don't remember other kids with patches on their patches. The only negative side to having to wear worn-out clothes most of the time, was a few of the other kids at school (who didn't know what hardship was) would take the mick and I was constantly bullied over this and it got quite relentless at times. That is the way schoolkids were and still are. They will find anything to zoom in on and just keep picking on you until you break or react. In most of my schooling I have defended myself, mainly physically, but that is how it was in those days and more than likely still is now.

One day while in my secondary school the mechanical engineering teacher ridiculed me in front of the whole class because of the state of my clothing. I never mentioned it to my parents. I saw no point in telling either of them anything about what had been said, as nothing would have been done anyway. I did mention it to my granddad in passing one weekend, about what the teacher had said. He came into school one day and complained to the headmaster who in turn got the teacher in his office. But that was like putting a target on my back for that teacher for the rest of my time at that school.

He was the only one who ever gave me six of the best and I was guilty of nothing. Someone had let off a firework quite near me in the playground and I got the blame for it. So throughout my secondary school and my life at home I suffered constant bullying from some of the teachers and other pupils.

Generally, my schooling wasn't that bad. One of my best memories was when I was in the primary school choir and even the secondary school one and I loved both. When I was about 11 or 12 our school choir was chosen as one of the choirs at St. George's Church one Christmas for a carol service and I sang a solo piece. There was easily more than 500 people in the church and I was praised next day by one of my teachers who was in the audience. Strangely, my first stepdad had no recollection of it even though he was in the audience with my mother. I'm quite sure that if it had been one of my sisters, he would never have forgotten any of the service.

While in secondary school I did morning prayers at assembly in front of the whole school until one day I said it wrongly. I was meant to be saying the longer version of the

Glory Be, but one morning I ended up saying the shorter version. The whole school just laughed me off the stage and since then I have a morbid fear of being the centre of attention, better known as stage fright.

It turns out that I was born with ten to two feet, it was no hardship for me at the time and still isn't now. It just means I wear my heels down on the sides of my shoes quicker than most other people. It was granddad who happened to notice it and told my mother to take me to the doctor to get it sorted, which she did. I was sent to group therapy and it turned out I was the eldest kid there. I had no problem with that, but it seemed my mother did. She kept saying to me on the way home that we were not going back there. I have never been so embarrassed in all my life. Good job it was not life-threatening or I would have been in deep trouble. I still have ten to two feet.

Another thing stuck in my mind that my mother often said to me while I was growing up and even into my adulthood. In the school holidays we would all go to the paddling pool at Astley Park, Chorley which was about ten minutes' walk from where we lived. I was so skinny my shoulder blades stuck out like little angel wings and again my mother would say it was so embarrassing taking me there. She said she would try to make out I was not her son and she was deadly serious. (It's always nice to hear just how much your mother thought of you and how you were an embarrassment to her as you were growing up. Really makes you feel good about yourself. Not).

Both my parents worked. My dad was a lorry driver and my mother worked at a local butcher's. It was there that my mother befriended a Polish guy. We all called him Uncle Fred. I can't understand or remember why. I think, if truth be known, my mother was flirting with him to see what she could get out of him because he was the butcher and he was always giving her parcels of meat on the quiet. But I'm quite sure he more than likely wanted to give her another kind of meat given half a chance. For years she kept sending us all (my two sisters and me) to him and most times he would give us all some money. I really have no idea why and I know my dad didn't know anything about him and more than likely still doesn't.

As I reflect now, it does seem she was quite good at using her sexuality to get what she wanted. She was a definite user and from what she has told me in the past, my dad badgered her into marrying him. I think my mother gave in because one-parent families were shunned and looked down upon in those days.

My name was changed by deed poll and everything seemed fine, even my mother changed to Roman Catholic from C of E, the same as my dad (my first stepdad) and for most of my younger childhood I was a good Catholic. We all went to church every Sunday. I went to confession in the week, although, that did frighten me quite a bit at the time, as we had a canon who always seemed to take confessions when I was going and he scared me rotten. But I still went to confession as a good Catholic boy should do.

I would always observe Lent. I had a small blue suitcase under my bed, it usually had my knick-knacks in, but at Lent I would put all my toffee in there that I would have usually eaten. Of course I always looked forward to Lent being over so I could make a pig of myself. One day I noticed that most of the toffee was missing. I had no idea who had taken them, so I told my parents who did nothing, which wasn't unusual. I suspected it was my younger sister, but I had no proof. I think that was the start of her thieving from me, even into my adulthood, but anything my two sisters did went unpunished and it seemed I would get the blame for things that were totally not my fault. I suppose I was just the whipping boy; the child that no one really wanted. That's just how I felt at the time and I still think the same.

I was the usual kind of boy, always fighting or getting into trouble of some kind, in fact, I think I was about six when the police first came to our door about me and I must admit I needed a change of underwear after the copper's visit. I was not alone. Another kid across the road from us also got a visit. I can't remember what his reaction was, but it kept me on the straight and narrow for a while and it would have stayed that way if my home life had not radically changed as badly as it did.

Because I was quite good at climbing and doing things I shouldn't have done, I was nearly on first names basis with all the nurses and doctors at Chorley A&E. I wasn't that good at climbing really, but as a kid, I had no fear of heights. I broke a few bones and had stitches all over, but it was what kids did in those days and there were times when I got in trouble at home. I thought nothing of it at the time as to the way I was being punished as I had no comparisons to go by, so I didn't know any different. It seemed how it should be at the time, but looking back now, I was definitely abused by both my parents and quite a few of these incidents have stuck in my mind, as I think they would have done with anyone.

When my mother was teaching me to read, every time I got it wrong I would get slapped hard across the back of the head and that happened until I could read. It wasn't easy trying to read and crying my eyes out at the same time. My dad saw this and did nothing. But as I know now, I was not his son. I took his name, so he should have accepted me as his own. I am a stepdad now and I show my stepkids respect in every way. My first stepdad never did this at all (but when I saw myself in the tabloids I suddenly became his son. He even called me son, which he'd never done until then. I wonder why that was? Was it guilt perhaps?) It was small things like that, which made growing up just that bit harder. Not feeling loved affects you in many different ways. For me, as I grew up I always had no self-esteem or confidence. I was painfully shy and very introverted, probably because I was being abused.

On one occasion I was fighting with a neighbour's kid like most kids do at that age and their dad came running after me. I ran indoors like you would do when a 6ft 6ins guy is racing after you, but the neighbour's dad started shouting at my stepdad at the front door. My stepdad had a poker in his hand, not sure why, but he struck it across the back of my legs. I'm not sure if this was in front of the neighbour, but I remember it hurt like hell and I was bruised quite badly for quite a while afterwards. I think this was abuse. At the time I had no way of comparing with other kids, so I accepted it as normal.

Then when my parents where splitting up when I was about eleven or twelve my mother told me that the guy I thought was my dad, wasn't. She told me my real dad died in a car accident shortly after I was born. It all seemed to make sense then, all the abuse and beatings I had suffered from who I then knew as my stepdad. I think I had just turned twelve and to say it screwed me up, would be an understatement.

From then on I know I effectively pressed my self destruct button. I was constantly fighting with other lads at school, so much so that I had what I think is known as boxer's eyebrows, meaning the bone under my eyebrows stuck out due to constantly getting punched in the face. Strange thing was I hated violence, but even now, I don't back down with bullies, because that is how I saw my parents. Nowadays I can never be a bystander to bullying.

Nowadays I can mostly talk my way out of trouble and I try not to use my fists. I think in my secondary school I had the cane or strap from all the teachers even the headmaster and throughout my time in secondary I was bullied relentlessly by other pupils. Having a big nose didn't help me one bit. It gave the knuckle draggers something to pick on, but I have since learned that if I had not had a big nose they would have found something else to zoom in on. That is the way bullies are and bullying is not just physical. It is mental, as I know all to well and I have found it does follow you throughout your life, as it did with me. I blame that on the people who were in my life. I firmly believe that you are only as good as the people around you.

My mother was going through a divorce from my first stepdad. She was back and forth from this younger guy who came from Standish and back to the guy who I had thought was my dad since birth and we were constantly moving from bedsit to bedsit.

One night when we went back to my first stepdad's, I was misbehaving while my mother was out on the town with my auntie. My first stepdad told me off and rightfully so. I turned around and said he wasn't my dad so I didn't have to do anything he said. That was wrong.

My first stepdad lost his temper with me, which was not unusual, but this time he threw his slipper at me and it was the kind of slipper with a hard plastic sole. It caught me a hard blow under the eye. Blood was shooting everywhere. My mother was more than likely shagging behind his back or more than likely blatantly in front of him, knowing my mother as I do now.

Of course, my stepdad was sorry straight away. The next day when I went to school with a very angry black eye, every man and his dog wanted to know what had happened but not one teacher asked me about it, so I had to make up some lie about getting beaten up by neighbouring school pupils. I'm not too sure if I was believed as I am the world's worst liar, but I must admit I did feel loved by my first stepdad. He hardly ever called me son, which hurt at times, but when I found myself in the newspapers he totally changed towards me. After more than forty years of getting nothing from him, suddenly he was so up my backside that only his feet were showing and even calling me son proved how fake the people were around me throughout my life. If I like you I show it and if I don't I show it. It's just the way I am. I think it's good to be genuine.

From what my mother has told me I think he was only interested in her, but from what she has said in the past, she wasn't really interested in him, because he was always working to make a better life for us all (I don't see anything wrong in that) but my mother was just a young housewife who seemed to put sex before anything else. My dad couldn't keep up with her in the bedroom, so at every opportunity, she would play around behind his back. Even she has said that there is doubt about my younger sister's paternity.

I do remember that she would go out with one of my aunties every Thursday night and it was on one of those nights that on the way to my auntie's house my mother hit a parked Jaguar Mark 10 on Lyons Lane in Chorley. At the time she was doing her make-up in the driver's mirror. So to me she was on the pull even then, but she paid the price for dolling herself up like a tart.

In those days it was not the law to wear seat belts, so she ended up going through the windscreen and was very lucky to survive. She was driving a Ford Anglia, which ended up having to be scrapped. The Jag owner kept coming to our door demanding money for the damage to his car and because of this we couldn't go on our annual holidays, which I moaned about to one of our neighbour's parents, who in turn told my parents. I must admit I must have been a spoilt brat for moaning as I did, but I was a kid and knew no different. It wasn't a bad life with my first stepdad on the whole though, a lot more bearable than with the second one.

I remember my mother going through a phase of making holes in the interior walls. Obviously she was ignorant that they could have been load-bearing walls or not, but I think it was an excuse for her to getting the builder to be constantly coming round. He reminded me of Yul Brynner as he had no hair at all on top. What stuck in my mind were the holes were downstairs, whereas my mother and the builder were always upstairs. I obviously did not know why at the time, I was far too young to understand all that, but I do know, they were decorating, or maybe filling holes upstairs.

One of my many weekend jobs was to go to the corner shop for the groceries. Because I was quite young I would take a shopping list and the money and the shopkeeper would drop it off in his car for us. One time I took a list, but no money, which I thought was a bit strange. The shopkeeper came as usual, although on this occasion, he came in and went upstairs with my mother and there were many more times like that with different men.

Then out of the blue, my mother and I did a

moonlight flit from Water Street to a bedsit at the top of Stump Lane, around half a mile from where we lived. She had just up and left my first stepdad. Not even my sisters knew anything about it until they came home from school and found my mother gone. She couldn't have been any crueller if she had tried. I was only told days before that we were doing a moonlight, but of course, I couldn't fully understand what was happening because of my age, so I effectively went with the flow. My mother had left my first stepdad for this younger guy from Standish.

This new guy seemed completely different to my first stepdad. He loved pets (my first stepdad hated them). He had a large Alsatian which I walked everywhere, every night. It was quite a frightening dog to most people because of its size, but it loved me to bits, so none of the bullies would ever come anywhere near me when it was with me and of course, I would have loved them to try it on. Bullies though are generally cowards.

From what my mother has told me, the first time my second stepdad and my mother made love was in a derelict house on Parker Street, Chorley. He pulled her into it as they were walking past one of the doorways. She thought that she liked doing it rough, but in reality, he raped her. That is how naive she was.

My grandparents were in no way happy about what my mother had done, by leaving my first stepdad as she did and both of them told me to put myself in care, as in their words, 'I would be better off in care.' It was as if they knew something about my second stepdad. It was debatable whether I would have been any better off in care, knowing what I know about kids' homes, probably 50/50. I think they were right.

I told my mother what had been said by my

grandparents and she demanded that I write to them, basically telling them to keep their noses out of our business. That well and truly soured my relationship with my grandparents big style and they never recovered from it, even though it wasn't my fault in any way. They didn't want to know me any more after that. I didn't go round as much and if I did, I never let my mother know and to be honest, it all added to the hurt I was already feeling that my real blood dad was dead.

I was about twelve while all this was going on and I went from a quiet lad to someone who just wanted to fight all the time. Emotionally, I was hurting. Fighting seemed to deflect it. I never won many fights. There was always more of them against me, never one on one, but I just wanted others to feel the hurt I was feeling inside even though I was nearly always the loser.

On one of my rare visits to my grandparents I thought I would confront them about what my mother had told me about my real dad being dead. They denied any knowledge, but I must admit I am not certain about what was said at the time, as it is all a complete blur now. I remember losing my temper with them and storming out. As I was going over the railway bridge on Brook Street to go home, I pushed a very large coping stone which in all honesty was ready to fall anyway. It could have fallen either way at the time, as I'm not sure exactly what had happened to the brickwork that was meant to be supporting it. I have since found out that a lorry had collided with it some days or weeks earlier and weakened the brickwork under the coping stone, (a gust of wind could have done the same as what I did at any time and like I said, it could have fallen either way at any time). I was only eleven or twelve and about seven stone, so it obviously didn't need much shoving over.

Unbeknown to me there was a stationary steam train right under that part of the bridge restocking with coal and water. The coping stone hit one of the guys working on the train and killed him instantly.

Even now it sickens me to think about what I did. In no way did I plan to hurt anyone and if I could, or even swap places with the guy, I would in the blink of an eye. Often, I have wished that the coping stone had fallen on me instead of him. It haunts me daily, even though I was never sent to prison or even charged for it because I was too young at the time. Now, I'm locked up in my own prison cell in my own mind and I carry what I did on that day with me everywhere and all the time. It certainly would have contributed to the way I started drinking as I did later on in my life. Even now that I am sober, it is never far from my thoughts. It is something that I will take to the grave and to be honest, I know very little about what else happened around that time. As I said earlier it is mostly a blur. I think it must have been too traumatic for me to endure mentally, so my mind has blocked out quite a lot of it.

I do remember me and dad going up what is known as the chapel steps near the town hall and someone shouting abuse at us. That is all I remember about that incident and I got beaten up quite a few times at school because of it, so all I can do is take this opportunity to apologise wholeheartedly to the guy's family. It was a childish tantrum gone tragically wrong.

My second stepdad and I were moving nearly every other week. The first was to a bedsit in Stump Lane, Chorley. It was just one room and one bed. Luckily for me, a middle-aged guy who lived upstairs let me watch his telly now and again. He lived with another guy and even on the same floor as us, a guy and a cross dresser were living in the next bedsit to us. I worked it out much later, but at the time it confused and disgusted me. It even shocked me, but I didn't fully understand anything about anything like that at the time.

It's not something they teach you in school. I never had sex education and had to play it by ear. Wives taught me quite a lot as well. No wonder my choice in women was a bit suspect at times, especially when I was a suffering alcoholic. The alcoholic blinkers have a lot to answer for, believe me.

When we were living in Stump Lane, our sleeping arrangements were that we had to top and tail, at least for the first few weeks. Then one night when I was half asleep, my new stepdad was in the middle of my mum and I and they were giggling and whispering. Suddenly I felt a foot in my groin, kind of touching me up, so I said in a loud voice, "Get your foot out of my fucking groin." It moved instantly. The next night I was on the couch. It was so uncomfortable I couldn't sleep. I was then moved to my auntie's the following night in Wright Street, Chorley, which was only a few streets away. Again, we were all topping and tailing because my auntie had four or five kids, so I slept with my younger male cousin. Neither of us was keen on that, but thankfully it wasn't for long.

One night when I got to my auntie's at my usual time, the babysitter was there. I'm not sure but I think she was one or two years older than me and quite attractive with fully formed breasts. She started chasing me around the couch, just in fun I thought, and while I was still trying to get away from her, somehow we ended up on my auntie's bed. She held me down by sitting on my face and she must have got my penis out and performed oral sex on me because that was the very first time I had experienced an orgasm. It was a very strange sensation, to say the least. Before that I thought it was just for p- out of and nothing more than that. After that, I started to masturbate.

Within days my mother and auntie were quizzing me about it, but I truly didn't fully understand what the babysitter had done, so couldn't say much about it. Soon afterwards we moved in with my stepdad's parents in Standish, but only for a matter of weeks.

My second stepdad's deviant side started to show its ugly face even more now. One night I was washing myself in the bathroom sink as in a top and tailing. I was completely naked and stood near the sink, which was less than a foot from the bathroom door. I sensed someone watching me and just by chance, I noticed through the reflection in the mirror that the door was open slightly. I knew I had shut it properly earlier when I came into the bathroom. I had to be careful not to make it known I had seen him and the fact that I knew it was my stepdad peeping through the gap at me.

I can only guess what else he was up to and to be honest I felt physically sick and very confused as to why he would want to watch me washing. I couldn't say anything to anyone as I wasn't sure at the time what to do or say to anyone as I didn't know how people would react. So, out of fear and confusion, I had to let it go, and I never said anything to anyone, until now that is.

Soon after that we moved back to Chorley, to Primrose Street, which was more central Chorley. My sister moved in with us. By this time my mother had left my first stepdad and my second stepdad's sexual deviant tendencies turned from me to my younger sister. I started suffering physical and mental abuse from my stepdad and

I was constantly being bullied at school as well as at home and sometimes I was even bullied in the streets outside of school hours. This went on for about three years or more and at one point I seriously thought of taking my own life.

One day after a really bad day at school I sat on my bed. My bedroom window was quite large and also quite low and I was facing the window, crying my heart out. I was seriously contemplating suicide for at least an hour or more. I thought to myself, *if I take a run at the window, all my problems will be over.* Then I thought I'm not letting those bastards win. After all the crying I felt physically and mentally drained, but also stronger in myself.

When I went back to school the next day I started fighting back. At first it was a no-win situation, as now instead of one to one fights, it was three or four to one, but even though I was losing I gained respect from quite a few of the other lads, including the bullies, who started to leave me alone more. Bullying is about control and because I was fighting back the bullies at school had lost their control over me, so most gave in and left me alone.

I realise now that the abuse I was getting from my second stepdad was his way of deflecting me from what he was up to with my sister and I must admit it worked as I couldn't do anything about my home life. That in every way was a no-win situation, but thankfully he was in and out of prison most of the time. When he came out, it was back to square one. He was a big guy, enough to frighten most people especially a skinny 12-year-old lad like me who at the most weighed 11 stones wet through, so in no way was I any kind of match for him. He was easily about 18 stones.

When he first came on the scene he was in the demolition game and sometimes when I was off school I would have to tag along with him. At first I was interested, then it got to where we would not go home after work. It seemed he couldn't wait to get in the pub at night and I was left outside in the van, usually parked up on the cattle market for hours on end with no food, no toilet and not daring to move in case he came out. Because of this I didn't get a chance to meet my mates for quite some time. I'm not sure what they must have thought.

One day one of my schoolmates came to our door, to see if I was coming out. I was there for about five minutes just chatting, when suddenly my stepdad came barging out, punched me full in the face in front of my mate and pulled me back in. God knows what my mate thought. I'm quite sure it would have gone around the rumour mill around the town or at least around my school.

At home, my stepdad would egg on my little brother to throw a metal candlestick holder at me, which always seemed to catch me at the back of the head and always left bruising. If I dared to tell off my little brother I would get a good hiding off my stepdad as well. It was his way of ridiculing and controlling me and it worked.

I don't remember my mother ever siding with me or defending me in any way at any time and I would just like to point out that I have no resentment against my little brother. He knew no difference at the time, it was more my stepdad's and my mother's faults. They seemed to get off on bullying people.

Then my stepdad had this novel idea of building a little extension at the back of our house with the block paving that was laid as flooring in our back yard, but the blocks were half the size in height as a normal brick, so, we soon ran out of bricks in no time at all. Then we cruised around Preston and Bolton in our transit van, with my mother and I in tow, stealing bricks, sand and cement from building sites.

I was always the one who had to gain entry while he and my mother stayed out of sight until the coast was clear. I found that by me assisting him in this way made him less abusive towards me most of the time. I suppose it was my way of people-pleasing or was it my way of self-preservation? When you are bullied or being abused you will do anything to stop the bullying and abuse and that is what I did to appease him.

On one occasion while we were building the extension, I was mixing mortar for him in our back yard. I had no board to mix on, so, I was getting dirt and soil off the floor in the mix. Not good if you are trying to lay bricks (as I now know) and he very quickly lost his temper with me (even though it was not my fault in any way if the truth be known) so for whatever reason, he threw a pointing trowel at me. It seemed that the pointer was coming at me in slow motion. Maybe that was a good thing as it turned out, because if I had not put my chin down as I did and taken it on my chin, the pointer would have stuck in my throat and quite obviously could have killed me. It cut me quite badly. I should have had stitches in it, but how would they have explained that in A&E? I still have a scar there now, it is a constant reminder of what he put me through every time I shave. I can't remember what my mother did about it. More than likely nothing, as per usual.

While walking home with one of my school mates one night after school, I opened up to him about what was happening at home. He told me his sister worked for the social services, so he would have a word about me to her and she gave him a phone number to give to me. The only time I could ring was after school. I must have rung the number at least a dozen times, but never got through. I was getting nowhere fast. It's a shame no one like Esther Rantzen was about then.

One dinner time I broke my collar bone on the school playing fields when another lad rugby tackled me and I fell awkwardly. I was about twelve. We were just mucking about. The pain was knocking me sick and I went to the headmaster's office. The PE teacher told me to grip my tie, as in a makeshift sling, and sent me home. I had to walk about a mile and I was in total agony with every step I took all the way home. For once my mother lost it with the school. It's no wonder I was a bad lad there because of how they treated us at times.

The worst thing I ever did was when I was winding this lad up before school. It just started as messing about in the morning in the cloakroom. For some unknown reason I grabbed the lad's tie and tightened it round his neck. I never thought for a minute that he was going to end up nearly choking to death. If it had not been for a prefect cutting his tie off he would have passed out or worse.

I remember the headmaster addressing the whole school that very morning in assembly and mentioning the incident and more or less warning me indirectly in front of everyone that I was on very thin ice. All I could do was put my head down in shame while all eyes were on me. Even now I have no idea why I did it, probably with my home life being the way it was. It may have been a cry for help in some way or hitting out because of my home life. If the lad is reading this, I am truly sorry for doing that to you. I was in a very bad place in my life at the time. Please forgive me.

Eventually, it came time to leave school. I was fifteen. I had no qualifications. In fact I think I was very lucky not to have been expelled and I'm not proud of that. My English is probably average at best and the thing that annoys me most is when I am on a social media site. I get criticised by some know-all who has never tasted hardship of any kind and they think it is amusing to take the meikle out of someone who was not wrapped in cotton wool like they were. If it was a face to face chat they would not dare say anything like that.

Within days of leaving school, I had to go working for my stepdad, so the bullying continued. In total, I worked for him for about eighteen months and I only got paid once in all that time and it was a fiver. I didn't know whether to frame it or what. While working for him I met some of his mates who worked with us, off and on. It soon became quite clear that even his mates hated him nearly as much as I did. I had no idea why, but I do now.

I realise most step parents have a hard time with their stepkids. I know from my own experience as I am a stepdad myself now, but there was something about him. When he was fondling my testicles with his foot when we lived in Stump Lane he didn't make me feel any better about him. He was constantly putting me down, humiliating and ridiculing me daily. When you're in the thick of it you can never truly see what is happening around you.

Once while working for him my mind was so messed up with all the abuse I was suffering from him, I accidentally backed him into a wall when he was backing the van up to load up some sand at a local builder's yard. He totally lost his rag with me, but as luck would have it, there was a lad helping us load up. He was quite handy, about 18 or 19 and as my stepdad went to go for me, the lad stepped in his way and because he was a coward, he backed off sharpish. I didn't get away with it for long. He punched me full in the face with his fist. It was always the full fist and that kind of thing happened a lot over the eighteen months I worked for him. Even customers witnessed it on a few occasions and it didn't do his business any favours either. He was quite well known in the Chorley area and most people hated him. I didn't know why for sure at the time.

I know now it was his sexual deviancy that every man and his dog knew about, apart from our family, but we were totally in the dark about it. I was picking up the signs of it, although it was not something I knew a lot about.

One day I gave him some karma back for his ill-treatment of me. I was having something to eat before setting off for work. My mother came downstairs and told me to get out of the house right then and not bother coming back until I had found a job and while I was at it to find somewhere else to stay.

I was about sixteen at the time. I hadn't a clue why this was happening to me, but my first call was the youth employment office, then on St. George's Street, Chorley and I signed on. In the process of signing on they asked me what I had been doing since leaving school, so (unwittingly) I told them that I had been working for my stepdad (not knowing that he was not legit) hence I dropped him head-first in the mire. As the saying goes, *what goes around comes around, is very true.*

I managed to find a job with a flooring firm from Upper Adlington. I had visited my grandparents before going on the job interview, as I had no money for bus fare and I also asked if I could stay at theirs. They had no room to put me up, they only had a one-bedroomed bungalow in Eldon Street, so, I had to go back to my mother's. She opened the door and welcomed me with open arms as though nothing had been said.

I was due to start my new job the day after. The next morning my mother begged me not to go to the new job and stay working for my stepdad. Eventually, I gave in, but very reluctantly. I had very little choice really as I had nowhere else to live.

Because I was working for my stepdad and not getting paid like I should have been for quite a while, I was frequently eating jam butties for every meal (as whatever money that came in, went on my stepdad's beer or my mother's fags. She easily smoked 40-plus a day). I don't think anyone noticed what I was eating but on the occasions I went with my mates, they had cars and nice clothes, because they had proper jobs with wages and I have to admit I envied them quite a lot. There was nothing I could do about it. If I had got a proper job my stepdad would have hit the roof and I would have been out on my ear.

I tried for the army, the post office, even the police force. I was only sixteen, but I never got any kind of reply from any of them, or was it that my replies were being intercepted by my parents? I think the latter. Going in the forces would have been my way out of their control and a way of getting away from the mental and physical abuse.

While working for my stepdad, one of our first jobs was to point the gable end of one of his mates ex-wife's house just off Pall Mall, Chorley. The ex-husband owned a carpet shop in Chorley and I must admit I took to pointing like a duck to water, which was probably a good thing because my stepdad kept leaving me on my own to do all the work. Over the years I have done tens of thousands of square yards of pointing. I have always found it quite therapeutic.

We even managed to get some good jobs such as a contract with the MOD, working on an army barracks, but he would always keep doing a disappearing act. On one job, we were doing the footings for a big Ariel and for some reason he got this secretary, who I must admit was a stunner, to ride round in the van with him. I think she lasted no more than a day because he had likely tried it on with her. I was seriously starting to open my eyes to what he was really getting up to, but in most cases like that, you need real evidence before you can act on it. Mostly, he kept his perverted ways well hidden.

On one occasion we had a small job to do for an old lady on her house in Fellery Street in Chorley. It was just fixing her front doorstep and a few bits and bobs, about three days' work in all. After the first day she wouldn't allow us back. I didn't know why at the time, but my mother told me many years later that the woman had accused him of trying it on with her. The woman was probably about 70 and could barely walk. It's highly likely he would have done such a thing, because he was a sick and dirty bastard.

Also around that time we started doing a job for a fairly well-known farmer in Croston and I must say I liked him and his wife instantly. I nearly messed it up though right from the start when I nicked some mole grips out of the farmer's toolbox and he noticed them missing. I managed to persuade one of our workers to take the blame, which he did, but it made me feel as guilty as hell when the farmer was telling him off. He kept looking at me and if looks could kill, I would have been long gone and with good reason.

We ended up terylening the whole farmhouse. It was quite big and my stepdad had underestimated how much scaffolding we would need, so on the gable ends we ended up building the easy fix scaffold on top of one of the farmer's trailers. Hardly safe or ideal, but it worked and made it easy to move as well. My stepdad was quite high up doing one of the gable ends and I was supplying him with buckets of terylene. In those days there was no such thing as plastic buckets. We had a heavy metal bucket. Of course I was doing all the donkey work and was up and down the extension ladder.

Finally, we got to a point where we had to lower the scaffold, which was quite easy even at that height. Just to finish off, I lowered the extension ladder and thought I had secured it on properly, but soon found out I hadn't. When I pulled on the ladder to move it across I got the bottom rung across the bridge of my nose and it knocked me easily six foot against a wall. It broke my nose and blood was everywhere and because it had jolted the scaffold quite violently my stepdad threw the empty metal bucket at me, even though I was holding my face in my hands with blood pouring from my nose. Thankfully, the bucket missed me.

The farmer heard what was going on and came running round the corner to see what all the shouting was about. He took one look at me and more or less threatened him that when he came down off the scaffold he would rip his head off and my stepdad s- himself (like a coward would) so much so that he stayed up the scaffold in case the farmer got hold of him, which even though I was in agony I found quite amusing, but I dared not let it show.

The farmer took me to his wife who helped to stop the bleeding and patched me up. Shortly afterwards my mother turned up with the van and the farmer told her all about it. I'm not really sure what if anything was said between my stepdad and my mother. I think at the time I was in a daze because of what had happened. I wasn't taken to hospital even though my nose was obviously broken and badly cut.

The most sickening thing my stepdad did around that time was to try it on with my grandmother when she was suffering from Parkinson's disease and was close to dying. The worst part was that I was with him at the time. We had been a bit quiet on the work front and he'd suggested going to my grandparents for a brew. I desperately needed to go to the loo leaving my grandmother and stepdad chatting in the front room. I never thought for a minute anything would happen, but I could hear my grandmother saying, 'get away, get away'.

When I came back into the living room, there was nothing untoward as far as I could see, but I could see my grandmother was very upset and was ordering us both out, which I found strange, but we left without question.

We parked up about half a mile away, down some back streets and he more or less persuaded me that nothing had happened and he begged me not to tell my mother that we had even been to my grandparents. I was very naive at the time and fell for it, hook, line, and sinker. It stuck in my mind, as most things do if I do not fully understand them, but I was getting more and more on high alert about him.

One day especially I was walking past my parents' bedroom, which, by the way, had no door on. I glanced in and caught my younger sister pulling her hand out from under the covers more or less round where his groin was. She came downstairs shortly afterwards and I confronted her with what I thought I had seen. She swore blind that nothing like that had happened, but I found out years later (in 1976 while doing eighteen months in Walton prison) that she was lying because she was s-scared of him. I know if she had of admitted it to me at the time, I would have run a knife through him for sure and I think she knew there would have been a lot of trouble if she had told me.

It pushed me into a deep depression and my only form of escape was to climb a very high fire escape at Chortex mill. It was easily three to four hundred feet up and I loved it up there. I would spend hours just watching everything around me and it was so peaceful and away from all my abusers and bullies. Because I knew I was breaking the law by doing this, I started to get a bit daring and started breaking into places, always commercial ones. I started doing simple things, places that were quite easy to break into and as I look back now I quickly got addicted to the adrenalin buzz it gave me. My *modus operandi* was gaining entry at height, through skylights, etc, even removing slates and at one time going through a fireplace to adjoining premises, as in those days it was a single brick wall and easier to get in. I quickly became a one-person crime wave in the Chorley area in the early Seventies. It lasted roughly a year before I got caught in a bank of all places, but they were nowhere near as secure as they are now.

I suppose I had this crazy notion that I could outwit the police. I think I had been watching far too much *Sweeney*, it did influence me a lot in my wrongdoing, as did *The Saint*. I learned a lot of my fight moves from Simon Templar.

It was just a matter of time before I was caught, but before then the closest was in the GPO sorting office in Chorley (as it was then known) in the early hours of the morning.

At that time I was quite skinny, about ten to eleven stone wet through and I had managed to get in through a very small, narrow open window, which at most was about 8″ to 10″ wide. I had a quick look around and couldn't find anything worth nicking. I knew there would have been workers knocking about on the night shift so I gave up on it quite quickly.

As I was making my way out, I had just got to the window where I had just gained entry earlier when this guy came out from nowhere and shouted at me to stay right where I was. I think he went to get someone else and I instantly thought, *why the fuck am I standing here waiting for him to come back?* So I quickly got back out of the window. I knew I couldn't go out the way I had got in through the yard. They would all have been waiting for me and I could hear people shouting in the yard below and I was sure the police would have been there too. So, as luck would have it, the bus station backed on to the post office. It was very early in the morning so there were no buses there. I did my best to check no one was around and hung from the roof and dropped about 10-15 feet to the concrete floor. It hurt my feet and legs like hell, but it was a lot better than getting caught and ending up in a police cell. Then I ran across the bus parking area and past where the library is now.

There is an old saying. I'm not sure where it comes from and it goes like this: *'Murder is easy to do, but hard to get away with. Burglary is hard to do, but easy to get away with'.* In other words once you are away from the scene of the crime there is not much chance you will get caught, but the police had a rough idea of what I looked like, which wasn't good.

A few days later I was out and about with one of my mates who knew nothing about what else I was getting up to. As we walked across the cattle market (as it is known), a copper was parked up and I did my best not to look at him or look guilty of anything. But I could feel him glaring right at me. I was so relieved when I got past him, but it worried me for a while afterwards.

The same copper more than likely remembered me from a couple of years earlier when he took me off the school bus for giving him the V sign nearly every morning for a week or so. He put me in his car and took me to the headmaster's office. The headmaster later caned me. At the time, I also found out that my stepdad was well known to the police but I didn't know what for.

It wasn't long before I was back out again. Neither of my parents knew what I was up to, because my bedroom was at the back of the house and I would sneak out of my window, then on to the PVC lean-to roof of the extension and off to do whatever I was doing and then sneak back in with my swag.

A couple of weeks previously I had managed to get into one of the banks in Market Street. In those days it was quite easy to gain entry to most places. All I had to do was break a pane of glass and smash a door panel.

The second time I broke in, I was only there for maybe ten minutes. I was just taking a look at the large safe door trying to work out how to get in it. Not that I had a cat in hell's chance of getting in it. I wasn't even tooled up. Suddenly I had a feeling I was being watched. I looked round and saw a silhouette of a helmeted head looking through the spyhole. As quickly as I could, I snook out the same way I had got in. I was wearing a white shirt, which isn't the kind of thing to wear when you're trying not to be seen. I really don't think I had thought it through much at the time. I was totally blocked in, but I managed to get out of the bank itself and hide in a doorway about six feet from the broken window. It was all situated more or less all underground, but with a very small alleyway. Two coppers climbed down and through the missing window pane into the bank.

I left it for about 30 seconds then as quickly and silently as I could I climbed up and on to a flat roof away from the remaining coppers who were chit-chatting among themselves and at first hadn't noticed me. I had got on to the flat roof when one of them saw me and came running after me. I quickly shinned up a drain pipe on to another roof and then on to the bank's main roof. It all happened in seconds. The copper was close behind me so I knew if I stopped he would get me. I had to make a quick decision to jump off the main roof of the bank on to next door's roof, which happened to be a flat roof. It was easily a 60-foot drop from the roof to the floor, but about a 15-20 foot drop on to the flat roof next door. To make sure I could get the distance I needed, I ran along the bank's roof to gain height and distance. The copper decided not to follow me. He must have thought better of it as he watched me go to another drainpipe and down to the ground into someone's back yard where I found that I was trapped by a barbed wire fence that was over a six foot wall.

Mind you, even if I had been able to get that way I would have been running right past the police station. Not a good idea and I could not go on to Market Street as the police were all around there too. I couldn't think of anything to do, so I hid behind a toilet door hoping the copper on the roof had not seen where I had gone. But he had and this massive traffic cop came barging through the door pinning me behind it and knocking the wind out of me in the process. That was me done. Caught!

The police station was two minutes around the corner. They had two types of cells, one for under age criminals (like me) and about five or six normal ones for the adults, which had toilets. I was only sixteen and wasn't in the cell long as the CID came down for me around 2 am to question me. It took them a while, because at first I wasn't saying anything. I suppose I had watched too much *Sweeney* in the past, but after an hour I started telling them what I had been up to. I knew what I had done and what I hadn't.

One officer kept trying to push other crimes on me and I knew for certain I hadn't done any of them and in no way was I going to admit to something I knew I had not done. He kept trying for a couple of hours. Eventually, he gave up and I was charged with three offences and around thirty TICs (TICs means taken into consideration) and I was then taken back to my cell at about 6 am and had the shock of my life, as I could hear my stepdad moaning to a copper about something. It turned out he had been thrown in the next cell to me. I think he had been arrested for fraud.

We had done a guttering job for this old lady in Leyland a couple of months previously and unbeknown to me he had charged her £30 and had tried changing the cheque to £300 and was arrested. I was left in the cell all day not knowing what was going to happen to me. My mother came visiting us both and the copper who had tried chasing me over the rooftops of Market Street was telling her how lucky I was not to have been killed. She must have been well brassed off visiting her son and her husband at the same time in the police cells.

That night I was taken to Red Bank remand home, near Warrington, by a social worker. It was quite late, so they fed and showered me and put in a cell on my own. That was when the situation hit me hard and I must admit I was really scared of what I might be facing the following morning. I had never been on my own like this before and I must admit that night I cried myself to sleep.

I had heard all about these places and I was scared thinking what might happen to me the next day. But when

I was let out the next day I was quite pumped up and ready for any kind of hassle that might come my way, but I'd worried over nothing. We had breakfast and only a couple of lads spoke to me, which I had no problem with at all, as I just wanted to keep myself to myself.

A little later on in the morning my social worker came for me and I was taken back to Chorley Juvenile Court and remanded for four weeks in custody. Later on, my social worker took me to Woodend remand home, also near Warrington. It was mainly for under sixteens, but there was around six over sixteens there as well. Once again I arrived quite late, so I had my tea on my own in the canteen with four screws watching me. I was just finishing off having my brew, (something I hadn't really done for two days). It was a big blue plastic mug and one of the screws told me not to use both hands to hold it. At the time I couldn't see what difference it made and I cannot remember what I said back. But I think that I very nearly ended up in confinement (block) on my first hour of being there, which is not hard to achieve in those kinds of places. The way I saw it, if I would not take that kind of thing from my mother, I certainly was not going to take it from him, even if he was twice my size and that I was easily outnumbered, four to one.

Once again, I kept mainly myself to myself most of the time, but at nights we had telly in a communal room and because I was over sixteen I was allowed three fags a night. As I didn't smoke I swapped them for Mars bars or some kind of sweets. While there I had all kinds of tests, ink spots, all kinds of questions. Because I was away from my family, I started to realise what scum they really were, especially my stepdad and how he had brainwashed and groomed me and the abuse had affected me. When you're in the thick of it though, you don't notice what is really happening around you.

When my mother and stepdad came to see me one Saturday afternoon on a visit, I refused outright to see them, but I was told I had to see them; it wasn't an option. So I sat in the visiting room in front of them and refused to speak. I think in some ways I was blaming them for me being where I was and in some ways it was their fault, but in reality it was my fault. I was the one who had done the crimes.

My mother started crying and my stepdad started threatening me with violence in front of everyone if I didn't start talking to her. He had showed his true colours. Eventually, they had to give up and go home. Some of the other lads who were in the visiting room at the time and had witnessed it, started asking me what it was all about and some tried to take the meikle out of me because of it. I told them more or less to mind their own business and most did. The bottom line was, it was just entertainment to them.

The only bit of trouble I had while I was in there was from a lad who was in the same dorm as me. One morning when I woke up, I caught him masturbating. There was only three of us in a four-person room and when we all went down for breakfast he decided to tell everyone that I had been the one masturbating, not him. Of course I was mortified. I was embarrassed and angry with him. My reaction made the situation even worse, because now the others kept winding me up over it. I didn't realise at the time, that it was just entertainment for them to help pass the time. Eventually, they got bored of it, but I kept having a pop at the real culprit. It was just friendly banter.

On the funny side of it though, while I was there the governor, who was the spitting image of the *Master from the Kung Fu* programme would wind up most of us, and say, "Once you take the pebble from my hand you can go." We all tried, I tried around a dozen times, but none of us could do it. Not that he would have ever let us out, but it was a much-needed laugh.

I went back to court and was put in the care of my first stepdad and at first, everything was fine. I found a job in an exhaust factory in Lower Adlington which was my very first proper job with proper wages.

In those days because I was only sixteen, my take-home pay was about £27 a week. I gave half to my first stepdad for my keep and managed for a whole month before going back to my old ways, thieving. I cannot honestly say why I started thieving again. I had more than enough money to get by. Perhaps I missed the adrenalin buzz it gave me and the fact that because the first time I had got in trouble all my friends did not want anything to do with me anymore and that did make me think, *perhaps I'm not doing what I should be doing.* Not like the present day at all, it's the opposite now. This time I was more careful and I was not doing anywhere near as many break-ins.

The strange thing is though, we got broke into ourselves and I knew it was my sister who had done it, because in my room there were these massive set of blue drawers (I bet they're still there now). They had a secret drawer and that is where I kept my money. When I found money missing I knew it was her. There was only family who knew about the drawer, but I didn't realise it was my sister straight away. So I told my dad about the money going missing and he said to go to the police. I know if I had said to my dad I think it was my sister who'd done it, it wouldn't have gone down too well. He would have more than likely kicked me out on the streets for saying it was my sister because in his eyes she could do no wrong. In reality, though, she was far worse than me in a lot of ways. In my book you never thieve from your own or tell lies over each other in any circumstances.

So I went to the police, but, all they said was "now you know what it's like" and nearly broke their ribs laughing at me. I was to find out that this was a very common thing when you break the law. Perhaps the police think it's all part of your punishment and quite a few coppers think they are judges. They also like stopping you in the street in front of everyone every two minutes like they did many times with me, in Chorley, Leeds and even London. They are mainly bent coppers who give you grief like that and believe me I have come across loads of them in my time, but also some decent ones too. When I say decent I mean coppers where the uniform doesn't go to their heads.

Going back to my job, when I first went for the interview, I had asked the foreman who interviewed me, if I could be trained up as a welder and true to his word they trained me for around two weeks. It was only MIG welding and I lasted a couple of weeks before I was taken off it and put back on my old job because the guy I had been working couldn't not cope with his workload.

I must admit I was quite annoyed with him, as I thought he was a friend. We had even met up one weekend and I went to Horwich Baths with him and his mate. I sussed out a few days later that they had a hidden agenda, i.e., they wanted my posterior. I realised this was when we started ducking each other like most people do in the baths or sea. They kept pulling me down under the water so that I was sat on their faces. I thought at the time that they were a bit over friendly, but I was quite naive about that kind of thing in those days. I guess they wanted to admire it more closely and who could blame them? But they weren't going to get it, so maybe it was sour grapes that he did what he did to get me from being trained up as a welder. Who knows?

To be honest, I wasn't that bothered about sex with anyone around that time. My head was so screwed up with everything that had happened with my parents splitting up and in some ways was still happening in the way my family were with me and because Chorley in those days, the early Seventies, was quite a small town. In no way am I trying to insult anyone from Chorley, but small-town people generally are quite small-minded. The reason I say this is that although I never knew anything until many years later (the early Nineties), there was a rumour going around Chorley that I was gay or bi. I believe my sister knew about it, but she never told me anything about it. I was only told by a girlfriend of my brother-in-law's, brother who knew me from one of my first stepdad's neighbours while I was decorating for her. It's no wonder I never had any luck with the opposite sex very often back in those days. Maybe if I had met someone half decent it might just have sorted me out much sooner. Things happen for a reason as they say.

Within a few months, the police had hold of me once again. I was caught in a clothes warehouse in Friday Street, Chorley and again I was remanded in custody, but this time I was put in a children's home in Chorley. I was only sixteen. For the first couple of weeks I wasn't allowed anywhere outside the house. I didn't even venture out into the back garden. I wasn't locked in. I could have done a runner at any time, but it never crossed my mind.

To make matters worse there was a girl there around my age and she kept coming on to me. On my attraction-rating scale she was a 15-pinter plus and her attitude matched how she looked. Once she was sat in the living room with me while I was watching telly and she was trying her best to chat me up. She was still in her short bedclothes in the afternoon and at one point she let out a loud fart, which nearly made me retch and her attractiveness went even further down the scale. She slept in the next bedroom to me and there was an adjoining door into each of our rooms. I was so glad that there was a bed in the way of the door, or she would have eaten me for breakfast.

A few months or so later, I was in Chorley Baths on my own and the same girl came in with a very slim attractive-looking girl who turned round to the big girl and more or less said she fancied me. The fat one turned around and said, "You have no chance there, he is gay." So I lost out there. I have found out throughout my life, there is no defence against backstabbers especially in my case when you don't have anyone half decent or genuine watching your back.

When I first arrived at the children's home my dad came to drop off some of my stuff. My other sister was with him and one of my aunties, my dad's sister and my dad's sister. We had a lot in common. We hated each other, big style. She made Cruella seem a decent person and she gave me a really hard time, telling me to say sorry to my stepdad for getting into trouble. By the time they all went, which wasn't long, I had to go to my room to get over their visit. It made me very depressed, even broken-hearted, but not suicidal and it just added to how much I hated my dad's sister. After a couple of days I was totally over it and back to my old self.

Thankfully, there was good news coming my way for once. I wasn't allowed to go back to my mother and my first stepdad certainly didn't want me anywhere near him.

When I went back to court I was put in the care of a friend, the farmer from Croston. After we had worked on his house we had become good friends and I would visit him and his wife a couple of times a week. At one point, when I was fifteen, very nearly sixteen, I tried to run away from home to them, basically to get away from all the abuse I was suffering. Because I was under age by a couple of months, I had to return home to the abuse.

It seems that in those days you could go into school with black eyes, all sorts of cuts and bruises and teachers and police seemed like they weren't bothered. The police sent me back home (even though I told the copper what was happening he simply didn't want to know) to suffer even more abuse from my second stepdad. If I had been allowed to stay on the farm, I doubt I would have ever been in trouble with the police at all. Of course I would say that now, wouldn't I? I should have kept walking and tried my chances sleeping rough in London. As I look back now, I think I would have had a much better life.

Thankfully, the court put me in the farmer's care. In return for my keep I would help around the farm, which to be honest I loved. I learned a lot from him. I think I even looked up to him as a father figure in some ways. I had never had a chance of meeting my real blood dad, because of my mother's lies. The farmer was certainly more of a father to me than my two stepdads had ever been.

He and his wife were genuine people with no hidden agendas. What you saw is what you got and apart from when I was in the depths of alcoholism, I have tried my best to live my life the way they showed me. I cannot stand mind game players, as in my family, their friends and even my friends and even the tabloids. I would not class any of them as genuine or trustworthy.

I lived on the farm for around six months, I was never bored. There was always something to do. Every Thursday morning we would all get in the farmer's Ford Zephyr and go to Chorley, While he and his wife would do the shopping, I would go to the bus station for my read of *Farmer's Weekly* and commercial news.

One day when I was going back to the car, I bumped into my sister on the cattle market. She seemed very upset and she was telling me, my mother was very depressed because I didn't want to know her anymore, which was not true. I didn't want to know them because of my second stepdad. I told my sister I would visit them only because my stepdad was in jail at the time. I didn't want to be anywhere near him. On reflection I should have stayed well away from my mother and sister as well, as in reality they were just as bad as my stepdad, if not worse.

When the farmer and his wife came back to their car and we were on our way back to Croston, I told them both what had happened with my sister and the farmer told me I should go and see my mother. It was not that I needed his permission. I valued his opinion. I had total trust in them both.

I visited my mother and it was worse than I had been told. She was a complete mess, the house stank of urine, because of the kids wetting their beds etc. and it was a complete tip. (When my mother was with my first stepdad she was very house proud). I stayed there for about half an hour before I went on to visit my first stepdad, for a brew and a chat.

I started visiting my mother every Sunday after that and on some visits, she was begging and pleading with me to come back home. I loved it on the farm, but every visit to mother's affected my mental health a lot. It was like a grenade going off in my head every time I visited her. Subsequently, I got very depressed about it all, so much so, I attempted to hang myself.

One early evening I went for a stroll round the fields and noticed this tree near a nearby farm. It was quite remote. A couple of days later I took a rope with me. I was certain about what I was about to do, but looking back now, my head must have been totally screwed up to even think about doing this. There were all kinds of stuff going round in my head, but the main thing was I felt I was never going to be free of my abusers (my family). I put the rope around a strong tree branch then put the noose around my neck and jumped. Once I had jumped I changed my mind. A bit late I know, when you're hanging by a rope, but thankfully, I was able to swing holding the rope as best I could until I could reach a branch and take the noose off. It wasn't easy and I think I soiled myself in the process, but it also left quite a large rope burn around my neck and I had to wear a scarf all the time for about a week in the middle of summer until it faded.

I didn't want anyone knowing what I had tried to do. The farmer kept asking me about the scarf. In no way do I blame the farmer or his wife. They were more loving than any of my own family had ever been put together throughout my whole life. I blame my mother for screwing me up as much as she did. As far as I can remember I never told the farmer anything about me trying to hang myself and this incident didn't do my mental state any good at all. I was now even more screwed up than before, but I gave up on the idea of suicide.

I realised that I needed to get as far away as I could from everyone, mostly my family, so I tried to join the Navy. That was a no go, as I had been in trouble with the police. I even tried the RAF, again the same happened. Once you get in any kind of trouble you carry it around like a ball and chain for the rest of your life and career and as soon as people find out about your past, there are all kinds of allegations thrown at you.

I now know that I was destined to have a lot of dead-end jobs and as I mentioned before, once people find out you have been in trouble, they resort to pre-judging you. They don't bother about finding out why you did what you did. Hopefully, someone who is reading this will think twice about getting into any kind of bother with the police because if I had a chance to change the fact I had been in strife with the police, I would do it in an instant. It does mess up the rest of your life, big style.

Within six months my mother won me over and I moved back in with her. The farmer and his wife were not very happy about it at all. I think they knew I was making a big mistake and looking back I was. Within a few weeks I was up to my old tricks, thieving and breaking into places and I know my mother knew what I was up to and she seemed to encourage me to do it at times and even gave me a drawer of my own in her room to lock my money away.

It was a set of three wooden office type drawers which you could lock and I was given the bottom one, I never suspected a thing. I didn't know at first that there was a thin piece of wood in between each drawer. One day I checked the drawer and money was missing. I, of course, kicked off wanting to know where my money had gone, but no one wanted to admit to anything, which was the usual thing.

I'm quite sure some of you might be thinking serves him right, but that money was my wages too. In no way have I ever been classed as a career criminal. I worked and my thieving was my way out of all the abuse I was getting from my stepfather and my family.

I found a way around what they had done. I simply swapped the drawers round so now I had the top one. This made my stepfather very abusive and it was not long before they found another way of ripping me off. They were like leeches. I admit stealing is wrong, but stealing from your own is more than despicable.

The mental/physical abuse from my stepdad made me go out burgling even more, mainly to get out of his way. I seriously thought about living rough for a few weeks at least.

If I had not had the family I had, I know my life would have been a lot easier. I doubt I would have ever been in trouble with the police. I'm glad now how my life has turned out. I am now in a much better place with only real, genuine people around me. They are all much more upfront people, but I'm always watching for the leeches I have banished out of my life. I doubt they will be far away. They will find a way of stalking me.

Sometimes we would have a rough sleeper working with us called Georgie Prez. I'm not sure that was his real name and I asked for his advice about living rough. He told me about the bins behind supermarkets. When I checked them out they were all locked up, so I changed my mind on rough sleeping. I doubted it would have worked out for me. I had no friends so most nights I went breaking into places, hardly ever people's homes, mainly shops or some kind of business. It was as if I was addicted to the adrenalin buzz and it gave me or some kind of escapism, maybe both.

The house we lived in at the time was mortgaged and I don't think my mother could afford the payments so we ended up moving to Lower Adlington, into a three-bedroom council house. It was a nice home, which backed on to countryside, which I loved. I had only been there at the most a couple of months before I was caught by the police in the council offices in Market Street, Chorley. This time I was in a lot more trouble because on the previous two occasions I had been given supervision orders and fined. This time I was put on remand and I was now heading for crown court and to top it all I was sent to grisly Risley as it was known then and believe me it lived up to its nickname.

At the time I was back and forth each week going to Chorley Magistrates Court. The first week I was in, I was padded up with a Manchester lad, who was quite a bit bigger and stronger than me and was about 20. I was 17 and I was scrawny. He had this novel idea that if I committed suicide he would get let out on compassionate grounds, so he was beating me up every night when the lights went out at 10 pm, but not in a way to show marks. Then he would start with the mental abuse. Luckily, I was only in that cell a week, but it took its toll.

I knew I was not in a nice, friendly place and if I didn't toughen up fast, my life would be hell, so I did my best to do just that, although being that I was classed as a woolly back or a country gobbin, I was seriously outnumbered on both sides. Mancs hated us and so did the Liverpudlians, but I soon got my head around what I had to do to survive. Even when I didn't stand a chance of winning a fight I would still fight. That way most people would not mess with me, only a few, but most inmates just wanted to sit on their pots and get through their bird as best they could and that is what I tried to do with mine, all four and a half years of it, in total.

I suppose all the abuse I had suffered from my stepdad had hardened me up quite a bit. Punches never seem to hurt like they used to, but I never once thought of suicide, it just wasn't an option. After the Mancunian pad mate, my pad mates were fairly decent, so positive can come out of negative. I was in there for about six weeks waiting to go to the crown court; it's always a bit of a wait.

It was not all that bad. Because I was a YP we were close to the women's wing and mostly when we were on exercise the women would be shouting rude stuff at us and hanging their tits out their windows. It was entertaining, the only trouble with that was neither side could get together, so some, if not all of us, had to stand our sheets up in the corners of our cells in the mornings, including me. I suppose you could say this was my apprenticeship into masturbation.

While I was in Risley there was a lad about my age from Blackpool. He had been nicked for making a pipe bomb, with weed killer and sugar. He was pleading not guilty because his intention was not to harm anyone. It turned out he was acquitted and to be honest I was pleased for him. He was even on *Granada News*. To look at him he wouldn't have harmed a fly. The police were bang out of order nicking him like they did. That's the way they are. No wonder they're called wooden tops.

My big day came to go to Preston Crown Court. I knew I was not going to get out. I was pleading guilty. I was up in front of Judge Openshaw, the last judge to sentence someone to death. I was filling my nappy waiting for him to put the black cloth on his head. I ended up getting six to two borstal and was sent to Strangeways for allocation. Again, I had a six-week wait. In the daytime before tea, we were not allowed to sleep on our beds, because we had our kit arranged neatly on our beds, similar to how they do in the army. I'm quite sure a lot did what I did and moved their kits carefully and had a kip. There was this screw who would creep around in slippers and if he caught you, you were nicked and lost pay or privileges. On one occasion while I was mopping our landing, a bit of the mop caught him and he went berserk. He was saying it was assault. If only we had been outside I would have showed him what assault really was. He was a complete idiot; some people abuse their authority. He was certainly one of them.

Because I was classed as a country bumpkin, i.e., not a Liverpudlian or a Mancunian, I kept myself to myself and tried to stay out of trouble as best I could. Within a few days though of being there a couple of lads demanded I give them tobacco, which I did because I didn't smoke so it was no hardship to me. I didn't realise at the time that they were taking the meikle, but, the penny dropped quite soon after. Thankfully, it was just a one-off. Being weak in those places is no fun and I certainly was weak and shy around that time.

I had three pad mates. The first one was only in on my first night. He was from Dewsbury and seemed a nice guy. The second one was from Manchester somewhere and the silly bugger was spitting out the window one night and managed to spit out his false teeth as well. To recover them he had to volunteer to go on parcel duty. The thing was I had to accompany him. I wasn't happy. The funny thing was he found his teeth embedded in a pile of faeces and I took the meikle out of him after that.

One night two screws came to see him. They ordered me out of the cell and they were with him for about ten minutes or more. When I was finally let back in I asked him what it was all about. He never really told me. I have seen screws do this since and it is usually with nonces, so, maybe that is what it was about.

My third pad mate was a Liverpudlian from Halewood and we got on well, in fact very well sexually wise. At the time it disgusted me. It didn't change things. I just told him it wasn't for me. He kept trying though, but I never partook.

Eventually, I was allocated to an open borstal not far from Doncaster. It was like going back to big school all over again. Most of the lads there were a lot bigger, stronger and older than me. I decided to keep myself to myself as much as I could. There was a communal area with a television. At first I hardly went in and after tea I would lie on my bed and read a book. It was my way of escaping from my reality and my way of self-preservation.

In the day I would usually be working seven days a week on the farm. At first I did every day jobs, such as digging ditches,etc., but within a month I was driving tractors, helping to plant stuff, which I loved, but I ended up damaging a couple of tractors and got the sack from that job. One of the accidents I had I was very lucky not to have killed myself because I jack-knifed a tractor and trailer into the corner of a concrete cow shed. I was going far too fast around a corner, lost control and managed to hit the corner of the cowshed totally bending one of the front wheels in on itself. It was quite a big tractor as well (Ford 5000), so it took some doing. I thought I will lose bird for this for sure.

Thankfully, I didn't. The governor was quite understanding about it all, which shocked me a bit, but it might have had a lot to do with the fact that none of the screws believed it was me who had done it. I think they had seen how I was being treated at times by other inmates. It wasn't physical, more verbal put-downs and constantly being ridiculed every day. Because I was quite a shy person anyway I seemed to dwell more on what was being said and I went into my shell more and more each day.

What didn't help was my mother and stepdad saying they were coming to visit me, but not turning up deliberately. I took time off work and stayed on the wings waiting for them. It was more than likely a silly mind game by my stepdad, to mess with my head. At times I got quite depressed because of this and with all the bullying I had to endure, although I was never beaten up, which is something I suppose, but to me, mental abuse is far worse than physical abuse.

Around the time I was there, they were in the process of building a gym and some of the lads from a neighbouring borstal were working on it as well. One day just before tea one of our guys asked me to come with him to look around the gym, so he said. We hadn't been there ten minutes when we went into this small side room, where one of the neighbouring borstal lads was. He pushed me hard against the wall and demanded sex of some kind from me. I, of course, refused and that made him angry. He was a lot bigger and stronger than me and I knew I would not stand a chance in a fight against him. When I broke down crying he gave up on the idea of raping me and let me go back to my wing.

Now, if ever I see the rape scene in *Scum*, it always reminds of what could have very easily happened to me on that day and to be honest it scares the daylights out of me and I cannot stand to watch it.

A few months later, I was in my cell, minding my own business reading my book, when about six to eight lads came rushing in on me, the biggest of them and the ringleader was a lad from Doncaster. His nickname was Donkey Dick for obvious reasons. They all had me pinned down on my bed and Donkey Dick was sat on my chest and was trying to force himself on me. One of the others tried something else. All this happened in a matter of minutes and I quickly broke free and they all ran off.

I went after them with a metal chair that was in my cell and I hit this lad who I thought was one of them. It turned out he had nothing to do with it at all, but it sent a strong message to the others not to come anywhere near me in the future, which they didn't. It all added to my hatred of rapists and nonces.

On another occasion in our dining room on the farm one weekend, we were waiting for our dinner to be delivered and to pass the time this big lad was wrestling with me. At first it was just friendly play fighting, nothing serious, but he wasn't winning, so he started losing his temper with me and at one point I was lying on the floor and he was just about to come down hard on my chest with his knee, which, with his combined weight and the force he was putting into it, would easily have broken my breast bone.. But as he was coming down with his knee I quickly rolled out of the way and he kneed the concrete floor hard. I'm not sure how much damage he did to his knee, but I know he would have broken his kneecap for sure. As I thought at the time, better his kneecap than my breast bone.

While I was doing borstal, I attempted my Duke of Edinburgh bronze award. I was genuinely wanting to do it, it was not a way of getting out of the borstal as some did, but you cannot blame them. To pass it we had to do first aid, canoeing, rock-climbing, mapreading, animal husbandry and tractor driving. I did it all, but I didn't pass on the mapreading. All the others, bar me, couldn't be bothered to do it.

A couple of months later, I succeeded in doing the

52.5 mile Crosses walk over the Yorkshire Moors. It is run by the army and out of the ten of us in our group, I was the only one to finish and the gym teacher who was with me. I'm not quite sure if he was happy about me carrying on or not, because he would have had to keep me company in case I absconded. It was never my intention, even though I was not that far from home at some points of the walk. If I'd done a runner I would have been constantly looking over my shoulder. I go for KISS every time (keep it simple stupid).

Before we had all set off on the day of the walk, the screw in charge of the kitchens told us all that whoever finished would get 10 Mars bars from him. I didn't finish it to get the Mars bars, I just wanted to finish it as an achievement. I did it in 20 hours and 25 minutes. When we all got back to the borstal and showered and went down for tea, the kitchen screw addressed the whole borstal in the dining room. He said he had seen how other inmates had been treating me in the past and being that I was the only one to have finished the walk, I had showed them all up for what they were: cowardly bullies. It mostly went down well and I gained more respect from the more intelligent ones.

The next day my legs ached and I had blisters on my blisters. I still went to work the next day. I was now the head stockman, but my main job was looking after the pigs, mucking them out, castrating them, etc. The worst part of my job was occasionally we would get a weak pig in one of the pens, where the other pigs would pick on it with no remorse. It was sickening to watch (humans are much worse, as I found out from 1985 until 1993).

The only right thing to do for the pig was to kill it, not something I ever enjoyed doing, but I knew it had to be done. If I'd had any choice I would have killed the bullies, but then there would have only been one pig left in the pen, but I hate bullies and bullying of any kind. All the abuse I went through as a kid, teenager, even as an adult, can follow you in life. It certainly has with me.

Eventually, my discharge hearing came up and all the screws gave me a glowing report and I ended up getting out four weeks earlier than I had expected. This proved not to be a good thing, because although I was a better person in a lot of ways while in borstal, I went back out to all the abuse from my stepdad and the rest of my family. Nothing had changed there. I found a job pretty quickly, but in those days jobs were easy to find.

My job was on a building site helping to lay main drains on a new housing estate in Clayton-le -Woods and mainly, I enjoyed it. The only down side was that it was two bus trips away, so I had to get up very early in the morning to get there. At least I was doing what I loved, driving a three-ton dump truck. By night, I was doing a very good Raffles impersonation, mainly because I could not stay in the same house as my stepdad. I hated him so much and didn't want to breathe the same air as him. Then, within six weeks I was nicked once again.

I had made the mistake of doing the same place twice and with the same MO (*modus operandi*). It was to break in at height and search safes, but by sticking to how I had done the place before, it didn't turn out to be a good thing. I committed the crime on a Thursday night. Next day I went to work as usual, but little did I know the police were watching my every move, until the following morning (Saturday).

On the Saturday morning, there was a knock at the door. Somehow my mother knew it was the police and she told me to hide behind the couch. The police searched the whole house and wanted to look behind the couch where I was hidden. My mother refused to move, but the police said, "We'll get him, so tell him to hand himself in", which I did a couple of hours later. Three CID officers questioned me for about five hours, each taking turns, one went out, another came in. I never had a break in those five hours.

When they searched my bedroom they found a camera and the main guy confronted me with it. The detective inspector said to me angrily, "What's this?" I turned round and said sarcastically, "It's a camera, of course." He smacked me across my face with the back of his hand, cutting the inside of my lip. I gave in after that and told them everything I had done in the last six weeks that I had been out.

I was taken down to the cells and within a couple of hours my mother came to see me and told me to deny everything, even though I had already admitted the offences. The CID bloke bodily threw my mother out of the police station.

I think the reason why my mother had said deny everything was that I had hidden £1,500 behind the Emerson heater in the bathroom. I know now my stepdad and mother would have helped themselves to it and they did not want the police taking it back off them.

When it came to charging me, rather stupidly I denied everything as I had been told to do by my mother. When I went to the magistrates' court, I pleaded not guilty. I must have been off my rocker to do anything my family told me to do. It is like they say, 'If you lay down with dogs you are bound to get fleas'. But everyone has 20/20 hindsight, don't they?

On reflection, apart from the money which would

have seemed like a pools win to them, another reason for my mother to say plead not guilty would have been that my stepdad would have thought the longer he gets in the nick the longer he is (me) out the way so he could mess with my younger sister. Believe me, if I had caught him at it, I know I would have killed him.

He had started messing with my sister from eleven until she was sixteen, but, for most of that time I was in borstal or prison so I was out the picture. If not, I would definitely have sussed him out and it would have been a totally different matter. I firmly believe my mother knew nothing about what he was up to with my sister, because most nonces are good at covering their tracks.

When I went back to Risley, which seemed to be fast becoming my second home, I had to wear a brown itchy uniform. That was the only downside to pleading not guilty. The good thing was I could get food and fags on visits, but that proved to be more hassle than it was worth, as other inmates got a bit jealous and jealousy makes people get very violent in prison, so I had to keep it down to just fags. I could hide them, so less hassle.

I was in Risley for six weeks on remand and again for the first few weeks I was back and forth to the magistrates, so I had different cellmates nearly every week. Thankfully, I only had one bad one and he came from a big family from Birkenhead and it seemed most of his brothers were also inside.

One day we had a bit of an argument and that night he told me not to fall asleep as that would be the last thing I would ever do. I think I was on edge all the time I was in that cell with him. I think he was totally in the wrong place, as he was a nutter. In the six weeks that I was on remand in Risley. I was also padded up with his brother, but he was totally different. In fact, he was a nice guy.

Because he could neither read nor write, I wrote his letters and read his replies out to him. Of course, once I had been committed to Crown I was given a job in reception, which meant I was out of my cell most of the time and no exercise yard at all, which I loved. I always hated walking round and round in circles for an hour. It was not as if we got fresh air while we were out. All you could smell were parcels or on a Friday the fish. Prison has a certain smell to it and it is not nice, so not going on exercise was a very big plus in my book. Working in reception was mostly good, apart from getting a black eye off a big Welsh guy one day.

It all started with simple banter. We were just messing about in reception and I happened to call him a bastard in jest. At one point he tried to ram my face into a wall. I was lucky to come away with just a black eye and a chipped tooth. He was another nut job, to say the least.

While I was still in Risley I had another pad mate from Wales (I know another Welshman). At one point he got so desperate for a fag he wanted to blow me, it was a no brainer in my book, it was either his mouth or my hand and I had the same thing from a lad who was from Preston.

Eventually, I had my day in the crown court. I was in front of Judge Kershaw this time and because I was pleading not guilty, I was back and forth to Risley. The trial lasted three days. I ended up changing my plea after that time, because the prosecution ran rings around me like anyone would have done because I am a terrible liar and in no time at all, I didn't even know my own name after he had finished cross-examining me. I managed however to worry the CID who had arrested me, because it came out that the one in charge had slapped me across the face. As usual in these cases I had no proof. It was my word against his so I had no chance at all.

Judge Kershaw was very upset by the time it came to sentencing me, because when you plead not guilty and you are found guilty, judges take a very dim view of it. He said at the time that if I had been eighteen or over I would have been looking at a long time in jail and he warned me not to come in front of him again, because he would throw the book at me. He then sentenced me to 6-2 borstal and I was later taken to Strangeways.

Three of us were in a cell. One guy was from Farnworth and another from Ince in Wigan somewhere. They were both sound guys, the only bad thing about it was we were all in for Christmas, so it was quite depressing to say the least. We got through it, no choice really.

The only bad thing that happened was one day we were all going down to the canteen and while we were waiting, I was mucking about with one of my pad mates. I pushed him back in fun and he accidentally rang the riot bell. I admitted to it straight away like anyone would do, but ten screws grabbed me and took me down the block. I kept trying to tell them it was an accident and not intentional, but they were having none of it. The screw who was in charge of the block got me out of the cell and started laying into me. It was as if he was using me as a human punchbag, but he had an audience which made it worse for me. Bullies love an audience. I used my arms to fend off most of the punches, but some got through. He then put me back in the cell for an hour, then two lads came to my cell door threatening violence when I was let out to slop out, which I thought was quite extreme. In prison you can get a beating just for looking at someone in the wrong way. It's all about power and control. Eventually, they let me out to go back to my cell on the wing with a stern warning and I must admit it did shake me up a bit and that was the first and last time I had ever been down the block. Getting out the block was like an early Christmas present for me.

After about four weeks I was allocated back to Gringley on the Hill. As you might expect the screws were not happy to see me back there and this time I was a totally different person. This time I knew the script and I knew what was what and what I needed to do to survive. I wasn't going to be bullied by anyone. I think I had come to realise, win or lose, you have to fight to gain respect although I didn't have that many fights while I was there.

I was a lot fitter than before. Quite a gym bunny! Most kept their distance, not because I was a bully. I just didn't take any rubbish from anyone. My thoughts were, *if I would not take it from my mother, I certainly will not take it from you.* In no way was I ever a bully. I suppose as I was not suffering the abuse from my family, I had more respect for myself now.

For the first few months I had a little sideline. I was a tobacco baron. I would give someone a quarter of an ounce of tobacco and they would give me half an ounce back when they got paid. All was going well until some smart boy refused to pay what he owed me, even when I threatened to throw him down the stairs. But it was only a threat. I have no stomach for violence. He ran to this bigger guy, who hated me with a vengeance. I didn't have the stomach for all that rubbish any more, so I just gave it up as a bad job. The down side of all that was that the screws noticed I was buying tobacco and they knew I was a non-smoker, so one day when I was buying tobacco they quizzed me about buying it, so now and again I would have a fag in front of them. Trouble was I soon got hooked on fags in no time. Karma can be such a bitch and thirty years later, (now) I am back to being a non-smoker, but it took nearly thirty years to put it down. I know, serves me right really.

One Sunday night I was called into the main office as my mother had sent me something that needed signing. One of the screws was quite adamant that I shouldn't sign it, but he did not or could not explain why. He could probably see I was going to get ripped off.

I found out why when I went back home on leave for a week. I made Chorley my first stop, because I wanted to go to the bank first to draw out some money. I was thinking I had about £400 plus in, but it turned out I only had 95p. Apparently my mother had forged my signature and withdrawn nearly all my money. I noticed they had certainly been living the high life while I was away. They had a Ford Zephyr and two vans. I made my feelings known straight away, but it was like water off a duck's back. They sat there and laughed at me. It was like that saying, *'What's yours is ours and what's ours is ours.'* Altogether they stole about £3,000 off me on that occasion.

OK, I know some of you might be thinking, it serves me right, but at least half that money was my wages and it was my means of moving out and being as far away from my abusers, the scum I had as a family and getting out of all the abuse I was suffering at home. There are always two sides to every story and there was a purpose to my wrongdoings. I have never been a career criminal in any way, more a persistent petty criminal, who was not very good at it as I kept getting caught.

Later on that day my stepdad gave me a fiver to spend, which, to be honest, I thought was an out and out joke, but I still took it and caught the bus to Chorley. I was quite angry about what they had done to me and getting drunk didn't seem to quieten my anger, so even though I was not really dressed or even equipped for it, I pressed my self destruct button and tried burgling a few places. I had no tools to get in anywhere anyway so I gave up on that idea fairly quickly.

As it was a nice warm summer's night and I suppose I was enjoying my freedom, I thought it would be good to take my time walking back home. To be honest I had no compulsion to go home at all. I think it was about three miles from Chorley to Lower Adlington, where I lived, but I was mooching around as well, so it took a bit longer or it would have done if I hadn't found an old banger at the back of some houses in Bolton Road, near Albany High School, Chorley.

It was a Ford Cortina and the owner probably left the keys in so some numpty (like me) would nick it, then he could claim on the insurance. So, looking back, I did the owner a favour. It started first time. I drove it to the end of the backs just as a police car was passing. The copper looked right at me and I couldn't have timed it more wrongly if I had tried and I knew he had recognised me. Most of the Chorley police knew me. I quickly turned the opposite way, but the car was an old banger, not what you would class as a getaway car. Somehow I reached my destination, Lower Adlington, without being caught.

Although I didn't realise it fully at the time, the copper knew I had nicked the car, so he could have gone to the station, had a brew, something to eat, a fag, toilet, shave and then come back and nicked me. In fact, that is more than likely what he did.

When I got into Lower Adlington, I thought that I should hide the car and I had this stupid idea, (nowt unusual there). I tried to go over the train lines (the main

Manchester to Glasgow line) and hide it on the other side of the tracks, but the car bottomed on the tracks and as much as I tried to move it off, it wouldn't move. I panicked and ran off back home. In no time at all my house was surrounded by police. I had not been out twenty-four hours and I was back inside. I spent my eighteenth birthday in Chorley police cells and I must say I felt a complete idiot and I had only myself to blame.

There was no point denying it. I was bang to rights and the police, for some reason, kept me in the cells for a week. They took all my clothes apart from my undies and I had to go to court every day with just a blanket wrapped around me. I had been charged so there was no reason to keep me in the cells so I had to keep going to court every day. For some reason they would not put me in a cell with a toilet. I know I had broken the law, but it was hardly a civilised way to treat anyone. You put a uniform on someone and they think they are judge and jury. I have no idea why courts came about, because some coppers think they are judge and jury and prison officers perhaps watch too many cowboy films and think they are sheriffs or something.

After a few days a British Rail transport policeman visited me in the cells. I think he just wanted to know if I had done it deliberately or not, as in, to derail a train, which I had no intention of doing. He told me I was very lucky that it was a big locomotive that had hit the car. If it had been the normal kind of passenger train, it would have derailed it and I would be looking at a very long time in prison, as people would have been hurt or even worse, killed. Of course, this shocked me to the core.

I doubt that if that had happened I would have been able to live with that on my mind. It's bad enough living with what I did on Brook Street bridge when I was eleven or twelve. Even though it was accidental, the result would have been the same.

I was remanded to Risley. I hadn't had a shower or been to the toilet properly in over a week. I suppose I just couldn't relax enough while in the police cells and the toilet I was allowed to use was one where I would have been watched by a copper. He would have been tutting and telling me to get a move on. It's not as if I could have gone anywhere else. Even now, if I have to go into public toilets I cannot bear having another bloke standing beside me.

While on the subject of loos, since spotting myself in the tabloids, I am always on my guard, as it is far too easy for someone to say I have done something, even though I know absolutely I have not, so I go in the cubicles where possible to avoid anything like that happening. Paranoid I know, but a little bit of paranoia does you good sometimes.

We got to Risley fairly late on, so we were quickly processed through reception. This time I was in a dorm with about seven other lads, but the thing was some idiot had dismantled one of the beds and by the time I had realised what was happening I was the one with it. I tried kicking off about it. The other lads ganged up on me and I had to let it go. I got my own back though, as quite suddenly I wanted to go to the toilet and it was very nearly past the baby's head alert time. I rang the bell to ask the screw. I had no chance. Even if I had been dying he would not have opened that door. I think the screws see it as part of your punishment.

So I had to do what I had to do, so I filled the pot so much that no one could use it after me so they had to do it out of the window and of course I shared the smell with them all. Karma can arrive pretty rapid at times. They didn't call it grisly Risley for nowt and that smell was grisly.

Very early the next day I was shipped out to Strangeways. I didn't even have time to slop out so I had to leave the pot to my ex pad mates. I wonder if they drew straws to empty it. When I got to Strangeways, it seemed that I was in reception for ages. I had to write a statement to the governor of Gringley on the Hill. What also didn't help was I couldn't get off the loo for most of the day.

I knew that I was looking at a long time in prison and it would be prison this time and not borstal. The fact I had hardly seen the light of day between sentences frustrated me quite a bit. I had to get on with it. I had no choice.

While in Strangeways I was banged up for twenty-three hours a day, seven days a week, so I just read books. It was my way of escaping. I met an old friend while in there. He was a cleaner so he kept popping round for a chat. After a couple of weeks I was shipped off to Stoke Heath, a closed borstal, and for the first couple of weeks I was hardly let out of my cell, so again I just got books to read off the other guys and more or less kept myself to myself.

Even though I was banged up I still made friends and even enemies with other inmates. One of them was a Welsh guy who had done a runner from Gringley on the Hill, my old borstal. For some reason, he was blaming me for what had happened to him, escaping and of course getting caught. Before he had done the runner he had asked me for advice. Why he asked me I have no idea as I have never done a runner from anywhere.

I remembered telling him this, but there are quite a few sick people in these places, believe me, and I think in reality, he was just wanting to take it out on someone and he picked me. He tried on a few occasions to beat me up. Thankfully, I managed to get away each time, which annoyed him quite a bit. So the next thing he did was to set a few of the other lads against me, which meant I had to watch my back, big style. On one occasion I was minding my own business in the TV room, just watching telly, when a few of the lads tried to wind me up. I gave as good as I got and they backed off.

I had long since realised that even when you haven't a chance of winning it's never wise to back down, because then the others will think you are a soft touch and you also lose respect. Anyone will have a go as well, which only makes life worse. I have found it is better to go down fighting than bottle it, which mostly I have had to do and have done quite a few times in the past.

I did make a friend who wanted me as a cellmate. He had a hidden agenda which I honestly did not see coming, but it didn't take long to suss out. When I moved into his cell, he was constantly trying to get me to give him a BJ. It was something I had not done before. I was on the bottom bunk reading a book and he would get out of bed in just his undies and pretend to be doing something to his bed. He had quite a large hard-on which was no more than a foot away from my face.

It took a few days at least before I gave in but it was not a BJ he got, he just got a hand-job, but he gave me head though, so I had the better part of the deal and thankfully it was just a one-off. I was starting to lean on my side more and more. You either fancy someone or you don't. It's not much different than being heterosexual and at the end of the day it is sex and in reality is just a different form of sex. Being bi for me means I am just a greedy person where sex is concerned and in my mind, it is up to individuals concerned who they go with. It is no one else's business but the people involved. As they say horses for courses. Just because someone else is disgusted by it does not mean I should feel the same and vice versa.

All in all, I was in Stoke Heath for about six weeks, but a couple of days before going back to Preston Crown Court, one of the screws interviewed me and before I sat down, he said, "Terry Anton(yes, this is my real name) this is your life" and put this large folder in front of me. I must admit I had no idea my file was so thick. It was easily two to three inches. The screw was making me aware mainly that I was facing a long time in jail and at the time I was thinking about three to four years. I have always found it best to look at the worst scenario that can happen, that way everything else is a bonus.

Well, eventually the big day came and to be honest I was bricking it. While in Stoke Heath reception, one of the gym screws said to my escorts, "Watch him, he is a very fast runner." But, even he wished me luck. Both my escorts looked at each other and were more than likely thinking, *O dear god, what have we let ourselves in for here?* We got to court and none of us knew how to get in, so we ended up going through the main public entrance and it was jam-packed with people as far as I could hear as for some reason, they put a blanket over my head. I heard the click of cameras, but couldn't see a thing.

I was put in a cell with two other lads. One was about my age, the other a bit younger. He was constantly whining, but he was very scared, as was I. I understood what he was going through though, so I grinned and bore it as best as I could.

It turned out I was back in front of Judge Kershaw. He had promised that if I was ever in front of him again, I would get a lot longer sentence, but in some ways, I was lucky. I got eighteen months and two six months all to run concurrently. It knocked me off my feet a bit though as I don't think I was fully prepared mentally for it, even though I knew I would not be walking out of court. It was still a kick in the nuts when I was sentenced. Unless you're expecting a serious amount of bird, then I suppose my sentence would have been laughable for what I had done and to be honest, it was.

Later that day I was taken with some of the other lads to Walton prison. We all got on a small coach and as we were pulling out of the back of the courthouse, there was a bit of a crowd. I thought at the time that my mother might be out there too, so I waved, even though I couldn't see her. A screw who was sat on the back seat came rushing up to me and smacked me full in the face. As I was handcuffed to the guy next to me, I thought that the screw was a very brave man to smack me as he did.

I asked him what was that about. He ignored me and went back to his seat, but didn't notice there were some people with cameras in the crowd. Perhaps the screw was bigging himself up in front of the cameras, and media, and would not be the first person to do that or the last. Uniforms should come with health warnings, as some people don't have the mental capacity to know how to behave responsibly while wearing them.

To say I was bricking it on my way to Walton was an understatement. I suppose it was fear of the unknown. I had heard all kind of stories about prisons, but it turns out it was nowhere near as bad as I had thought. I met an old friend who helped the screws allocate cells. I had worked with him on Risley reception, so I ended up with a good pad mate, who was from Barrow-in-Furness. He was about my age and at the time I came to his cell, he was chatting to one of the cons on another wing, by shouting out of his window. When I told him what I was in for, he shouted to his mate on the cons wing, "Guess who my new padmate is?" Apparently I had been in the newspapers and TV news, but I didn't see or hear a thing when I had been in Stoke Heath and my family was very quiet about it too. The three wise monkeys syndrome had started early methinks.

As in most places I was tested by the other inmates and for the most part I defended myself verbally and sometimes physically, quite well mostly. I only met my match once while in there, which wasn't too bad and that fight was basically over a few slices of bread. Believe me, people have fought over a two's up before now (in case you don't know what a two's up is, it is a few draws on a roll-up). Some guys will literally do anything for a smoke.

My first job was stripping large electric cables in what was called the Manies. It was a dirty smelly job as you can imagine, but I didn't mind. There were about four to six of us to one bench. One day, this little Liverpudlian kept trying to wind me up (mainly because to them I was a woolly back, so, he assumed I was easy pickings, but I soon proved he and his mates very wrong). He kept pushing my buttons till I snapped. He was still taking the meikle from across the workshop and I think he thought he was at a safe distance from me, but I threw a lump hammer at him from about 30 foot from him and I missed his shin by a couple of inches. Luckily for him, he moved just in time otherwise it would have easily broken or even smashed his leg I threw it that hard. It now meant most people kept well away from me and didn't try to wind me up, which wasn't a bad thing. It made my life so much easier.

In nick and even outside you have to set boundaries and if people don't respect them then they have a problem. In those days because I was in the nick on occasion I felt it necessary to use violence. It is what you have to do. There are no other options, it is how other guys see it. Outside, it is different and nowadays I am able mostly to defend myself verbally. It's a longer and more frustrating way of sorting people out, but it keeps you out of prison and that is paramount.

I was in the Manies for a couple of months. I had applied to go on a bricklaying course when I first arrived. I was quite a good bricklayer already, but I wanted to better myself as best I could while doing my bird and maybe get a City and Guilds out of it, but they didn't give certificates out at the time. I also started doing night classes and studying the French language. I was also doing art classes, not just to get out my cell, but I wanted an interest apart from lying on my bed reading books all the time and it broke the boredom of doing bird.

On the wing, most of the other lads left me alone. I had made friends with a couple of lifers or I should say they had befriended me really and I think that scared off most of the other YP's. My friends were both from Leeds and had been done for murder. When they told me what had happened, I thought it was more them defending themselves than murder, but they had gone a bit too far.

Some lads attacked them for no apparent reason while they were on their way home from a night club. One of my friends managed to knock one of his attackers to the ground. He went a little bit too far and while the guy was down on the ground, my friend stamped on his head, so much so, the lad's head was shaped like a rugby ball, obviously killing him (my friend's description, not mine) so most of the lads on the wing knew all about this and kept well clear of them and me.

While I was in Walton, I had to see a woman once a

month. I'm not quite sure what she was, maybe a psychiatrist or something along those lines. I think it was due to the nature of my crime that I was in for and how much more serious it could easily have been, but I kept attending even though I didn't fully understand why she was asking me all kinds of questions.

Because I was there for a year minimum, I had a few pad mates. I think I had only one bad one who had some kind of mental health issues due to drugs. On the outside he was a Hell's Angel or so he said he. One of the best pad mates was a lad from Blackburn (only because of his oral skills). We got on well mostly until I received a letter from my mother one tea time, telling me that there was a good chance I would be bumping into my second stepdad because he had got three years for messing sexually with my younger sister.

He had been sexually abusing her since she was eleven until she was sixteen. When I found out, I went totally off it and had to have my pad mate moved out. I wasn't angry with my pad mate, I wanted more than anything to have ten minutes with my second stepdad. I hated him so much I could taste it.

My stepdad was on the adult wings and I was on the YPs ', but I was on a bricklaying course and there were adults on the same course, plus we often walked through the cons' wings to get to our course and I only bumped into him a couple of times.

I offered tobacco to the lads on my course to throw him off the landing. No one was interested and after a few weeks I gave up. It turned out we had the same probation officer and because I was nearing the end of my sentence I had to see the officer. After about twenty minutes, my stepdad came walking into the same waiting area. We were all locked in so I had no escape. I told the screw I didn't want him anywhere near me and I told him why. The screw was having none of it, even when I said I wanted to go back to my cell. He just walked off. I didn't consider beating my stepdad up there and then. I wasn't that concerned about the extra bird I would get. I wanted to hurt him badly.

It turned out he had befriended this guy, who was also from Chorley and in for ABH and he was sixth dan at karate. The guy must have sensed I was going to kick off with my stepdad and for a while sat in between us, plus a couple of screws were knocking about, so, I stood no chance of getting to him and doing him some proper damage as I wanted to. I would have been lucky just to have smacked him the once and I wanted to put him on at least a life support machine or dead. I truly hated him that much.

So, I was trapped in the same room as him for about half an hour or more. He kept pleading his innocence saying that my sister had led him on, but I told him exactly what I thought of him and the more he tried to talk me round, the angrier I was getting. He must have noticed this because he changed the subject.

He then started talking about my real dad. My mother had told me when I was about eleven or twelve that he had died in a car accident when I was very young, but my second stepdad was telling me that he was still alive and well and who he was and he filled me in on what my mother used to get up to on her Thursday nights out, as in being gangbanged in a graveyard, somewhere in Chorley. He told me so much I could not get my head around it all and it certainly put my mother in a different light and with everything that has happened since it all seems very plausible now.

Eventually I got out of Walton. It is one of the best

feelings ever walking through those big gates; my only problem was the outside world. Because I lived in a small village, i.e., Lower Adlington, the world and its mother knew me or knew of me and what I had been in the nick for. Quite often, the corner shop owner (a fat, red faced guy, aged about 60) would make some snide comment when I went into his shop and of course others wanted to judge me while only going off hearsay. Must be a common trait of so-called normal people.

I bet in reality they were or are far worse than me for stealing or wrongdoing in general. No one is whiter than white, the only difference is I got caught and in my mind, if you know someone who has been in trouble with the police, there is quite a big chance they will know they are being watched so will not do anything, so they are not going to thieve off you. But that is a common sense approach and generally, in small towns and villages common sense is in very short supply. Mind you, saying that it was not true with me when the newspapers were circling overhead like vultures, (I suppose everyone has their price, but some have a lower price than others).

Within an hour of getting home, I asked my mother about my real dad. She couldn't really say a lot. I think she was in shock that I had found out so much. I have got to admit when I am looking back now, I do resent my mother for putting me through seven years of believing my real dad was dead. Because of my mother telling me that, I totally went off the rails aged twelve. She effectively ruined everything in my life and I ended up doing a lot of bad things and in prison because of it. I am not proud of it but in no way can I change any of it. I can only blame my upbringing for the way I was (I say was because to date I have been out of trouble for three decades) and I have achieved this by keeping my nose clean and distancing myself from negative people, i.e., my family and most of my friends and my family's friends and one major factor is my sobriety. The saying, 'You can choose your friends but not your family' is very true from my experience because of what I endured throughout my teenage years.

When I was about sixteen, I tried to get a job at my first stepdad's place of work. I had seen the job advertised in the Jobcentre and I thought I would give them a ring and mention that my stepdad worked for them thinking it might give me a better chance of getting a job, but I didn't say stepdad. I said dad, to be honest. At the time I thought of him as my dad, as he had been more one than anyone else (until this point, that is) but the guy on the other end of the phone told me he didn't have a son and the guy was adamant as he never mentioned ever having a son.

I think the worst part of this was that it came from a complete stranger. If my first stepdad had been totally straight with me throughout my childhood, life etc, and simply said you're not my son, so go away and don't bother me again, it wouldn't have hurt so much. But right from day one I had always felt there was no love there. I could never understand why he was like he was with me; the penny never ever dropped. I never understood as a child why he treated me the way he did with the physical abuse and being far too quick to lose his temper with me over mostly petty things. But back then where I felt pain, I did my best to distance myself from it, mostly by putting a mental block on it. Just not thinking about it at all seemed the only way I could cope at times.

Even now I do the same, more or less. Now I put on my automatic blinkers and a hypothetical mask to hide behind and carry on regardless. It has always been part of my self-defence mechanism and I also use my sense of humour to get out of bad situations.

I could see all the business between my second stepdad and sister had had a very negative effect on my mother's mentality, so, I didn't push any more about my real dad. In no time at all it was as if I had not been away and the issue about my real dad was quickly brushed under the carpet. It was never far from my thoughts, but at the time I had no desire to find him, basically, because he had never looked for me, so I just added him to the ever-growing list of people who didn't want me in their lives.

Quite quickly after getting out, I started working on a nearby pig farm. Of course, there were comments from some people from the farm about me putting the car on the tracks, but it is something you have to learn to live with and ignore, which I did easily.

When you do wrong it is not just a prison sentence you get, you have to contend with people pre-judging you and knowing the hearsay side of things and the made-up lies about you. All the time I had been inside I had to watch my back all the time, (strangely even now forty years on I do the same). Usually when I walk into a room, I notice more than most the little things. I think I would have made a good copper in some ways, if there is such a thing, allegedly.

Because of the way my mother had been treated by my second stepdad, it seemed that she had totally gone against white guys and so had my sister. When I was inside they had both started going out with West Indian guys, one was from Chorley and my sister's boyfriend was a black guy from Bolton. My sister had moved in with the guy from Bolton, before I had got out of prison. At first I wasn't too keen on my mother or for that matter my sister going out with black guys, but the more I got to know my mother's boyfriend the more I accepted the situation. I never had the chance to get to know my sister's boyfriend. Mind you in no time at all my sister moved to Liverpool 8, Toxteth and ended up marrying a one-legged African guy, who was very violent, to put it mildly.

My sister would sometimes visit us and she would help herself to my stuff and my mother would cover up for her by lying. It was a constant battle to keep hold of any of my stuff. The minute my back was turned and being as I was the black sheep, nothing I said made any difference to anyone but myself. In some ways it was like being a ghost.

It was quite amusing to see both my mother and sister mimicking black women, as in kissing their teeth and saying cha man. I kept my amusement to myself though, but, in reality, I was not that impressed and that was before they became working girls. I cannot say for sure if their boyfriends put them on it or if they did that off their own bat and that is in no way being racist. That is just saying it as it is or was.

At home it was just my mother, my younger brother, sister and me. Looking back now, my mother's drinking was getting quite bad, but most people around me drank to excess. I think that all started due to what my stepdad did to us all.

His main trick with my mother was to get her drunk every night so that she would pass out. Then she became oblivious to what was happening to her daughter behind her back and he would then abuse my sister. My mother discovered what was going on, when she had woken up one night to go for a drink of water and stumbled on them in the kitchen and saw my stepdad having sex with her daughter. I do wish it had been me that found them.

I very nearly caught him at it myself once, but I couldn't get my sister to admit what was happening to her. I threatened her with violence if she didn't tell me. I was that angry, but she wouldn't tell me. If she had told me I know I would have surely gone at him with a knife. Because of what he did, my sister ended up on drink and drugs to mask the suffering he had caused her. My mother ended up being an alcoholic and five years later I started on the same alcoholic road. He ended up getting three years for what he did. Nothing compared to what we all went through.

My sister, mother and I all started a nightmare path downward on the alcoholic, addictive spiral. Most people would say getting drunk every night would be brill, but, believe me, being an alcoholic means you are compelled to drink. You need a drink like you need air to breathe. Giving up is nothing to do with willpower when you try to stop. The only way I stopped was to give up on drink. You stop fighting it and accept that it isn't an option anymore. It isn't as easy as it might sound. I had to convince myself. Even today, that is how I see it and for me now fags are the same, as I have given them up too.

My mother and sister were not so lucky. My mother died when she was 57 of cancer and I firmly believe that she died early because of her drinking, which I think brought on the cancer. My sister died because all her organs just packed in when she was 47 leaving two teenage kids behind. So sad and such a waste of a life and I am saying this after all that they have done to me throughout my life.

To me, blood is thicker than water and always will be in my book. All told I have done four and a half years in prison, but only once when I was quite young have I stolen from my family and that was 50p. It's absolutely nothing to what my family have stolen from me. In my case it was not just the money they stole from me, but they even stole my good health. I would love to know their reasoning behind what they did to me, but I seriously doubt I will ever find out.

While I was still living in Lower Adlington, after work I would go out cycling and sometimes just out for a walk or run. You tend to realise when you lose your freedom just how precious it is. We had a little park at the end of our road, off Park Road. One night I was just minding my own business having a swing on the swings and chilling out. It was quite late at night. I was not breaking any laws, but suddenly I could see car headlights heading in my direction across the park. As luck would have it, there was a small wall about forty foot behind me. I ran for it.

I have never thought it wise to wait to find out if someone is after me or if they were just messing about on the park. It is always best to assume the worst when a car full of people is heading your way. Of course, I easily got away from it and I carried on running home which was only a few minutes away. Funnily enough, while running through the fields to get home, I accidentally stood on a guy's posterior. He was having sex with his girlfriend, so at least she got it a little deeper for a second, but she never thanked me for it though (sic).

Because of all that had happened between my stepdad and my mother, they were quite rightfully going through a divorce and he was constantly writing vile, threatening letters to her, which was not doing my mother's mental health any good. So we ended up moving to Bramley, Leeds. The novelty soon wore off though, when our neighbours found out where we were from, Lancashire. (It amazes me sometimes, because the War of the Roses happened at least more than a century ago, but there is still resentment. Perhaps some people need to get a life).

My brother was being bullied at school because of where we came from. I told him that if you cannot beat them one way you try another. I have done the same thing many times and still do, but now I use my mouth more, not my fists. No one is worth doing bird for.

I also got a bit of abuse from some of my co-workers. I was working for a builder in the Pudsey area and I soon learned to keep my mouth shut about my being in the nick. In the past when my boss found out I had been in the nick, he near enough sacked me on the spot. Instead of sacking me, he said one little step out of line and I was out on my ear. So much for people trying to put their past behind them and move on with their lives. But after a couple of months, it was all forgotten about.

This was late 1977 and looking back I am quite sure my mother was definitely a suffering alcoholic by this time and it was mainly down to my stepdad getting her drunk every night so he could abuse my sister. I know from my own alcoholism, it is a very, very fine line from heavy social drinking to alcoholic drinking. In my case, it was so fine a line it was invisible. One minute I could put it down and no problem. Next minute I would rather die than put it down, but to a so-called bigoted "normal person" it is self-inflicted. How little they know.

After a few months in early 1978, my mother turned around one Friday night, just after tea time and said she was going to London. Her boyfriend already lived in Clapton, East London. I thought she meant she was just going down for a couple of days. By Sunday when she had not returned, I had the problem of, 'do I stay at home,(lose my job)and look after my younger brother and sister or do

I go to work as usual'?

I decided on going to work as normal and hoped to god that the kids would not burn the house down while I was out. I must admit I was desperately worried. I virtually ran home from our drop-off point but thankfully all was fine. I had warned my younger brother not to turn on the fire or cooker, but he ignored me. I told him off, but I didn't know what to do for the best, so, the next day I did the same, and I was hoping my little brother would listen to me this time. Luckily, I had a dental appointment, so I finished work a bit earlier than I would have normally. When I got home, two social workers were waiting for me in the living room. They gave me the option of either staying at home and looking after my brother and sister or they were taken into care. As much as I didn't want to be making this decision and it broke my heart to make it, I thought I can barely look after myself let alone two young kids, so I told them to take them into care. This is one of many things that haunts me daily. I will never forget watching the social workers taking them down the path to their car. My younger sister was crying her heart out and begging for her mummy and I think my brother couldn't get his head around it or he was just in shock. It took me quite some time to get over how depressed this made me feel and it has affected my life ever since.

What didn't help was about a week later my mother paid a flying visit (her boyfriend was a long-distance lorry driver) and even the two social workers stopped by. I'm not sure how they knew my mother was going to be there, but she angrily blamed me (in front of the social workers) for the fact my brother and sister were in care. This was like having my heart ripped out and stamped on and then replaced. In reality as I look back now, it was absolutely my mother's fault. She was the one who walked out on us.

OK, she was in a bad place at the time, but in my mind, a mum or dad should do everything they can for their kids. Of course, within reason. Years later I found out it was my second stepdad's fault, as he had moved to Leeds jail, which was quite a local jail to where we lived in Bramley and he was threatening my mother by letter even though the prison censored prisoners' letters going in and out. So what happened there? Mind you, he was a nonce and they do look after nonces, allegedly.

It was only a matter of weeks before the debt collectors started knocking at my door and demanding money. I was not in debt myself, it was all my mother's debts but I was so naïve and quite gullible that I took my mother's debts on thinking I had to pay them to help my mother out and also because the debt collectors told me that is what I had to do as well.

Firstly, it was the electricity board. They ended up taking my cooker away and when they checked the meter, my mother had rigged it with a long darning needle. She had totally forgotten to tell me anything about it, so that was added to what my mother owed. Then there was the rent arrears and the landlord was threatening to kick me out because they were saying I was squatting. As I told them at the time, did they know many squatters who paid rent as I was paying at the time? They could not argue with that.

Because I had given up my job to go on a course with JCB, I was hardly eating. In fact I was eating three or four days out of seven, so eventually I had to give in and go out thieving and once again I was caught (that night my mother, for whatever reason, paid me a flying visit from London and more or less persuaded me to go out thieving).

I was caught and thrown in prison for a few weeks and because I was from Lancashire it didn't go down too well with some of the other inmates and while inside my mother took quite a lot of my belongings and shared them with everyone she knew in London. I asked where my stuff had gone and she said she was looking after them for me. But I never got any of it back when I was living in London although I noticed that my third stepdad was wearing a t-shirt of mine that had gone missing. This was quite common. I think my family thought they had the right to do this.

While I was inside, very few of the other guys bothered me. I presumed it was because I knew the script about what I needed to do. I even had my twenty first in there and I should have been transferred to an adult prison, but for some reason my mother had written to someone saying not to move me to Armley (Leeds jail) as my second stepfather was in there and there was a good chance that if we met there would be a lot of trouble, which looking back, wasn't that far from the truth.

By the time I got out, my probation officer and the council ended up moving me to some high rise flats. My flat had a cooker, but the caretaker conned me out of that by saying the previous tenant said he could take it. I bumped into a neighbour who knew otherwise and she tore a strip off him to say the least. I still had no cooker, so, although it was against the rules I had to get a little gas camping stove and I managed quite well with that all the time I lived there. Obviously I was limited to what I could eat or cook. I had to cope in whatever way I could. That's life and looking back I think I coped quite well.

When I first moved, I was on the dole and because I was a total novice at living on my own. I paid all my debts first, then bought food. It meant I was only eating four days a week and because I had no friends or family around me, I got quite lonely and depressed at times. I even got to the point where I would walk round the streets of Leeds picking up dog ends very late at night, just to save money on fags. I was spotted doing it a few times and gave up. I didn't want a reputation like that.

So once again, I was forced into going back to my old burglary ways, so even though I wanted to stay clean and out of trouble with the police, I ended up going out thieving. It was petty stuff and didn't really put food on the table, but now that I was living on my own and having to look after myself in every way, I was always mindful that if I was caught again, I would lose my flat and all my belongings with it and would be homeless. It slowed me down quite a lot, but didn't stop me completely. You have to do what you have to do to survive in life.

As luck would have it, while walking back from the DWP in Pudsey which was two miles each way from where I lived, I got a lift off one of the drivers from my old building firm. I had made a really silly mistake by resigning from my old job to go on a five-day excavator driving course with JCB at their base in Uttoxeter and the driver told me this in no uncertain terms. I thought I was bettering myself and had resigned to thinking that I could easily find work.

All would have been well if I had had some means of transport. It wasn't practical to try and do it, so I had shafted myself.

We got chatting and he asked me what I was up to now and once I had told him that I couldn't find any kind of work, he suggested asking for my old job back and gave me the number. I was seeing my probation officer later that day, so, because I had no money to ring anyone, I asked if I could ring from his office. My old boss was OK with taking me back, but I had to go back as a labourer instead of a bricklayer. The way I saw it at the time, at least I had a job and money was coming back in. It turned out I was still bricklaying etc, so I had gone back for lower pay and doing the same job as before. We have to do what we have to do to survive.

So I was back eating properly. My boss even ignored that I was the last to take on when he had to lay people off around Christmas time and it upset a few guys that he had kept me on and not them. I suppose it was because I had quite a few more skills and I was a hard worker. I didn't have any time off at all, even when I had accidentally scalded both my ankles.

I had blisters on my blisters and most of the time I was in complete agony when walking because I was wearing boots which rubbed my ankles where the blisters were. The way I saw it at the time, if I did not go into work, I would not get paid and then would not be eating. Apart from that I would have been bored out of my skull at home and going into work took my mind off the pain I was going through.

I worked for this builder for about eighteen months and life felt good, although I still had no friends or family around me and it did get quite lonely at times.

I did my best to support my brother and sister by going to visit them every Sunday in the children's home in the Roundhay Park area of Leeds. I walked it there and back for about six months until my second stepdad latched on to me on my way home one night. I couldn't get rid of him, no matter what I tried to do and I didn't want any trouble of any kind from anyone.

So I just went with the flow. I had no choice but to let

him stay overnight at mine. He must have been mooching around after I had gone to bed because when I returned from work the next night, my diary which had a lock on was broken. It had all my phone numbers in and all my addresses, including my mother's, so he now knew where she was and even her address. The next morning I got up extra early and left for work to avoid him.

While still at work I had managed to phone my probation officer and he put me in touch with a solicitor. It ended up sending my second stepdad a solicitor's letter and the solicitor rang the local police station who gave me a phone number to ring in case he showed up at my door again. A couple of nights later, my stepdad did just that. He came round with a guy I had never met before. I was in the middle of cooking my tea, so I made an excuse to go to the shop for something, but I phoned the police as well as getting some shopping, so it wouldn't alert them in any way to what I had done.

Only one policeman came, but he soon fired them off. As soon as they'd gone the policeman asked me a load of questions. I suppose it was to fill in the background as to what was happening with my stepdad and me and I must admit I broke down while explaining everything. It must have been the stress of it all.

Most of the time in Leeds I hardly ever drank. Months would go by without alcohol, mainly because I was not the type to go in pubs alone. I always sensed when I walked through the door of a pub that everyone turned round and stared at you as you entered. This always unnerved me and I felt like I had two heads. I suppose I was a bit paranoid at times, I had tried going out to the local pubs when I lived on Broad lane, Bramley, (of course I now realise that people look round to just see whose coming in, nothing more than that) but because I was on my own I got hassled a few times. Some people can't have a drink without wanting to fight you, so I gave up on that.

Then after a few months, I think through loneliness, I started drinking whisky. I quickly found it gave me a warm sensation and it helped me like myself more and best of all, I forgot all my abusive past, all my wrong doing. The more I drank the more I drowned it all out or at least that is what I thought it did at the time.

That was not the last I saw of my stepdad though. One Sunday afternoon he came around. He was very angry. Obviously, he had received the solicitor's letter and he was threatening to break my legs if he got his hands on me. I lived on the seventh floor of a block of flats and I went out on to my balcony at the back of my flat and I was seriously debating whether to climb down to another balcony or even down to ground level. I was that frightened of him getting hold of me. My thinking was if he gets in, he will more than likely throw me off the balcony anyway, but as luck would have it, one of my neighbours (a little old lady of at least 70) had heard all the ranting and raving from my stepdad and even though she was in her seventies she sent him on his way with a flea in his ear. She obviously didn't know him like I did, because in no way was she scared of him. I think I was scared of him because I could remember how violent he used to be towards me when I was a kid and you never really forget that.

If I had thought about it properly, I could have easily sorted him out, as I was no longer the little kid he use to punch and abuse. But at the same time I didn't want any more time in prison. Looking back, I 'm not sure if I was more fearful of ending up back inside or of him. I know I felt in no way he was worth it.

Months before while living at Broad lane, I managed to get a pistol and I thought at the time, if he should ever turn up at my door I will shoot him dead. I had the gun for a few months, but then I thought to myself if I kill him, I will get done for murder, because it would have been premeditated. So I broke up his gun and got rid of it, but it didn't stop me hating him. There was a long list of people who hated him, because no one likes paedos.

While living there I used to go to a shopping parade just down the road from me, and for some reason, I was banned from one of the shops because the shop owner's Mrs kept coming on to me and I must admit I was quite interested in her too. But this didn't please her hubby one bit. I think he was a bit on the jealous side or he just did not trust her but it wasn't a hardship as there was another shop, a launderette, a few doors down. I was washing as many clothes as I could before moving down to London.

Who should come in but the woman from the shop from where I'd been banned. She sat right near me and we chatted for at least half an hour and she told me, more or less, her hubby was a bit on the jealous side and that I needed to keep my head down. But I knew that already.

I told her that I was moving to London the next day, so did she think that was low enough in keeping my head down? I think if I'd stayed around our friendship could have easily grown to more, so, I think at the time it was the right thing to do.

So in mid-1979 I gave into my mother's nagging and moved to London. She had painted a very rosy picture of it and had found me a bedsit right next door to hers (literally) at Evering Road, off upper Clapton Road, E.5. As I look back now, it was totally the wrong move for me. I would have been far better off staying in Leeds, but, we live and learn, I also packed my alcohol problem in my suitcase and took it with me down London, trouble was I never remembered packing it in my suitcase and my drinking got a lot worse quite quickly.

A few months after moving in with my mother she moved to the Stamford Hill area and also around the same time my sister left her husband and moved to London from Toxteth.

Every time I had chatted with my mother on the phone when I lived in Leeds, she was always banging on about how London was so great and that I would make loads of money. But if I had listened to my head rather than my heart I would have realised she wanted me there so that she and my sister could carry on ripping me off and continue controlling me like they had been doing for most of my life. Alas, I'd never noticed.

The reason I say this is a few months later when I did move down, my sister more or less moved down at the same time, within a few months in fact. My mother and sister started ripping me off all over again and like I said earlier they were both very controlling as well, although I didn't realise straight away, but it was all done in very subtle way.

So subtle that because of my drinking I didn't really notice it, because I loved all my family without question and unconditionally. I must have turned a blind eye to a lot of the stuff they got up to. I knew full well they were mostly up to no good most of the time, but they were still my family. Not everyone who smiles at you is your friend, but sadly, the people I should have been able to trust and rely on, I shouldn't have done, but for reasons best known to themselves they were all my worst enemies and as I look back now, this happened throughout my whole life. But it took alcoholism and seeing myself in a tabloid to show me how bad they all were.

My sister left her husband to move to London. He had just got his compensation from the shipping company he was working for when he had his accident. When she left him she stole a couple of blank cheques out of his bank book and drew out £2,000, but I had been guilt-tripped into cashing them through my bank.

I must be honest. I took take a small cut for myself. It was a ploy on my part because I didn't want to cash any cheques for them at all, but they (my mother and sister) agreed, after a bit of arguing, so I thought I can't back out now, so I wrongfully went with the flow.

At the time I was getting more and more reliant on alcohol. I was now drinking every night, but I didn't see it as a problem, as most of my family, in particular my mother and sister drank to excess and up until then I had not done anything wrong. That was partly why I gave in to my mother wanting me in London. I thought I was drinking like I was through loneliness. I had no one in Leeds and I had one friend who it turned out wanted to get into my pants and I never saw it coming. He had a stunning girlfriend too, but I wasn't that lonely to go with him. The girlfriend most certainly, but not him, so he was hardly a friend. I never did find out what he wanted to do, but I can hazard a guess.

So this leads me on to what I call my alcoholic nightmare. In total, I was a suffering alcoholic for around eighteen years, so I know a lot more than these people who study it in uni and give advice and more surprisingly I know more than some doctors. They may know the terminology of things, but that is all they know. They seem to know very little about alcoholism.

As a way of giving back what I have received I am now on a counselling course at a local college and I also volunteer as a listening volunteer for the Samaritans. So far, I have learned a lot about myself and I have found out what true empathy is with the Samaritans.

By listening we sometimes hear some terrible things, which in my case puts what happened to me into more of a perspective, which is a positive thing to do I think. So although I know quite a bit, I don't know the whys and wherefores, but I'm quickly finding out.

My Alcoholism

Like most people, I started drinking mainly at weekends on Friday and Saturday nights or on nights out, but I was never keen on the feeling of being drunk or out of control. I never once told my careers teacher at any time that one day when I am in my early twenties, that I wanted to be an out of control alcoholic and believe it or not I never sent away for it from a mail-order catalogue like so many bigots and know-nothings seem to think. It was never a conscious decision to ever become an alcoholic.

It most certainly was not a lifestyle choice. If truth be known I had no choice in it at all, I simply stepped over that invisible alcoholic line one day into a nightmare called alcoholism. Addictions are not chosen, they pick you, as I know now. Alcoholism is no respecter, be you male, female, black, white, rich or poor. It is, without doubt, a great leveller.

As kids, we once found alcohol stored behind a nearby local college. It was just a one-off and to me it didn't impress me at all about being ill and feeling sick and being sick.

It was the same with cigs. I tried them once when I was about seven because all the other kids in our street were doing it one day. The taste was vile, but I already knew what they smelled like, because of my mother's habit of more than 40 a day, which all the family shared with her. By rights, that should have been enough to put me off cigarettes for life.

I even tried my dad's bitter once when we went out for Sunday dinner to a local pub and to put it mildly it was s- and I can honestly say I have never touched it since, even though I had an 18-year-old problem with alcohol which very nearly killed me. I find it quite strange that I never drank bitter. Maybe it was that I never got that desperate as nothing alcoholic was ever safe around me. If my mother were alive now she would back me up on that one.

I want to clarify that in no way am I bragging about any of what I am about to tell you and I am in no way recommending anything I have done. The truth is that I feel more ashamed about some of what I have done. Most of what has happened in my life has been done through ignorance or being under the influence of alcohol or just the product of bad parenting. Maybe what I am about to tell you just might give the "normal" people an insight into why us alcoholics are like we are and I use the word "normal" very loosely.

There are and were mitigating circumstances throughout my life and two sides to every story. This is my side, which newspapers never tell you about. They have their version of events, so nothing else matters in their bigoted world. They never let the truth get in the way of what they call a good story, as they are constantly banging on about. Their way is the coward's way.

I am quite proud of what I have become and by rights I should only be judged on how I am now. I think most people with a past like mine would want people to forget their past as well, but that is just never going to happen no matter what I say or do. I have found what you do for people you cannot make them like you and mostly what I have found is you never know who your friends until trouble looms.

In my case, my so-called friends and family were still there, smiling at me as if nothing was happening behind my back. They were not my friends. In reality, they just fed and stole from me like leeches and sadly that included my own family and their friends. All the people I should have been able to trust were in fact my Achilles' heel as it proved to be. All this brought me to my knees and pushed me into trying to commit suicide at least a dozen times.

The only problem I have ever had was alcoholism. I don't admit to ever having a drug problem. The most I have done is pot and weed. I have never been addicted to any drugs or abused any of my medication, which is what a family member told the tabloids or maybe they invented that. I'm not too sure.

Not one person who was around me at that time was hardly an expert witness. To my mind, you have to have walked in the same shoes. To someone who has zero knowledge of 24/7 pain and is watching a person constantly having to take heavy duty pain relief because the pain was so bad, it might seem that they were abusing their medication. But that doesn't stop the tabloids printing what they print even if potentially it ruins someone's life.

Sobriety is the best thing I have ever achieved. I have made a lot of enemies and made a lot of foolish mistakes but I don't fully blame being an alcoholic for most of my mistakes. I have nearly lost my life on a few occasions. Sometimes it has been my fault, but always drink-related. At other times it has been other people's faults, but my fault for mixing totally with the wrong kind of people, and not having my wits about me enough to suss out bad company from good.

When you are trying to run your life looking through the bottom of a beer bottle things can only get worse and the myth that when you're a suffering alcoholic, you forget everything is total b-. It is quite the opposite. As most intelligent people will know and of course other alcoholics (same thing really) your problems are there before you pick up your first drink of the day and still there in the morning. A common trait of an alcoholic is that they will dwell on the smallest of things and build mountains out of molehills.

Our minds never shut down. AA calls it a racing brain. It is not a medical term as far as I know. I still get flashbacks even now, but it's all part of my recovery. I suppose it's a good thing when I am trying to write a book.

I think my alcoholism started while I was living in Leeds. I was about 21, but I did a lot of stupid and some quite serious things when I got drunk even before I stepped over that invisible line from normal drinking to alcoholic drinking. There is quite a list.

At first, I could go months without drinking alcohol, mainly because I didn't have the money to buy it and mostly because I didn't want to drink anyway. One night I thought I would have a drink of whisky. I didn't intend to drink the whole one litre bottle, but surprisingly, I finished it all. No problem. I drank it like water, it never really touched the sides.

Instantly it gave me a warm glow. I felt that I loved myself more, despite all my past. It also helped me forget the bad parts of my upbringing and the abuse I had suffered and I didn't give a monkey's what people said or thought about me. You could say it turbo charged my 'I don't give a fig filter'. It was like alcohol had given me a suit of armour from all the nastiness in my life.

Naturally, I felt quite ill the next day at work, so that night I tried some more, as in the hair of the dog and it soon became a regular thing. Every night I nearly always felt that warm glow and it seemed to make me forget all the abuse of my childhood and as an adult and seemingly all my worries went away only to return the next morning. I know growing up is not easy for most people. I grew up never knowing my own dad from the age of 12, (I resent my mother because of this). She was a bully throughout my life. My sisters were very two-faced users and thieves, who thought nothing of telling lies about me to anyone who was stupid enough to listen to them.

It seemed that my whole family were control freaks and that is being very polite, so in some ways being on my own was OK with me, apart from me being lonely. I now know there are far worse things than being lonely. I could be with the wrong one, which looking back has happened quite a few times (I blame my alcoholism for this) and sadly that includes my family, which is something else I can blame on the drink. I was only attracted to people who were attractive on the outside or so it seems looking back.

I lived in Leeds for 18 months and in the last couple of months I had started making friends and going out with them. I should never have moved to London. My mother painted such a rosy picture. London's streets are paved with gold is the expression but the truth to me is that it is quite the opposite; more like paved in dirt. The place itself is quite beautiful, but the people, let us just say, very few are nice deep down or was I just a magnet for the wrong types?

When I moved there I carried on drinking the way I had been in Leeds, but only ever at night. This had lasted eighteen years. One night while doing some paperwork (invoices) I'd decided not to have a drink, but the craving got so bad I just couldn't concentrate on what I was doing. I gave in and popped to the off-licence down the road for six cans of Special Brew. I'd never even heard of it before, but we soon became very close friends, although it too, turned out to be another false friend. That was the start of my drunken path through life and I must admit it was never a happy one.

To say I made a fool of myself at times would definitely be an understatement and by the way, that old myth about drunks showing his or her true colours while drunk is total rubbish. It isn't true that all alcoholics are not to be believed or trusted. That is what the Jimmy Saviles in our society rely on to get away with their wrongdoings against vulnerable people. For me I would not trust a so-called "normal person"at all and I use the word "normal" very loosely. I have seen how vile and toxic so-called normal people are with others.

I trust very few people now because of them (I would rather be an alcoholic than a so-called normal person). I have seen what normal people do and to me they are far worse in some ways than us alcoholics and I have met a lot of genuine people in AA and even for that matter in prison too.

If by chance, medical science ever came out with a pill that would let me drink again I doubt I would want it, because I am totally happy not touching anything at all. I don't even smoke normal cigs any more, although I am a bit annoyed that I have put on loads of weight since putting the fags down (at present, I am nowhere near going into AA or putting the fags down).

Moving to London was one of the worst mistakes I made in my life. I had no problem with my mother moving to the Stamford Hill area. It gave me back my privacy, which to me is priceless.

Just to get a bit of pocket money I did odd jobs for my landlord. I'm not sure if he was Indian or Pakistani, but whatever he was, he wasn't a very nice person to be around. I used to sit with him while he collected rent from people. In some ways I was a bodyguard or minder, I'm not sure what. Any trouble and I had to kick out the troublemaker, but I was only getting pocket money and in no way would I have put my liberty at risk for that. I worked for him for about six months and in that time I kicked out one guy. I never used violence. I didn't even lay a finger on him. Although the landlord told me to hit people a few times, I refused point blank and the stories I had heard about him trying it on with tenants, male and female, in a sexual way even made me less likely to defend him. I hate nonces no matter what race they are. In the time I worked for him the local CID called a few times about tenants and even the *Hackney Gazette* paid us a visit one night and I even got a mention in the newspaper. They never named me (perhaps it is the way the newspapers conduct their business or was it because I wasn't silly enough to tell them my name when the journalist had asked me for it)? Even if I'd given my name, they would have changed it in some way like the tabloids did quite often with me from 1985 until 1993. It must be how cowardly they all are.

Within a few months, while I was doing house repairs for the landlord, I met my future son's mother. At first it started as a bit of fun, as she was married to a Turkish guy.

The first time we met she came to the front door in quite a revealing negligee which took my mind off the job I was there to do. I could tell she was quite interested in me, so I just went with the flow, so to speak.

A few weeks or so later my future son's mother was in my sister's bedsit in Lower Clapton. My sister lived in the same house as my future son's mother and at the time she was coming on to me very strong, so I arranged for her to come around to mine one afternoon in the week.

On our first meeting we only kissed. The second time

we had sex and on our third meeting she moved in after leaving her hubby (I didn't think I was that good in bed!) and as you would expect, her hubby was not too pleased about this and at one point threatened to break my legs. I ignored his threats, as he was only good at beating up women, so nothing to worry about really. We lived together for around two years, and in that time I soon found out why her ex-husband had beaten her in the past.

She was always causing trouble with her lies. Once it led to my friend's boyfriend nearly stabbing me. If it had not been for my friend stepping in the way it would have happened. In the time I was with my son's mother she hardly ever worked, not even housework. She was always complaining about severe headaches or bad period pains.

She even told me she had been gang raped by four blokes who drove a scrap lorry, so for a couple of months I would go out around the streets of East London at night, looking for the lorry that she had described to me. Guess what? I never found it. I think it was just a ploy to get me out the way so she could put it about behind my back. I know now not to trust people who cheat. She cheated on her hubby with me.

For the first few months, some girls who were her so-called friends and friends with her hubby kept beating her up when they saw her in the street. I'm not quite sure why. I had to step in between them a few times and ended up warning them off. Eventually, they took the hint and left us alone.

I was working all hours just to keep food on the table. Some days I was so tired I was falling asleep even while working on a bandsaw in a foundry on Ridley Road, Hackney. It was only a matter of time before I had an accident. It was no one's fault, but my own, that I nearly cut off my finger. The union guy called it God's will, so I didn't get any compensation. Mind you, I should have got something for putting up with my son's mother for six weeks, 24/7. That is how long I was off work.

She was constantly telling me about her hubby and his friend who had seen us out walking and because I had my arm in a sling and all my hand bandaged up, she kept saying one day they're going to jump out of their car and give you a good beating. I replied, "It is the only time they will ever manage to beat me while I only have one good hand."

I must admit I was relieved to get back to work and away from her awful remarks, mainly because I was skint. She even cashed in my last sick money giro behind my back and did not bat an eyelid when I was quizzing the DWP and everyone else in the house as to where it had gone. I have never been able to steal off someone I know and look them in the eye afterwards. But that is just me. It seems a lot can.

While I was with her I had not drunk for around six months. My thinking was that if I drank like I had been doing before meeting her, she would run a mile, but because of the accident my drinking started up once again and back to how it was over six months previously.

Alcoholics don't need an excuse to start drinking again. The fact is if there is a Y in the day it is more than enough of an excuse to drink. To my surprise my son's mother didn't run a mile, more's the pity. She started messing me about every time my back was turned, not that I was aware of it at the time. She even tried it on with one of our neighbours in one of the bedsits we lived in. That really is doing it on your doorstep. Mind you, I was just as bad at times, but when I did it she was in Inverness after we had broken up for a few weeks, so I was not cheating on her really.

Once again, because of our shortage of money, I really had no alternative but to go out thieving and in no time at all I got in trouble with the police for burglary on an electrical shop in North London and back in Pentonville for three weeks for reports. I was then taken to court and sentenced to 250 hours community service by Old Street magistrates. I had to do my stint at an old people's home run by nuns in North London and while there I met this guy about my own age.

He was also on community service. We got on all right, so we went out to the pub quite a few times together. Although I didn't know it at the time he was helping me out with my son's mother, sexually, which was quite helpful of him, so much so I am not certain that my son is really mine. But at the time I put my son's mother getting pregnant down to the fact I was more fertile because of not having sex for three weeks through being in Pentonville (but I was totally in the dark about what she was up to until we had finished).

Then it seemed everyone came forward with all kinds of tales about her when she was safely out of the way. I think people left it until then because she was quite a volatile person, even quite violent at times, (some would even say not right in the head and some have said it quite often, but that is their view. I will sit on the fence while nodding my head).

At the time I thought I had had a son to her and for months I would come home from work and have to start doing all the housework, including washing nappies, all the baby's clothes, her clothing and my clothes and I had to wash them all by hand in the bath.

My mother had hated her ever since my son was born (I was in the Scrubs at the time doing a six months' stretch). She attended the birth and when my son popped out the first thing my son's mother asked in a panicky way was what colour it was. Although my mother didn't believe the excuse she gave that my son's mother sister had had a Down's syndrome baby she said what she said because she was worried that if the baby was blue then it was Down's syndrome.

My son's mother seemed to be forever faking epileptic fits. I put it down to attention-seeking and did not believe her most of the time. She even faked a fit in the dock of the Old Street Magistrates Court right in front of everyone. That was while I was getting remanded in custody for three weeks for reports. You can't beat that for seeking attention.

Once again I was sentenced to 250 hours community service and because she still didn't want to work, we started getting into debt pretty quickly. The only way I felt we could get out of it was for me to going back thieving. There was more work in a sick note than with her. In no time at all I was caught and once again thrown back into prison for another few weeks for reports. This time I ended up getting two years' probation.

When I got out within an hour of me getting back home, a black guy came to our front door. He was carrying a pretty full holdall and asked for my son's mother by name. I asked him who he was and he said he was her boyfriend. As you can imagine I went ballistic with him. That's not something you want to hear just after getting out of nick. My son's mother and I argued for the rest of the day and into the night, but within a couple of days things settled down again.

She still didn't want to work and because the police had arrested me at my place of work, I ended up losing my job. When I went to collect my wages and any money that they owed me, they told me that my mother and my son's mother had both been there on separate occasions and were both trying to get my wages. I should have taken this as a kind of warning sign about all my family, as well as my son's mother, but I just let it go over my head rather foolishly as I look back now.

Silly I know, but I couldn't see how bad all my family really were. I would have been far better off just firing off my son's mother and family then and there. She was a total waste of skin and air.

Although I didn't realise it at the time, while I was living in London this behaviour was a regular thing that my mother and sister would regularly steal from me every time my back was turned. Even some of their friends and even my own friends were at it too. So now, I was out of work and no money and my son's mother still didn't want to work.

So I started helping out one of my stepdads but the problem was because he was connected to the family he saw fit to underpay me too and even once blatantly stole all my tools from me, so I was hardly quids in. Once again I ended up going thieving and again in no time at all I was caught and once again ended up back in prison for another three weeks for reports. This time I got another 250 hours community service.

Luckily though, I found work a couple of months before Christmas, at a sewing machine shop in North London. We were now living in the N16 area and our rent could not have been any cheaper. We were now paying £6 for two rooms, but I was still up to my old tricks, (thieving) but, nowhere near as much as in the past. A few days before Christmas a citizen's arrest was made by a black guy. That was a bit of a surprise and I am not being in any way racist by saying this. But in the early1980s in the N16 area, it was quite a bad place to live and being arrested by a black guy, would have been unheard of back then.

Once again I ended up back in prison. This time though when I returned to Highbury Magistrates Court, I got six months' jail. That meant I was in the Scrubs for four months, but I was lucky enough to get a job in the kitchens, which meant working from 5 am until 5 pm, seven days a week. I was out of my cell and it was a well-paid job too.

While I was in a prison in South West London my probation officer came to see me. I could see she was a bit nervous when she told me she was leaving the probation service to have a baby. Of course I was happy for her.

She told me that she was very relieved to hear that as my son's mother had told her that I would kick off with her because she was leaving the probation service and to watch herself with me, as I would get violent with her. I think my probation officer had forewarned the screws that something might happen to her. To say that to a pregnant woman is, in my book , a very sick thing to do.

Looking back, it would seem, my son's mother was only happy if she was causing some kind of trouble with other people. This wasn't the first time she had done this kind of thing. When I worked at a babywear warehouse in Lower Clapton Road, she told a couple of the women who worked with me to watch themselves as I could get violent with them. One of them who was the receptionist, had the decency to ask me about it but, of course, I reassured her that in no way was I like that. My son's mother was a very sick person, mentally. It had been totally uncalled for.

I was obviously thinking with my nuts, as in the early days when we first got together, my son's mother had invited one of our other neighbours from another bedsit upstairs for a cup of tea and a chat. She was a black girl, 18 to 19, and very, very sexy. She was still a virgin and I looked at her virginity as a challenge. It wasn't long before we ended up in bed together, but we only went a couple of times.

When my son's mother found out I think she felt threatened. One night when I came home from work, I found she and one of her mates beating up the black girl. Of course, I stopped it straight away. Then my son's mother started lying saying she was pregnant. I had to let my new friend go, which was a big mistake, because my son's mother miscarried a few months later. So looking back, it was all lies. I had been conned by the oldest trick in the book. I was very naive in those days and I totally missed out being with someone as decent as my new friend. But things always happen for a reason, as they say.

While I was in the Scrubs I had a good think about where my son's mother and I were going and by the time I got out, I felt I needed to end it with her. She was toxic in every way. I had decided months earlier to tell everyone that I was getting out the day after the actual day I was getting out, because if I wanted to catch out my son's mother, then I had good reason to fire her off.

When I turned up at our door after going out with my mum, stepdad and sister that night I found out that she was out with my son. This was at 11 pm, hardly a safe time to be out and about with a young baby in London, so I knew she was up to something, although I couldn't prove anything. If there had been a bloke with her when she came home, I would have, more than likely, been in the police cells that night for sure. By luck, she was alone.

A few weeks before we separated, I let her go out on her own while I babysat one Friday night. My thinking was to give her a break from our son. I found out a couple of days later from one of her friends, she'd had sex with a guy on her night out and she even wanted sex from me when she returned home.

I must admit I went ballistic and I hit her a few times, but not full fist. I am in no way proud of that. I was driven to it by all her lies and with what she had done behind my back. The following day when I got home from work, she had packed up and gone. To be honest, I was glad to see the back of her and I got on with my life. A couple of days later, however, when I was visiting my sister, my son's mother turned up at my sister's door saying that my son was in Great Ormond Street Hospital and that I was needed as soon as possible because a dog had attacked him. By the sound of what she was saying I thought he was on a life support machine or something.

I, of course, got there as soon as I could. It turned out she had gone to stay with a friend who had a pit bull kind of dog and they had left the dog alone with my son in a room and for some reason the dog had attacked him. When I saw him there were no marks on him at all. He looked perfectly healthy. Rather stupidly as I think about it now, I went along with her story.

Later I found out that this was all lies to get me to the hospital. We visited my son every day and after a few days I met at least a dozen other people, who it turned out were from social services or doctors. They started accusing me of hitting or abusing my son in some way. I, of course, denied it, because it was a blatant lie from my son's mother and it was the last straw for her. I packed her off within a week after that. In no way was I going to put up with it, she was not only wasting the hospital's time, but the professionals too, which in my mind would have been better spent on someone who had been abusing a child.

When I put her on the train back to Inverness, there was a group of rowdy lads in the same train coach she was getting on with my son. I could see she was in her element and I'm quite sure she would have got up to something with at least one of them, judging from past experiences, allegedly.

When she was trying to keep us together, she said she would go on the game for me (like I have always wanted to be a pimp, not) and she would give me all the money she would earn, as long as we could stay together. This put me against her even more. It was like calling me a pimp or a leech of some kind and that is something I am not and never will be.

I didn't miss my son's mother one bit. But this didn't do my alcoholism any good. I had more money, so went out more. I wasn't looking for sex, I needed a break from all that, after all that my son's mother had put me through, plus I felt my way was a much safer option. As a parting shot she stole quite a bit of jewellery of mine.

A few months later, one night when I was in the Three Crowns in N16, I met my future daughter's mother sister. I have always been attracted to long haired ladies and she had long natural mousy blonde hair down her back and was quite good looking. As I got to know her I found that I could strongly relate to her, as we had very similar family backgrounds. Like me, she had also suffered abuse from her family while growing up, but neither of us wanted to open up fully to each other about it probably because I was self-medicating my skeletons by my alcoholism, but we cannot hide from our skeletons forever, as I now know.

I was a suffering alcoholic, where she was a self-harmer, although, I didn't not know this at first. We went to the Bronx night club after the Three Crowns. I got the impression that she was just using me to get into the Bronx, because when I came back from the toilets, she was dancing with this big black guy. Stupidly, I kicked off with the guy in front of the club owner (who I found out later was the father to her daughter) and a club full of black people. It wasn't a wise move for a white guy to make. This guy was saying, "Do you know who I am?" I replied, "I don't give a monkey's who you are." The club owner soon calmed it down, but by that time I had decided that she was not for me, so just left her to it and left the club.

I was still annoyed about it the next day, so I wrote a quick letter to her basically telling her what I thought of her. Unwittingly (maybe out of habit) I put my address on it.

I was not expecting a reply, but a couple of days later I got a letter apologising and asking me round to her place. So, I went around to hers and was greeted by her whole family and her sister and her kids. Her sister was sat quite near to me and kept getting closer and closer. I was friendly towards her, but I was more interested in my daughter's mother sister. My future daughter's mother was at one point sitting across from me. She had her legs apart and was showing me her crutch through her knickers. I easily saw the spider's legs round the edges of her knickers. I was trying hard not to look at her at the time.

I thought this could be some kind of test or trap, so I didn't give into it, but if we had been on our own it would have been a totally different matter. I don't perform in front of an audience, not even while drunk or on drugs. I had gone round to my daughter's mother's sister thinking that we would be having sex. With everyone being there, I thought no chance, so gave up on the idea and made my excuses and went home. As per usual, I called at the off-licence, like you do.

I kept trying to get inside my daughter's mother's sister's knickers as time went on, but because she knew about my son's mother and I'd packed them off back to Inverness, she was not happy and I suppose she did not trust me or for that matter trust any men in general. She kept blowing hot and cold with me. It did my head in at times, as I never knew where I was with her.

Then one day my son's mother turned up out of the blue, obviously trying to get back with me. Being one not to pass up on sex on a plate, I went with the flow, so to speak. My son's mother had only been at mine a couple of days when one morning, my daughter's mother's sister turned up unexpectedly and I thought oh hell, here we go. She was a little upset at first, as was my son's mother, but within minutes it all calmed down and they seemed quite OK with each other.

An hour later we all went to my daughter's mother's sister's place. She was living in a mother and baby hostel in Green Lanes, near Manor House. I was sent out of the room to make us all a brew and when I came back it had been decided that we were going to look after her daughter for a couple of days. At the time both of us didn't know for how long. This was on the Wednesday afternoon and by Friday I was getting a bit worried so I nipped round on my bike. There was a woman caretaker on duty as usual and I asked her about my daughter's mother's sister and she told me she had attempted suicide by taking pills. I had to sit down because I couldn't believe what I was hearing. The woman asked me if I knew where her daughter was. I told her she was at mine, then the woman told me I would have to speak to the police.

The copper asked me a few questions over the phone and even asked me if I knew my son's mother and he mentioned her by name which shocked me, as until that point I knew nothing about the pills. They had got her name from the pill bottle my son's mother had given my daughter's mother's sister. I had to deny knowing her because I didn't want nicking for something I'd had no part in. I knew though I could easily be implicated and at the time that is what I thought might happen, so I ended up covering up for my son's mother even though I was not at fault in any way. I knew the police could easily fit me up with something. It was well known in the circles that I mixed in at the time that the police could easily do that.

The next day Social Services came round for my daughter's mother's sister's daughter while I was at work. They said that the baby had a full nappy and had not been looked after properly. When I'd left to go to work that morning everything was fine. At the time my thoughts were that I was relieved that the police had not nicked either of us, even though I knew I had not done anything, but it is well known in the circles I used to knock about in that if the Old Bll wants to nick you, they will find something, allegedly.

(I've never been innocent when I've been sent down, yet, maybe when they see this comment it might happen. I've even had an MOT at the side of the road before now. It was in Preston one night and the copper must have been well wound up when he couldn't find anything to nick me for).

The next day my son's mother had gone without a bye or leave, obviously with her tail between her legs. The baby was taken into care and of course, my daughter's mother's sister was distraught about it all. She had to accept that what she had done was wrong for her daughter's welfare and as a friend I helped her as much as I could do. I felt that in no way would we ever become more than just friends, although at that time I did want more from her, but I had to accept that being a friend was better than nothing at all and I gladly accepted that as a true friend would do.

Then in mid 1982/1983 I started seeing my future daughter's mother. She had sent me a letter telling me that her sister was not interested in me sexually, but after a few more letters we arranged to meet one Friday night. I wasn't sure whether her address on the letter was 8 or 81, as the comma looked more like a 1, so I had a lot of trouble finding her as she lived on a large council estate not far from Tower Bridge and it was not in a good area.

While I was wandering around trying to find her flat, I met Mad Irish Tom, who asked me in no uncertain terms what I was up to. Luckily, I had the letter on me and I showed it him. I was friendly in every way with him, but he still warned me off. I ignored him. I just thought he was a pretend gangster (but, I was to find out just how he lived up to his nickname of Mad Irish Tom). I gave up trying to find her that night and decided to go back home and get p-, as you do.

We ended up meeting about a week or so later and at first, things were fine. She was also a drinker like me, and loved to get drunk on Emva Crème, every Monday night when she got her family allowance. Things got very volatile at times between us. On one occasion we were arguing and she came at me with two pen knives with three inch blades, one in each hand. She was attempting to slash my arms, so I slapped her across the face and that quietened her down.

She never tried that again.

I put the volatile nature of our relationship down to the fact that we both had cancers. She was a bit of a dartboard where sex was concerned

And once while we were making love and in the throes of passion she was biting my neck with what little front teeth she had (she'd had an iron deficiency while being pregnant with one of her kids). I had a large boil on my neck and it was ready to burst. By the end of our session my boil was gone, drained, so she was a good cure. I know that's gross, but it's very true.

On one of our many drunken nights she invited one of her neighbours and the neighbour's son from the ground floor flats around for a drink and also a few members of her family were there too. For some reason as the night went on and we were all getting drunker and drunker, for no apparent reason, we all started to throw eggs at passing buses.

In my very drunken state, I climbed on to the scaffolding outside her flat and was just joking around. By accident, thinking that I was looking through my girlfriend's bedroom window, I was so drunk I couldn't focus properly and was completely disorientated. It turned out it was Mad Irish Tom's bedroom window. That soon sobered me up and I quickly got back inside.

They were still making a nuisance of themselves, so much so that one of her other neighbours, my daughter's mother had nicknamed him Heart Attack, as he'd had a heart attack in the past (her family and her were not the brightest of people) started to shout at us through his window and he offered me out. I took him up on it, not even thinking twice about it as I should have done and I went downstairs to confront him. But I soon found out that this was a bad move on my part. It was a set-up; a trap.

He was on the next floor down and we met near the steps. I think by this point we were both angry. His wife was there to and to be honest all we did was have a bit of a scuffle. Nothing too serious. Afterwards, he said he would like a word with my girlfriend.

So as we were virtually at the top of the steps, Mad Tom came out of nowhere and attacked me from behind with a pickaxe handle, which I thought was very brave of him. In no time at all I was on the ground and he was just about to hit me over the back of my head , when the guy I'd been scuffling with shouted 'no' and covered the back of my head with his back. He took the full force of the blow on his back. It must have hurt him like hell. I heard him cry out in pain.

I have no doubt in my mind now and even soon after it happened, Tom could have easily smashed my skull and I am quite certain he would have killed me or put me in a wheelchair at the very least. He definitely saved my life that night and I am of course very grateful that he did like anyone would have done.

After Tom had finished with me I limped back to my girlfriend's flat and within 10 minutes I went out to try and sort it out, not in a violent way, but verbally. Nothing more than that. Mad Tom came out once again with the pickaxe handle in his hand and I backed off sharpish, heading back to my girlfriend's door. Then, from nowhere, I felt a blow to the side of my face and that was the last thing I remember. Apparently, three other big, brave guys had joined in with hammers and bottles and I was knocked out. When I woke up my girlfriend was over me and within minutes so was a paramedic.

When I was walking to the ambulance I noticed four

policemen sat in an unmarked police car on the car park, who had witnessed everything and did nothing to stop it.

I approached their car and asked if they were going to arrest them. One of them, I think he was a sergeant, turned round and said I deserved all I got. Considering Tom had very nearly killed me, I thought his comment was totally out of order and I didn't know exactly what he meant by it and to be honest, I still don't. I have no idea how I deserved it, as in my eyes I had looked through the wrong window by accident. Nothing more than that.

I didn't press it any further and I didn't want to add getting nicked to my troubles and that was a big possibility. A few weeks later Tom had hold of me once again in a local pub toilets and if it had not been for another customer trying to calm it down, I would have been badly beaten up again. In fact, Tom and his mate rounded on him. I should have stopped and helped the guy, as he had helped me, but I fled the scene. Later that night I went to the police station and when I told the desk sergeant what had happened he just laughed and said 'so what'? It makes me think that perhaps Mad Tom was some kind of informant.

I have seen in the past how the police protect them and turn a blind eye to whatever they get up to, (allegedly). They did much the same with my second stepdad and he was a known nonce. Quite often the CID from the local police station would keep popping round for coffee. I didn't know what the script was at the time though, as I was too young to understand, but it dawned on me how close I had been to being killed that night in South-East London.

I was taken to Guy's Hospital where I had an x-ray and generally checked over. I was given the all-clear and sent home with some very strong painkillers and believe me I needed them. Everywhere, I had bruises on my bruises.

CID questioned me that night, but conveniently they seemed to forget to tell me that I needed to press charges within three weeks.

I must admit looking back, I might have done the same thing as Mad Tom had done, but maybe not try to kill them. Certainly beat them up, not with a pickaxe handle though. Only cowards use weapons. I was in the wrong place at the wrong time and quite obviously in the wrong company. There was most certainly a lot of bad feeling against my daughter's mother and her family by her neighbours and most people in general.

I was stupid enough to get involved with them. At the time I didn't know the full extent of what was happening around me and to be honest, I still don't because of my drinking and maybe a few rumours that were flying around about my daughter's family. Either way, I didn't and don't not know the full story where they were concerned and more than likely never will.

I fully realise and accept that what we all did that night was wrong. In my defence I was very drunk and out of my head. I'm sure I' m not the first or the last person to do wrong when drunk.

A few days or so later I found out that two press guys had come to see me. I had no idea what newspaper they were from or for that matter that they were even journalists at the time as they did not even introduce themselves as journalists. It must be the norm with them. I thought they were some gangster friends of my daughter's mother, as they looked the part.

I later found out that my girlfriend and generally all her family were trouble and I had unwittingly got involved with the family from hell. They could have caused an argument in a cemetery and in no way should I ever have trusted any of them. For some stupid reason I thought, as the saying goes, *honour among thieves* and I turned a blind eye or ear as to what was happening around me. The saying is total rubbish, well regarding them it was.

I was once told by my daughter's mother that when they were visiting her sister in North London, they had broken into her neighbour's flat which was above his night club (The Bronx) in Casanova Road and taken a briefcase with all the owner's takings inside. I think there was a grand at least so I was told the owner could not prove anything. Its been said that there is no such thing as the perfect crime, as people will always brag about what they have done and they were bragging when they told me as if they were some kind of master criminals.

On another occasion, we were all staying at mine one Saturday night. Everything was fine or so I thought, then she told me out of the blue, that she was going home and started getting her stuff together. We began arguing because, for the life of me, I didn't understand what the hell was happening. Why was she suddenly wanting to go home and not in any way going to tell me why? It was like some sick mind game. The argument spilled out into the street as I followed her out and for some unknown reason I grabbed her eldest daughter and held a bread knife to her throat. It wasn't a very sharp knife.

I was very drunk and I had no intention of harming her. Of course I was the only one who knew that it was just a threat. Looking back, I should have helped her go instead of trying to stop her. We live and learn and I did eventually learn.

The police were called and I was taken to the local police station. I got the fright of my life when the murder squad started to interview me. I thought here we go, a 15-

year touch. Even though I was innocent of killing anyone, you still tend to worry when the murder squad is sitting across from you. Your bottle starts to twitch, to say the least. They quickly saw it as it was, that it was just something done in the heat of the moment by someone who was off his head on booze and the CID bloke actually stood up in court and spoke up for me.

I recognised the same copper who interviewed me from a couple of months or so earlier. He had come round to my daughter's mother one Saturday morning to ask about her Turkish husband. Until that Saturday morning, I hadn't had the slightest idea that she was married. It turned out my daughter's mother and another of her sisters had married for money and the Turkish guy whom she had married, was already married in Turkey and when his Turkish wife came over to find him and find out what was happening, he murdered her, obviously to keep her quiet and stay in the country. Apparently he stabbed her to death and to escape capture by the police he jumped off a bridge into the Thames and drowned. I doubt he wanted to drown, he just wanted to escape, but being that the Thames is far too dangerous to swim in for most people, he drowned. (I must add my daughter's mother told me all this).

I must have had somebody watching over me, because, after a lengthy discussion with my probation officer, he told me in no uncertain terms, the best thing to do was burn my bridges where she was concerned and what he said all made sense. I took notice of what he said and cut all ties with her. That pleased my mother very much. Since being attacked by Mad Tom and co. she kept saying one day she would get a knock on her door by the police saying I had been found dead. I think my mother was relieved I had made that decision. God knows how I managed to survive what was going on around me at the time.

I tried to get on with my life as best I could, but with the drinking being an every night routine, things were getting worse. The amount I was drinking was still the same and the effect it was having on me was getting worse or so it seemed at the time. Alcoholism is one of those illnesses that your head tells you you're fine and all the people who keep telling you that you need to put it down are all wrong, but in reality, it is more the other way round as most people know.

It is the compulsion to drink and I have been told in some ways it is worse than heroin to come off. I have never been on hard drugs at all, so, I cannot comment on that and hard drugs have never ever been an option for me and never will be, by the grace of God.

After that incident, I noticed that my neighbours had less tolerance of me and started judging me adversely because of my alcoholism, and everything had gone downhill. Not many people understand why alcoholics do what they do, but alcoholism is a serious mental illness.

I had to wear my alcoholic blinkers and my hypothetical mask, so I really did not give a monkey's about what others might have thought or could be saying about me. I know that all the time I lived in Dalston, East London, there was all kinds of comments and rumours which were mainly behind my back and in some cases whatever was being said was so dressed up that only the person saying it was the only person who actually knew what they were on about, as in some sick mind game.

What people forget quite conveniently is I never asked for my alcohol problem. It found, picked me and it would not let go of me for eighteen years and as much as I would like to change my past, it isn't possible.

Months later, I found out that my ex had fallen pregnant. After having a conversation with her sister I did some quick sums in my head and thought it could be mine. I knew she had not been faithful in the past by any means. To me, we could have drawn straws as to who the father was, so I brushed it off and never gave it a second thought. I even thought it could be Mad Tom's, as he had been sniffing about (that is no disrespect to my daughter, she was the only positive thing to come out of that relationship and I loved her to bits). Anyway, six months down the line, one Thursday night I was watching one of Bernie Winters' shows called *Whose Baby?* Unbelievable, I know.

My ex turned up at my door with her mother, saying this is your daughter. I, of course, was over the moon about it. We tried to rekindle what we had had in the past, but, it was not to be. I have found that it is never wise to backtrack where relationships are concerned.

Apart from that she was still seeing someone (a Liverpudlian) and quite a hard nut where women and kids were concerned. Once again she just stopped coming round and she gave me no excuse as to why. She was good at playing mind games like that and around that time I fell for all her tricks. She was very egotistical in a lot of ways.

Around that time I fell for most people's tricks and mind games, because of the drink. I was very gullible and I only saw things at face value and only really saw the good in people, not as they really were (I definitely wore rose-tinted glasses). I would have made friends with Ian Brady, I was that gullible.

A few months went by and my resentment came to a head. I had found out where she lived and on one Friday night, I nicked a three-ton box van from a local haulage firm, not far from where I lived and took it down to Tower Bridge. I wanted to confront her about the baby. I was off my head on drink and quite angry, not a good combination. When I got there, there was a guy already there. I think he was her eldest daughter's dad.

I kicked off big style, mainly because they were both taking the meikle out of me from an upstairs window. I think they thought I couldn't get to them, but I soon wiped their smug grins off their faces when I was kicking the door down. I couldn't get anywhere near them, so in a stupid drunken moment I decided to go on a wrecking spree with the three-ton truck and wrote off a minivan and a Triumph 2000 Estate and a transit van, all belonging to her neighbours and as I tried to run away I was caught by the local police easily and quickly. I was that drunk I could barely walk.

I was breathalysed at the station and was found to be twice over the limit. I was arrested and thrown in a cell to sober up. I honestly thought I was going down for it, even my probation officer thought so, and looking back I should have. While appearing at the magistrates court, I bumped into one of my victims, i.e., the Triumph 2000 Estate owner.

I didn't know at the time that he was the owner and he was the guy who had saved my life when he'd taken a blow from Mad Tom.

He had a young mate with him and they were not best pleased about what I had done to their cars. They were more or less threatening to throw me over the balcony in Tower Bridge courthouse and I believed they would have done given the chance, which of course I never gave them. The thing is I never intended to destroy anything of his. After all, I owed him my life, but I was so drunk and so angry at my daughter's mother that night. I just didn't know what I was doing.

So the next time I went to court I had a friend of my sister's with me. He was an ex-boxer and was built like a brick outhouse, so I felt a lot safer with him. I think I went to court about half a dozen times and thankfully I had a very good solicitor. If I'd gone down for it, it just might have sorted my drinking out, even though prison never did anything for any of my problems in the past. Prison in those days and probably even now was, and is, for banging you up from society, so it keeps you off the streets for x amount of time. It does nothing to sort you out, as it should do. It just preserves your thinking and in the way you are and maybe even makes some people even worse. It certainly did with me most of the time.

Eventually, when I was sentenced, I got 250 hours community service, a five-year ban from driving and around £400 in fines. Southwark Council had tried to get £1,000 to rebuild a small wall I had demolished when I hit the two vehicles I wrote off and virtually shoved them through the wall.

The magistrate said to me at the time that I could pay for the damage to the wall if I ever came into any money and laughed as he was saying it. This comment puzzled me, but it was less for me to pay so I just went with the flow. By not getting a non-custodial sentence, I thought to myself, nothing to lose now, so drank more. I didn't want to know her at all now, which was a positive thing.

I had kept in touch with my daughter's mother's sister though, so I started seeing her, but only as a friend. We went out around North London on Friday and Saturday nights. Usually, we started at the Three Crowns then on to the Bronx night club which was just around the corner. Although I was still drinking I think I still had all my faculties. I had a good job, but my timekeeping was rubbish to say the least. I was working seven days a week, five at my 9 to 5 job and at the weekends on my two bosses' houses. I think if it had not been for the fact that I was doing work on their houses, I would have lost my job far sooner than I did, but I was saving them a lot of money, because they were paying me through the business, as in, wages and I was getting taxed on it too and not cash in hand like a decent boss (person) would have done. In other words, they were taking the meikle out of me in every way and the taxman, but then again, I was taking the meikle out of them with my timekeeping.

For some reason the penny finally dropped about my main boss. I sussed out that he was bi. How I knew this was around the time I answered the job advert, I used to answer adverts at the back of *Time Out*, in the personal section. I was mainly looking for women, but, men too. I never sussed out it was him until quite a bit later. We met one night outside Streatham tube station. I didn't realise I was meant to be meeting him. When I bumped into him at the station it never clicked it was him I was meant to be meeting. So I just let it go and assumed I had been stood up.

While I was working on his house, he kept making gay remarks, but I thought he was just joking and left it at that. The penny finally dropped when another guy whose advert I also answered around the time, visited him while I was doing work on my boss's house and the guy was not best pleased to see me there. That was when I realised that my boss was bi.

When I met the other guy a few months earlier I turned him down, as he was just not my type at all. Whoever I have been with in the past, man or woman, there has always been an attraction of some kind. I had none for

him or my boss for that matter. Even his wife kept making
a play for me, because I think my boss had suffered from
angina, and she was having to do without. Mind you, if I
had gone there I might have got angina too.

Their daughter was stunning. She also looked a lot
like her mum when her mum was younger. But, seeing how
her mother turned out, it kept me away from the daughter
too, even though she was stunning at the time,

Then, weeks later, I came home after work at my
usual time of 6.45 pm and at first I noticed two panes of
glass had been broken in my front living room window.
Then to my horror, when I entered my flat through the front
door, I noticed smoke coming from my bedroom door. The
door was shut and I foolishly ran to the door and opened it.
The room was thick with smoke ,so much so, I could not see
my bedroom window at the other side of the room. Straight
away I ran to the pay phone across the road and within
minutes the fire brigade was on the scene and the police
followed shortly afterwards.

I noticed that my next door but one neighbours (the
druggies) were taking the meikle about what had happened
to me, but I didn't let on that I could hear them. They were
druggies and dealers and always causing some kind of
trouble with people. When I eventually got in, I found that
all my clothes had been piled up and set alight so I was left
with only what I was stood up in, (my work clothes). The
seat of the fire was only a foot away from a calor gas heater,
so both my neighbours and I were very lucky not to have
been blown up.

One of my neighbours, a Pakistani family on the top
floor, had witnessed what had happened and it sounded a
lot like my daughter's mother (years later when we briefly
got back together in late 1988, she told me she had set my

clothes alight because she had found knickers under my pillow). I seriously doubted that this was the truth. I never found any knickers there and if there was I have no idea whose they could have been. About that time I was sleeping around quite a bit and one morning I woke up in my own bed and it took quite a while to work out where I was.

Throughout my drinking, on average I would drink six cans of jet fuel (Tennent's Super) per night. I was totally off my face most nights and in no way would I recommend it especially with what was about to happen, although to be brutally honest, I don't blame drink or drugs totally for what occurred to me in late 1985/early 1986.

I blame my family, their friends, my neighbours, my so-called friends and not forgetting the tabloid press, for simply not being decent enough people to be upfront, genuine and honest.

In November of 1985 I started decorating my living room on the nights that I was not going to college or playing badminton. Normally, I do a proper job with most things that I do, but because all my furniture etc., had to be piled up in my bedroom, I couldn't relax enough to chill out at night, so I rushed the decorating in my living room and didn't put my front curtains back properly like I should have done. When I say properly there was an inch or two gaps in the smaller one of my front curtains. From the inside, it looked small, hardly noticeable (my view), but from the outside, which I never really saw, it looked a lot bigger and obviously very noticeable to anyone outside.

Most nights I would chill out by having a bath then I would sit around and walk around my flat naked, obviously unaware that I was being watched and had gained quite a large audience outside. I also got into the habit of sitting in my front room masturbating, (it is quite a natural thing to do and most single people, male or female do it. It was something I'd picked up in nick. You either pull the head off it or turn bi. I did both, while in nick). Then and even now I don't not see any harm in either. I was also drinking and smoking weed, not all at the same time though, it would have been a bit too sticky and would have hindered rolling joints or fags.

I was unaware that I had gained a large audience at the front and even at the back of my basement flat. It took me seven years to find out just how big an audience I really did have, but I will come to that later on.

At the time I put the crowd at the front of my flat down to a local pub that was a few doors down (apparently a famous comedian did a gig there once, so it was quite a popular place) and the fact I lived on a busy main road very close to a bus stop added to the fact nothing stood out of the ordinary. At times the pub got quite busy. One night I was coming out of my flat to go to badminton, when some guy in what I thought was the queue to get into the pub called me over. When I went over, all of a sudden someone he took a photo of me straight in my face. The flash from the camera hurt my eyes and my instant reaction was to lash out. I think I smashed the camera in the guy's face, for which I am sorry, but there was no warning and I thought it was someone's idea of a sick joke.

To be brutally honest though, I don't know why there was so much interest in me. After all, I was a drunk sat in his living room making a prat of himself. How is that in any way in the public's interest or newsworthy? It's not as if I had a twelve-inch penis. Perhaps there was nowt on the telly, but at least I know now how a panda feels or even a goldfish, in constantly being watched. You could say I was seen coming (cumming), but I must say I am amazed that there was not one decent person among the watchers or my friends/family in the seven years it took for me to find out.

From what I know now, it turns out that in my drunkenness, I had stumbled on a law that did not exist in this country. I had found a loophole by accident or apparently, where there was no privacy law in this country around late 1985. From what I now know someone could look through your curtains (which they did) and it was not an offence.

It also seems that I found flaws in some of the ways newspapers go about getting their stories. It seems they expect you to know what is in their newspapers even though you are not even reading any (I must have missed those lessons at school) and if you do not respond (like you would not if you were not reading the newspapers) they deem it true. In my case, I had the family from hell and for their own reasons (money or maybe they did not want their shady pasts coming out) they decided to keep it all from me. Like they say, you can pick your friends, but not your family.

I hardly ever read newspapers. My thoughts on that were and are, I am depressed enough without reading other people's bad news. Apart from that, it is mostly rubbish or lies most days (and only once has a journalist been to my door). In fact, there were two of them, but although they said they were from the national press, they started the conversation by calling me by another name, which at the time I was not remotely impressed about and I shut the door on them. It was a silly thing to do on my part and even on their part, but in my defence, I was a suffering alcoholic. What was their excuse?

I must not have been thinking properly at the time,

but why come from Manchester or wherever they had come from to my front door and treat me in such a way? Everyone deserves respect and calling me by another name was a blatant joke and that happened in early 1993.

Another thing that the tabloid in question has done to me in the past was to knock on my neighbours' doors but never at my door. Apart from being next door to my neighbours my other neighbours knew or know very little about me. At the very most they will only know hearsay, so how can anyone form an opinion on someone fairly?

I can honestly say at no point have I ever cried wolf, as a family member once said I had done. There were no cross conversations. My family and friends and all their friends knew for certain that I didn't know about the newspapers. You have to be aware of what is happening around you to cry wolf if the truth be known. I was doing a very good impersonation of a mushroom or toadstool, thanks to my family, their friends and my friends and of course the gutter press who kept me in the dark as much as they could and would occasionally throw dirt (hearsay) at me. I feel sure this book will go in some way to prove what really did happen.

From early 1986 until I found out in 1993, there were some very weird comments made towards me. One night (early 1986) I went to an Irish pub across from where I lived in Dalston. I had been in the pub a few times before, but not that often. The manager came over to me and said, "We don't serve w- in here," so I replied, "Well, in that case, I will just have a pint of Guinness then" and laughed as I said it. He was not too sure how to react to my comment, so he just served me and we ended up chatting all night and had a lock-in. Trouble was I got that drunk that I was still drunk the next day, so, I didn't go into work.

The bar manager's comment never really stuck in my mind at the time, but I can still remember it must have gone somewhere in my head. This was when the curtains were still partly open and I was completely oblivious to having an audience, so the penny never dropped (fully) about what he was really talking about.

In the same pub a few weeks later I went in because my telly had broken down and I needed to get out of my flat, as I was getting stir crazy, so I went to the pub to watch telly. I wasn't sure what was going to be on, but by luck, Clint Eastwood was playing in *Any which way but loose*. I didn't think I was bothering anyone by watching telly. It seems I was because after about half an hour I got up to go to the bar for another pint. Just by chance there was a mirror behind the optics. I knew there had been four blokes playing pool and just by luck I saw in the reflection of the mirror that they had their cues the wrong way round to be playing pool and were heading in my direction. I picked up my empty pint glass that was on the bar and turned round to face them. I think they caught on what would have happened if they came any closer because they backed off sharpish. After that, I got my pint and carried on watching telly. Nothing was said either way.

(I am not saying there were not other times. Quite often people came to my door asking very bizarre things. I will cover them later). It took about three months for me to find out about the curtains and when I did I didn't think I had broken any laws. I know there is a saying that the law is an ass and in my way of looking at it then and even now, the law cannot be that good if a drunk can find a law that doesn't even exist.

I feel sure that some tabloid somewhere would have put a spin on it, in that I was showing my private parts to the world. But in reality, I was the victim of peeping toms, nothing more, nothing less. I am in no way a rebel of any kind, not then not even now and the fact that a tabloid was sniffing about and that they are meant to be in the business of circulating information around the world, but didn't have the common decency or common sense to inform me. It beggars belief. Mind you, the newspaper in question has a reading age of five to seven and more than likely has adult infants as journalists.

I mean as far as I am aware there is no law against masturbation in private and also apart from it making you blind (allegedly). What is the harm? Everyone does it and if someone says they do not do it, then they are either lying, have no genitals or no hands and to be honest I have no reason to be ashamed of being caught doing it.

Although I was made to feel ashamed by people around me, who by rights should have supported me or at the very least informed me as a decent person would have done, instead they decided to rip me off and rip the tabloids off.

As I see it now, so I got caught masturbating, so what? I was also smoking weed, but not sure about that. One day it is legal, another day it isn't. In my view, what happens behind closed doors should remain there.

The only thing I did that was a bit perverted or out of order in any way and I am of course ashamed of, is that I tried to have sex with my mother's dog. In my defence, I was a suffering alcoholic and as high as a kite on dope and weed. I think anyone in that state would have been capable of anything and to be honest I have been with plenty of the two-legged variety of dogs on many occasions and drink and drugs leads to all kinds of problems. Perhaps I confused the two-legged dogs I had been with in the past with a four-legged one.

You only need to go to any A&E on a Friday or Saturday night to see what drink does to people. It is far more harmful than most people think it is. Weed and pot mainly just gives you the munchies where you will more than likely eat something you would not normally eat unless you have a whitey, but that is a different matter. I have had a few whiteys in the past. They can be quite scary. Once I ate a cheese on toast sandwich with jam on it, only the once though. My ex-wife looked at me like I was going mad and thinking back I must have been off my head to make the mistake of marrying her. Also I must add in some cases, even my own, it can cause mental health problems. It is not as harmless as some people make it out to be. It's like horses for courses, what suits you but might not suit me and so on.

Anyway, no journalists or police were knocking at my door in 1985/1986 or even until 1993, even though there were questions in Parliament about it, it seems. Apparently, one MP came out with, "He deserves everything that happens to him," (meaning me) which as I look back now, was quite big of him, as no one had even asked me anything or asked for my side of the story. They had all gone off a third rate newspaper's views, which in turn had been fed information, by low life drug dealers, takers and working girls, (not the nine to five variety). So, well done all, you all deserve a pat on the back for how good you all are doing your jobs, but the pat I am referring to is not the hand type.

I can honestly say that I have never had anyone at my door at all while I was living in London. The nearest I have ever been to being made aware of my curtains was one time when I was walking back from the off-licence one night (this happened in early January 1986, when my curtains were still slightly open). A helicopter was flying overhead. It was quite low, not an unusual sight in London, but for some reason, it shone its searchlight right on me (it was like the intro scene to *Mr Bean*)and someone on a loudhailer told me to shut my curtains, which I thought was quite bizarre and a very strange thing to happen.

I thought at the time that I was going off my head, maybe I was suffering from the DTs or maybe the spliff I'd had, earlier was a bit too strong. It certainly wasn't something that happens all the time. That's why it has stuck in my mind. It's not every day someone in a helicopter shouts at you or even shines a light on you. Something to tell the grand kids I suppose.

Then, on another occasion, I came home from work to find a board up at one of my front windows. It had a police stamp on it, but I thought I had been broken into again so I decided to check the window from the inside. There was nothing wrong so I thought that it was someone's idea of a joke, although I didn't understand fully why someone would do that kind of thing. I sawed through the wood holding it in place and threw it all to one side of my front garden and never give it another thought.

To me, you would have thought that if it was the police (which, looking back it must have been) and they had put it there and that by going to all the trouble of wedging a board up at my window, that they would have posted an official warning letter as well or had a policeman knocking at my door or stood outside my door. But it seems even though I was not reading the newspapers, people (including the police) thought I knew what the newspapers were saying.

Late one night a very sexy Greek woman said to me while she was serving me in a kebab shop, which I frequented, "You can't read English, can you?" I said, "Of course I can." As usual, nothing further was said. Then also around that time, after I had noticed what the newspapers were saying (early 1993), I had been writing to my ex some quite raunchy letters, an off-licence owner whose shop I had been in loads of times over the years before, said to me, "You can't read can you?" I replied, "I can write, but, not read."(I was joking, of course, I can read and write, but strangely I find it impossible to see things I am not reading like the tabloid seems to think I can). I think it made him scratch his head over that one. Obviously by that time I knew what he was referring to, unlike the many times over the seven years previously when people said strange things and I didn't have a clue what they were talking about.

To be totally honest, both were not far from the truth. I wasn't reading the newspapers. How do the tabloids make people aware if they cannot read, either through lack of education or being blind, etc? It seems to me that they assumed someone would tell me. In those previous seven years the tabloid reporter would quite often go to my neighbours' doors but never knock at my door and the tabloid would be constantly changing my name, obviously to keep me off the scent. So looking back, I stood no chance.

I say this because a couple of times when I was reading the newspaper in 1989 when I was in prison, I could identify a bit too strongly with some of the things I sometimes spotted. If I mentioned it to any member of my family though they knew nothing about it and called me paranoid.

I must admit while being a suffering alcoholic I assumed my family would be there for me. I was mentally ill at the time. Perhaps the tabloid in question was so up themselves that they couldn't or wouldn't see the real truth.

In early 1986, apparently one of my neighbours also put his penis on show. He was an old black guy. The difference between us was his was a deliberate action and mine was accidental. He was black and I'm white. The reason I mention this is because a young black guy confronted me one night when I was on my way out. He was shouting at me saying, "You wouldn't have got away with the curtain incident if you had been black."

To be honest, if I had been black I would have at least been aware from day one and I would have been brought in for questioning. Of course I would have been fully aware of my curtains being slightly open a lot earlier than I really was and also that the press was involved. I would have known the full extent of everything that was happening which was solely all behind my back and I would not have had to go through all the violence and abuse I had had to endure before I found out in 1993. I think I definitely got the worst part of the deal. This might sound like I am being racist; I don't think I am. The young guy was right. I would not have got away with it and that is the way it should have been no matter what colour or race I am. Not knowing was the worst option.

A few weeks later (in early 1986) my southern sister and her work colleague came to my flat late one Thursday night. It was about 11 pm and basically they told me about my curtains being slightly open and said, "People can see what you are up to." They didn't mention anything about the newspapers or media being involved. I thought it was confined to around the Dalston, Hackney area at the very most.

The next night, which was Friday, I managed to stay sober, although I had a few spliffs instead. I didn't have any telly. That had broken down at least a month before, so I listened to the radio as quietly as I possibly could. So much so, I could hear someone ranting and raving outside. He kept shouting, "Who's told him, who's told him?"

He sounded very, very angry and from where I was sitting, I kept looking at the gap in my curtains and to be honest, I got quite scared, I was half expecting my front windows to come crashing in at any second. The next morning I found clumps of grass outside my front window that had been pulled up and thrown at my windows. Thankfully, there were no bricks to hand, otherwise I would not have had any windows left, so, it was quite obvious to me, that me finding out had p- someone off, big style.

I knew, without doubt, I was going to have the meikle taken out of me, but I quickly learned to ignore most of it. I think because of my abusive and rough upbringing, I had learned very early on in my childhood to put the blinkers on automatically if I found myself in a situation I didn't like or was having trouble coping with. Of course my drinking helped in its own way. Quite often it acted as a cushion or a shield and tricked me into believing alcohol was my friend, whereas it was just one of my many false friends.

At the time I was still babysitting for my southern sister's friend on Thursday and Friday nights. I was doing it for extra cash for my alcohol habit. My sister and my mother were all working girls, so I knew at times they would have quite a lot of money to hand. My sister's friend seemed to be doing very well for herself. She was buying all kinds of stuff for her flat and herself and her son and one Saturday morning she asked me to go to an electrical store in a taxi to collect some stuff she had already paid for.

While I was picking it up she wanted me to say to the

shop staff that all the stuff was for me, which I thought at the time was quite a strange thing to say. As usual I went with the flow, because I trusted her, but when I mentioned it to the staff they all looked at each other as if to say what the heck is this guy on about.

A few months or so later, she bought herself a small yellow BMW, which broke down within six months of her buying it and had to be scrapped. With what I know now, it must have been karma, but at the time I was pleased for her like any genuine friend would have been. I didn't think for a second that she was feeding off me.

My southern sister was also quite flush too, as out of the blue she had had a nose job done in Harley Street and I am quite sure that would not have been cheap. I thought that they were doing well at their chosen profession and thought nothing more about it. I had no reason to think otherwise. My sister has since kept insisting her boyfriend paid for the op. because he broke her nose in an argument. I doubt that very much, but I do think she cashed in on my misfortune, as a vile, toxic person would do.

Just to clarify, in no way did, do I agree with what job they were all doing. I couldn't do anything to change it, although I hated it. I mean who would want their mum and sister to be doing that? Quite a few times I was disgusted with the way my mother went about things, but mostly I blamed how she dealt with her alcoholism. If I had not loved her like I did I would have walked away very early on in my life. But because my love for all my family was unconditional, I never judged them and I obviously thought they would not judge me on my past either, but I was way off the mark.

Occasionally, I would go to London to visit my mother and on one occasion we went to the Hilton Hotel. I was totally unaware of what she was really up to at the time. We sat in a bar quite close to the entrance of the hotel and I assumed it was just like anywhere else and when you need another drink you go to the bar. I even got told off for going there so I unwittingly brought attention to myself and I soon gave up on having a drink there and sat in the lobby minding my own business or so I thought. Two youngish Arabs kept looking at me, then at each other and they seemed to be saying something in their own language and laughing and looking in my direction. Before I could find out what the crack was with them, these two big security guards got hold of me by the arms and threw both my mother and I out the hotel. I didn't have a clue why.

Unbeknown to me, mother had started a new career as a working girl (not the nine to five type though. This was in late 1978) and for some reason she had dragged me into it as well, maybe for protection, I'm not quite sure. This was the same mother who, when I was a kid, was very houseproud and it seemed that butter would not melt. Well, on the surface that is what it had looked like back then.

Now she was having sex for money. It all seemed to coincide with her arrival in London and moving in with her boyfriend. I am in no way saying it was his fault, but it was a bit of a coincidence that she had only just moved to London six months previously and she was doing this.

On one occasion while I was living in London, one Friday night in mid-1988 around 8.30 pm my mother came home with one of her girls she was working with (my mother at that time was a madam, which for those of you that don't know, is a manager of a brothel) and they had brought with them a very drunken punter. I don't think he could see very well. He was that drunk.

To say I was angry would have been an

understatement. I didn't show it until the punter had gone. I just tried to ignore it as best I could. Because the punter was very drunk he obviously could not perform, but I think that was part of my mother and the girls' plan. It was Friday night after all, the guy had £400 on him, more than likely all his week's wages, but he didn't have it for long though. They picked his pocket, called a cab and bundled him in it. They slipped the cab driver something as well to help get the bloke out of the area.

I was livid. After all, they had put my niece and myself at risk, but I was more worried about my niece. Even now it disgusts me. I am far from an angel with some of the stuff I have been nicked for in my past, but I would never dream of doing anything like that. If I wrong someone I cannot give eye contact to them afterwards. It's just the way I am. I recently spoke to my niece through Facebook about what her mum and her nan used to do for a living.

Apparently, she was bullied because of it by one of her neighbour's kids and her mother and her nan, knew all about it and why she was being bullied and did nothing to help her. To me it just shows how callous and selfish they both were.

My southern sister sometimes would blame my mother for her turning to prostitution, because, my mother looked after her daughter for quite a few years when her daughter was quite young, but, my mother took all my sister's family allowance to help look after my niece, which left my sister with no money at all, so she turned to prostitution and my mother did not bat an eyelid. Really good parenting skills for both of them, not.

This is what I believe happened about my curtains. Around 1986 a tabloid newspaper got hold of the story. I say this, because it took around three months for me to find out about the gap in my curtains. I'm quite sure that a decent person would not have gone to the press. They would have found a way of telling me or would have gone to the police, who in turn would have told me (even though the police have never questioned me about it ever), but the press blew it out of all proportion, which is the usual case with them. So, thanks to the person who instead of phoning the police or pushing a note through my door, phoned the press instead. The reason is quite obvious: money. The police don't pay for information and I would have said thanks for letting me know if someone had been decent enough to tell me.

The tabloid in question must have thought to themselves it is in the newspaper. Everyone reads newspapers, so it seems people were more than likely talking to me through the newspapers, because every time they spoke to the press, they would have been paid. They would not tell me, because that would have stopped their meal tickets. The big problem was, as I said earlier, I was not a regular reader of any newspaper and I am still not, not even free ones. I would rather read a good book than a newspaper, but that is my personal choice. The tabloid in question should have been decent enough to come to my door, but it is part of the gutter press.

Also if I'd been watching the telly (1985/1986) I would not watch the TV news. Not that I had a telly at the time anyway, so, I was totally unaware of what was happening behind my back because effectively that is where it all was.

My sister from Chorley rang me one Thursday night while I was babysitting for my sister's friend. My northern sister told me to "close my curtains", but just prior to phoning her I'd had a very strong spliff, so I didn't take her seriously and I laughed it off.

I thought that it was some kind of wind-up or joke. I even told my southern sister's friend what had just been said by my northern sister and she laughed it off too. I had no idea that my northern sister was talking about my own curtains at home. I assumed she was talking about my southern sister's friend's curtains, but my southern sister's friend lived on the sixth floor so she didn't really need curtains.

Though I was losing touch with reality at times, I was totally incongruent because of my drinking and drug taking. I was always off my face at night and recovering through the following day, but I must add, my ears and eyes worked perfectly well. If I'd had one decent person around me at that time who would have given me a proper heads up, I'm quite sure I would have known.

On a couple of occasions while babysitting a guy kept phoning up and calling me a w-, but I just told him to f-off and put the phone down on him. I mentioned it to my southern sister's friend who just shrugged it off. I thought it was some half-wit friend of my southern sister's friend or a punter who did not have the courage to speak to me in person, but she knew a lot of low-life, pimps, punters, and the like so I thought it might have been someone like that.

A lot of what I would call strange things were said to me around that time. Quite often, I would bump into one of my neighbours and on one occasion she told me that another of our neighbours was blaming me for their fence falling down and she was more or less blaming our next door but one neighbours(the druggies).

It never really struck me then, but I now know what she was really saying was that the fence fell down because my next door, but one neighbours(the drug dealers) were letting peeping toms, journalists, etc through their house to get round the back of my flat. They would only have had to climb over two fences, one was a chain link fence and the other (the one that fell down) was a six foot board type. There was no other way round.

So as I see it now, they must have been pretty determined to get to the back of my flat and I would bet that my next door but one neighbours (the druggies) would have been charging the peeping toms, journalists, etc. Hence the bloke ranting and raving on the Friday night, the night after I had been informed about my curtains. He would have been quite p- off about losing his drugs money and the night after I was told by my sister and her friend about my curtains when he was ranting and raving trying to find out who had told me, I think he was ready to kill someone by the sound of his voice. He had lost his way of funding his drugs habit, which was more to the point and it is true to say that most, if not all addicts, would sell their granny's teeth for a fix. Sadly, this includes my own family, mainly my southern sister, who was an addict and a suffering alcoholic.

My southern sister's friend had a very unusual request in mid-1987. She had managed to talk me into looking at her son's penis, as according to her he was uncut and his foreskin had gone back to far over his Helmut,(bear with me, I am not a doctor)she wanted me to pull it back to where it should have been. It goes without saying that I was not very keen on doing this to say the least. I think most men would have felt quite awkward unless it was their own child.

I couldn't fully understand why she could not do this herself. I would have thought with her line of work (prostitute) she would be used to all kinds of foreskins and

I asked why she wanted <u>me</u> to do it, but she never explained why.

I went around one Saturday afternoon. We had a brew and a bit of a chat then she called her son into the living room from his bedroom, where he was playing. The living room door was very close to the kitchen door and as her son came in he stopped in his tracks and said, "Mummy, why are those people in the kitchen?" I gave my sister's friend a puzzled look, as I had not noticed anyone in the kitchen when I entered the living room. I was just about to get up and have a look for myself, when she grabbed me by the arm and ordered me out of her flat. In less than a minute I was outside her flat, bike and all.

From what I know now, I think the people in the kitchen could have been the press with a camera and you can imagine the photos they would have taken. They say the camera never lies, total b-. I believe my sister's friend's boyfriend beat her up over this, so I was told much later on, which to me would have been right. To me, using your child like that to gain money is something only nonces would do and a few weeks later my mother tried to blame me for my sister's friend getting beaten up with her boyfriend, but, as usual I was never told why it was my fault and as usual no one wanted to explain.

My mother and the rest of my family were just as bad. They knew I was ill because of alcoholism and they all saw the abuse I was suffering. I have to admit that because of all this, I was and am suffering with PTSD and alchol addiction. I'm quite sure genuine people would have helped me out, not take advantage of the situation like they all did.

That includes the tabloid in question who in their own way totally disregarded my basic human rights, as in my right to reply and my right to defend myself. To cover their lies they apparently said I was refusing to talk to them, but as they never came to me for any response at any time bar in 1993, it just goes to show how cowardly they all are/were. I am talking about a low life newspaper and it is quite well known for being part of the gutter press. Someone told me that although the newspaper in question is mainly for adults, its reading is five or six years old. That just about sums it up as I see it now. Perhaps adult children were writing for them too. It would explain a lot.

My mother was in Jamaica at the time the curtain incident was going on. She arrived at Heathrow airport one Sunday afternoon. My sister's friend and I picked her up. I couldn't hear exactly what was being said because they were whispering in the back of the taxi. Then, my mother smacked me round the back of the neck and called me a "dirty bastard". My sister's friend calmed her down quickly and nothing more was said about it on the day or even to this day. I can honestly say I have never had a proper conversation about it with anyone, apart from my wife, but she was more of a sounding board because she genuinely didn't know.

If I could have read between the lines of the verbal abuse earlier or if the people who were attacking me had had some kind of message on their knuckles perhaps I would have known sooner. I must have missed those classes when I was at school.

When I finally found out in 1993, the tabloid in question came out with," Had I not noticed the writing on the wall?" Hypothetically, of course, anything I noticed, I would have mentioned to members of my family or my friends. It was like asking the three wise monkeys most of the time and to me, if the journalist had been taking proper notice, they would have realised that the main reason I was not talking to them was that I didn't know anything about them sniffing around. So really good journalism skills don't you think? I have never ever said no comment so how these so-called highly skilled (allegedly) journalists came up with the notion I did not want to talk to them beggars belief.

I nearly always went to my mother's for Sunday tea and most of the time my southern sister would be there with her friend and all their kids. My mother always bought a Sunday tabloid and I would read it too, if I was given the chance. By the time I got the newspaper there would be bits missing, sometimes even full pages and I asked my sister who always seemed to get to it faster than anyone else why this was (I now know why). She would say there was an advert or something she wanted to keep and foolishly I believed her. I had no reason not to.

In the outside world I was suffering from all kinds of abuse from strangers in the street. I couldn't go anywhere without being verbally or quite often violently attacked. This made me more introverted towards people outside the family circle and my trust was zero. That included my workplace friends and my family up north. My mother would often drum it into me not to trust any of my family up north or their friends, as in her words they all had "hidden agendas", and I should not take any notice of anything they might say. In reality, I should not have trusted any of my family, (north or south) at all or any of their friends and even my own friends in London or in Lancashire. They were all as bad as each other. It is very much like they say, "not everyone who smiles at you is your friend". They could have wind.

In early 1986, I had been subscribing to a singles magazine, called *Singles* and I started dating a West African woman from Manchester. At the time she was living in

Kingston upon Thames, although she originally came from Ghana.

I didn't realise at the time that she seemed to be very pushy about wanting to get married. I thought it was love, as I certainly loved her, so, we were married within three months of meeting each other. My work colleagues and bosses were happy for me, or so it seemed. They even had a whip round for me and bought us some towels, but some took the meikle, saying it would only last six months at the most and that I should ask for money from her now before she did a runner, which of course angered me quite a bit. I can take a joke, but I didn't class what they were saying as funny. It was mainly one bloke who kept saying it and we didn't get on anyway. I put it down to racism on his part.

On one occasion when my wife and I were walking to my mother's one Saturday night, a car full of West Indian guys started shouting abuse at us. We ignored it. We had no choice but to ignore it. Four against one is not good odds really and people say white people are the only racists. Total bull.

One Sunday morning when my wife was on her way to the bus stop, to go back home, shortly after leaving mine she was attacked by a couple of West Indian guys, I didn't witness it, but she came rushing back into my flat and within half an hour I walked her to the bus stop. No one came anywhere near us while I was with her. I suspect it could have been something to do with my next door but one neighbour's. It was something they were quite capable of, plus, whoever it was more than likely objected to the fact she was a black lady and I was a white guy and so again, obviously the true image of racism.

It really should have dawned on me when my future Mrs and I first met. We would walk around the shops in the

West End, Oxford Street, etc. after going out for dinner and to walk off our food. At one point in Regent Street I tried to buy her a golliwog doll dressed in a guardsman uniform. I must not have realised how sensitive black people are over a doll. Normally, most black women or men would have been insulted and run a mile, but she must have been very keen to get a British passport because she did nothing. I could see she was annoyed, but I didn't make the connection. Ater all, it's a doll, nothing more than that.

Also around that time, my niece, who I think was egged on by her mother, was calling me an African botty cleaner. She was only about six and I thought she was being more than a bit cheeky. It seemed that what she was saying was more what an adult would say, not a young kid, but I know my southern sister and my other sister up north were good at hiding behind their kids. In fact, it was quite a common thing for them to do.

As for my home life, I was smoking weed like I would a normal fag most of the time and drinking half a dozen strong cans of strong lager at night. The only positive thing around that time, was that all kinds of women were making a B-line for me. I couldn't understand why, but I didn't grieve for too long over it. I just filled my boots. It got so bad at times that one morning I woke in my own bed and didn't realise where I was for at least ten minutes. The only downside was men were coming on to me too. Not good.

One Saturday afternoon when I was in the launderette in Kingsland High Street a couple of black guys were getting far too close for comfort virtually shoving their backsides much too close to my face and smiling at me. If it had been a woman that would have been a different matter. Being bi doesn't mean I will go with anything that moves. If there is no attraction there, it is a no go. It's no different than being heterosexual.

There was no change in how my workmates treated me, But, I think the drug dealer/welder tricked me into signing something I should not have (although I have no idea what it was). Generally, it was one of my many jobs to unload delivery lorries. I thought it was an invoice of some kind. Within ten minutes of me signing it, he was running round the workshop with the bit of paper held high in his hand up as in some kind of celebration. I thought what a strange thing to do, but apart from being called w- which even at school and in most of my work life situations is what most people call banter. That is how I took it and you have to give and take. Some would call it a form of bullying, it didn't make me think O s- I must read the newspapers. Nothing or nobody from 1985 until 1993 ever signposted me in that direction, not even to date. Not even the tabloid in question had the decency to give me a heads up. It just shows how genuine and decent they all were or not as it turns out.

On a few occasions I had stuff nicked from me by my workmates, even my wages once, but I must admit some of my other workmates tried telling me about my family. What made it so hard to believe was that my mother, sister and myself had been through hell together because of my second stepdad and it didn't seem plausible at the time that they would do anything like what my workmates were trying to tell me they were up to. It also didn't help the way my workmates were trying to get it over was not the best way of doing it.

They kept saying that my family were not fit to burn. In no way did I believe any of it and sprang to my family's defence, as a proper son, brother would do. Without solid proof I wouldn't accept it, (but in March, 1993 I had no alternative, when I saw my photo in the tabloids. It was the worst moment of my life).

One day in one of the loos at work someone had scratched on a wall a naked person with a spider coming from his nose and they had even written my name near it. To me, that was how childish, gutless, and cowardly they all were, because I knew not one of them would have said that kind of thing to my face. I ignored it and never let on that I had even seen it. I didn't want to pander to their childish egos.

I also noticed that most people's tolerance of me had gone down quite a lot. It seemed that they had no confidence in my ability to do my job, even though they knew I had done it hundreds of times before. It seemed that they thought because it was in a national newspaper everyone, including me, must know and I appeared to be surrounded by abuse, which only clouded or deflected my vision even more. The abuse became a distraction.

I did my best to ignore most of the abuse and condescending remarks as much as I could, simply because at that time I had confidence mostly in my abilities. My drinking or drug smoking had not really taken full effect on me health wise. Maybe it had mentally, but it hadn't dawned on me properly just how it had affected me.

Only once did I get a heads up from a co-worker (Ted Brown). One of my many jobs was unloading steel deliveries and for some reason I had got into the habit of just leaving my tobacco on my bench and going out to sort the deliveries. By rights I should have been able to do that if you have genuine and honest people working alongside you.

I mean I have done four and a half years in the big house on the hill, but no matter how desperate I have been

I have never stolen from friends or family, simply because I would never be able to look at them or anyone I have wronged in the eye again. I think I must have been an old school criminal.

On this occasion one of the welders came to tell me there was a delivery. On my way out to get the forklift, Ted called me over. He nodded his head in the direction of my work bench and when I looked round, the welder was blatantly helping himself to my tobacco. I went ballistic although there wasn't a lot I could do. The bosses would have sided with my other workmates before me and one boss had told most of the other blokes that if they had any trouble with me and it kicked off, whether it was their fault or mine, I would be the one getting the sack, not them. So, it was open season on me. Soon after that incident, the welder had an argument with me over something and we were toe to toe at one point.

One bystander noticed that the welder was holding a sharpened hacksaw blade from a mechanical machine, but because I was so close to him I didn't notice it. The welder was sacked soon after. I think the bosses must have found out about his sideline. The incident shocked me to the core a bit; it was not something you expect to happen at work.

Also, around that time there was an oldish guy who started working with us. I think his name was Burt and to put it mildly, he was very unpleasant and was forever trying to touch me up. He even told me once that he had been sniffing my bike seat and he did look the type to do that kind of thing. The thought of it made me retch and I just tried to do my best to keep away from him. He disgusted me. He was a definite pervert and always smelled of stale fags and stale beer (I realise now I did too at the time) but he must have been even smellier than me, because I could smell him from feet away.

I had a new family move in upstairs to me. She was a bit of a chav, to say the least, but she was very good looking. She was a one-parent family and had two sons, who were the noisiest kids you could ever have as neighbours. One of her more regular boyfriends was in no way to be trifled with. Thankfully, we got on, mostly. In no time at all my new neighbour had me babysitting and doing odd jobs for her and kept nipping down for sugar, etc. Her boyfriend noticed and pulled me up one day about it. But I reassured him that nothing was happening between his girlfriend and me. To be honest, though, you would have had to be gay not to want her.

Once she and her sister (who was also a looker) came down to mine naked, but for towels they were wrapped in. It was a hot day and they said they had been locked out. They did four circuits through mine, back through theirs and round again to my front door. I wondered what was going and knowing what I know now, I think the press were in some way involved. Once again in my experience the camera does seem to lie.

I did quite a bit of decorating for her off and on, but after the last job I did for her, her boyfriend told her not to pay me, because, according to him, I had loads of money. Where he had got this idea from I don't know because I can assure everyone absolutely have never knowingly gained any money from the newspapers, although, I am sure my family have.

My neighbour or someone to do with her broke into my flat in broad daylight and smashed down my front door down to gain entry. No one it seemed did anything to stop them and I lived right near a bus stop on a busy main road.

I think it was my nearest neighbour who noticed my smashed door and phoned the police.

Common sense tells me that if you are locked out for some reason, you look for a small window to gain entry, not smash down your front door. Even the police suspected my neighbour, but with no proof, what can you do? To rob your own neighbour after all the favours I'd done for her, really showed her true self.

Obviously, I had good neighbours (but it's not surprising where the IQ of some people living around me or in London in general was around that time). As far as I am aware I have never given anyone the impression that I knew about my curtains. Quite the opposite if the truth be known. More than a few people blamed me for it, but even if I had bricked all my windows up the peeping toms would have found another way of spying on me. It got that bad at times.

I got to know one of my neighbours' friends. Her nickname was Gnash-er. People called her that because she'd had a little accident while performing a 69 on a guy where she got a little overexcited. I'm quite sure you all can imagine the rest of what happened. Thankfully, I didn't make the same mistake.

Once when I was with Gnash-er, although I didn't realise it at the time, a radio station rang me and started the conversation by calling me a w-. I wasn't impressed to say the least and I thought he was more than a bit rude to him. I knew he would not have said that to my face. At the time I didn't realise who they were or where they were from. I thought it was a chavvy mate of hers, so I told him to go and f- himself and hung up. Gnash-er said nothing to put me straight like any genuine person would have done, but no matter who they were/are, no one has the right to treat you like that.

Although I had never noticed it before, across from where I lived in Dalston, someone had opened an amusement arcade around the time my curtains were slightly open. Obviously they had seen a way of making money out of my demise. It was situated where the carpet shop once was. One night he came over to me as I was crossing the road on one of my nightly trips to the off licence.

He was angrily demanding that I give him money because his arcade was not doing so good. I asked him what it had got to do with me and why he was asking me for money. He walked off without another word and I never saw him again after that.

One Sunday all my family and I went to Hackney baths, strangely we only went there the once. I think the baths had just opened for the day when we got there. It seemed we were the only people in the swimming pool at first. We were in there for about an hour until suddenly about half a dozen mid to late teen black girls came rushing into the baths. I was told by my mother to get out of the pool, quickly, which I did. But I didn't understand and not being told why I should do things became quite common. I was never given a warning about anything.

While we were waiting for a taxi to take us back to my mother's flat, this quite sexy black lady started chatting to me. I think my family were getting a bit paranoid and twitchy and maybe thought this lady could spill the beans and tell me what they were not telling me.

So we ended up walking back to my mother's flat, which was maybe half a mile away. As we were walking at the side of Downs Park, we were surrounded by more black girls, but all my family walked around me, as in some kind of human shield so as none of the girls could get anywhere near me. This confused the hell out of me even more and at the time I truly couldn't understand what the hell was going on around me. When we reached my mother's flat I asked what that was all about, but as usual I got no kind of explanation at all.

It became the norm and because I was drinking like I was, it gave me the memory of a goldfish and I soon forgot all about it and moved on with my life. No matter though how much you try to forget or drown out things through drink or drugs as soon as you put it down (like I did in March 97) it all comes flooding back.

Even now, which is nearly thirty-plus years ago, I have still not had a sitdown conversation about this with anyone who knew anything about it or so they keep insisting. It was like having the three wise monkeys around me, (even quite recently when I was having an argument by text on my mobile with my sister from Chorley, she totally denied knowing anything about the newspapers. This was the same sister who sat in the audience with her hubby on an *Upfront* programme in early 1993, where I was meant to appear. At the time I was far too ill and my sister and her hubby did not even offer me a lift or any kind of advice or any support, but gave me loads of abuse instead, just to make sure I wouldn't be going anywhere near the show. That's how I see it now, and with a sober head on my shoulders).

While I was still living in London, from opening my door for work until getting home at night, I was constantly getting abuse from people in the street or some knuckle dragger trying to attack me. The majority of times I fended it off quite successfully and the verbal I just ignored.

Even at my own home, I had hassle. Some guy was

shouting filth through my letter box one night, like "show us your a-, etc." I thought this could be some kind of trap, so, instead of going out and sorting it out like I would have normally done, I waited for the letter box to open again and when it did I gave him some deodorant in his eyes and he went on his way. On another occasion, I was minding my own business in my back garden, when I saw what I thought were some workmen on the roof. It was a very hot day, so, I was sunbathing and for no apparent reason, I started getting abuse from them so I started throwing stones. They soon got fed up and moved on, but it spoiled my sunbathing so I went in. Knowing what I know now, I think on both occasions it could have been journalists.

My actual thinking at the time was like the saying goes "*today's news is tomorrow's fish and chip paper*", but I seemed to be finding things out months after the events. I can honestly say my family and their friends and my friends have never helped me in any way, but from what I know now they were more guilty of helping themselves and if the press had used a less aggressive way of approaching me or at least used a bit of common sense when asking me anything and telling me who they were and not assuming I knew what name they were calling me that week, they and I might have found out what we were looking for a lot earlier.

How was I supposed to know they were journalists? If someone is ranting and raving at you and aggressively coming towards you, you get the first punch in before they get the chance to punch you. Past experiences in the big house on the hill taught me that much. You do not let anyone get too near you if you think you are going to be attacked, ever.

On a couple of occasions, I had trouble at my front

door. The first time I had a black guy demanding money from me. He said I owed some money to someone I had never heard of before. I had to get out of the bath and go to the door wrapped in a towel and full of soap. He was all for kicking the door down and I was just about to give him what for, but thought that wouldn't be a wise thing to do, as he was built like a brick outhouse and had all kinds of scars on his forehead, as if he had been head butting something a bit harder than his head. The fact that I was in a bath towel and full of soap saved me I think and I was so glad he was not gay, well, as far as I know he wasn't gay.

On the second occasion I was fully dressed. It was a different black guy and not as scary as the other one. This guy was ranting and raving like his friend before and again he was saying I owed money to someone I had never heard of, but once again, I stuck to my guns as I knew I did not owe anyone any money, so they were not going to get any.

On other occasions I was threatened on a bus, once with a knife and then with a Stanley knife. Both times I couldn't do anything because I was with a female friend and her daughter and it would have put them at risk as well as me. They were threats, nothing more than that.

While on my bike coming home from work, I always went down the same back streets of Kingsland High Street to avoid the busy roads and traffic lights. This car was waiting to come out of one of the back streets and for no apparent reason he set off and knocked me flying over the bonnet of his car. As you can imagine I wasn't amused in the slightest. I quickly got to my feet and with both hands on the bonnet of his car, I shouted for him to get out (at this point I wanted to rip his head off). He got out and when I saw the size of him I thought o s-. He was massive, not fat and looked like he did a lot of gym work,, i.e., a chicken winger. It calmed me down quite a bit. I no longer wanted to rip his head off, but I thought he might rip mine off.

It turned out that he was as nice as pie. He gave me his address and said he was sorry but when I went round a couple of nights later to get money for the damage he had done to my bike, I found out that he had given me a false address which was on a very rough housing estate, near Cricketfield Road, Lower Clapton. So, I was done up like a kipper, as they say.

I think he was in league with the two black guys who came to my front door months earlier, but at the time I didn't think much about it although it was quite bizarre that he didn't see me. There was a van on the other side of the road and the driver who hit me said that the van had flashed him to let him out. Nothing about the incident seemed plausible. This might sound paranoid but I think it could have been an attempt to either fit me with some concrete boots, the one size fits all variety, or just to give me a good hiding. It was all very strange for it all to happen in broad daylight, and how could he not have seen me?

The only positive thing to come out of it was I met a nice-looking Indian/Pakistani woman who invited me into her flat the night I went looking for him. Say no more, and her husband just watched, like you do. Each to their own, I suppose.

Workwise, it seemed to be getting worse. My bosses were becoming abusive towards me and they were openly egging other employees to do the same. One of them was (I nicknamed him, the Fat Controller, others called him Metal Mickey, because of the way he walked like Metal Mickey with his arm movements). For some unknown reason he had got it in his head that I didn't want to do any work on his house and he had spat his dummy out. He had said if I hit anyone no matter whose fault it is/was they would not get the sack, but, I would, so, it was open season on me.

Mainly, I get violent only in self-defence situations, no one could/can call me a bully or troublemaker in any way and on a couple of occasions I was smacked in the face at work for no apparent reason. I didn't react at all, I just fended off any more punches with my arms. I knew what the script was, but it was not a good situation to be in. It seemed that my bosses had put a target on my back for my co-workers.

Around that time, an oldish Bangladeshi guy started work. We already had a young Indian guy and they didn't like each other at all. I learned it was because of the countries' hatred of each other. All I saw was that the young Indian kept egging on others to hit the old guy. I sided with the old guy, as I do not like bullies or bullying of any kind, verbally or physically.

That did me no favours with everyone else though, including the bosses. One of the main bullies even tried to get me sacked. I suppose he wanted me out the way to bully the Bangladeshi guy whenever he felt like it. To be honest, no matter what their differences, no one should bring bigotry to the workplace. At the end of the day there is no excuse to bully anyone.

The guy who tried to get me sacked came to me one day to borrow my file. It had no handle on it, just the pointed end where the handle should have been. It turned out that he wanted my file to puncture some drums of hydraulic oil that were stored in the washroom and blame me for it. Within an hour I was called into the office where I was accused point blank, of stealing £1.50 out of a colleague's trouser pocket and puncturing the oil drums.

I told the main boss straight. "Do you honestly think

that I would put a £200 a week job at risk for £1.50? And as for the oil, I know nothing about it." It dawned on me later that the guy who had borrowed my file could be responsible, so I told the boss who he was and they sacked him. Just before he went he came over and shook my hand. I thought was a bit of a p-take, to be honest, but I let it go and shook his hand.

All my boss said to me when I was in the office was, "You either buck up your ideas or you're sacked." He also gave me another option: resigning. I knew my timekeeping was terrible, to say the least, so I only had myself to blame. He gave me a week to think it over.

In that week I cut my hand quite badly, badly enough to have to go to the hospital and when I was called back into the office a week later, for some reason he/they were under the impression that it was not an accident at all. They seemed to think that I had tried to self-harm in some way, which is something I have never ever done, before or since. I am far too squeamish for that kind of thing and it is not very nice being prejudged in that way.

I put all the hassle from my employers down to the fact that I had stopped working for them at the weekends, on their houses. It was my own fault, because of my time-keeping, but I knew it had p- them off big style me refusing to work on their houses, as they were both paying me through the firm ,i.e, it was simply a tax dodge on their parts.

I was also not happy that the main boss's wife had tricked me into eating dog food one time when I was working on their house and the fact she went around telling everyone about it really annoyed me even further. Only sick people would trick someone in such a way. Perhaps she felt scorned, as she kept making a play for me, but her nickname in the workplace was the Bearded Lady, for obvious reasons and her hygiene was very questionable to say the least.

On one occasion she found a stray kitten and she took it into the office and looked after it. But after a few months it just disappeared out of the blue and she was going around the workshop asking all the staff, "Have you seen my pussy?" The bad thing about it was just before dinner time and I was having sardine butties and the image of her pussy was stuck in my head. The smell of my sardine butties was not a good combination either.

My reasons for not working on the boss's house were quite simple. I wanted to spend more time with my wife, as I only saw her at weekends. In fact, being married to my ex-wife, was quite weird at times. I knew that she was not into fellatio at all, but one weekend, we started having sex in the living room. As usual, she removed her knickers but kept her knee-length skirt on. I found it quite a turn on, as we were in the 69 position and with her still wearing her skirt it was in a way like being blindfolded, something I'd never done.

Normally, she would have just played with me, but I soon realised I was being sucked off and it was so good I didn't stop her. When we had finished I found that my curtains were partly open and not as I had left them before. My front door was open too. I didn't ask her about it, but I thought it strange and I couldn't work out what the game was. To be honest, I still don't know for sure, but of course, I can guess and once again the camera does seem to lie.

My ex-wife had hair on her chin and I knew she would cut it short sometimes, but never shave it off completely. Sometimes she wouldn't have hair at all, which makes me think now. As mad as this might sound, it was maybe another woman. As most white people say all black people look the same, and vice versa, it could have been one of my ex's. Around that time I was still drinking and having a couple of spliffs at night, but never in front of my ex-wife. She hated anyone smoking near her, even normal fags.

That was why I wasn't that bothered when she was only coming around at weekends, but I never once two-timed her and I had quite a few opportunities. I threw myself into my work, although it was far from happy.

One day I got into an argument with one of my co-workers. It started with him calling me a flasher, which was unusual, as it was mainly w-etc. I turned on him and said I knew nothing about my curtains. It was an innocent mistake on my part and he just laughed at me and told me that there had been a debate in Parliament about it. How could I have not known? If you don't read the newspapers or watch the TV news and the powers that be are not decent enough to ask you for your side, how would you know? The people (my family and friends) who knew were not decent enough to tell me anything and everyone else assumed I knew. I was in a total no-win situation.

Although this might sound as though I am being conceited, perhaps I was a victim of my success, as in, people assumed if it is in the newspapers you must know, but if you don't read them for whatever reason, then you have to rely on the honesty of the people around you. I wasn't blessed in that way.

I had been listening to the news one day while I was in a chippy just down the road from my workplace in Blackstock Road and an MP had been saying, 'He deserves everything that he has coming to him.' I had no idea he was referring to me and as I mentioned earlier <u>no one</u>, no police, no journalist, had ever approached me about anything to do with my curtains. Then I knew what the MP was talking about when my co-worker said what he said, but for the life of me, I can't understand why no one asked for my side of the story before finally finding out in March 1993. To be honest, it certainly makes a mockery of what the MP was saying at the time. I would say it is only common decency and common sense to have spoken to me first before judging me and at least asking for my side before commenting as he did.

A few months later, one Saturday afternoon while I was clothes shopping, I had an argument with a security bloke at a Burton clothes shop, in Kingsland High Street. The security guy was being very disrespectful towards me for no apparent reason and I stood up to him. It nearly came to blows at one point, but the manager stepped in. I also noticed that two young black girls were looking in my direction and laughing. It all added to the ridicule I felt at the time, but it made me realise that I had to do something about my drinking, although I wasn't drunk at the time. I was more suffering with the DTs, which, take it from me, is a terrible feeling in itself. I was not feeling right most of the time. I was shaking when sober and nearly having panic attacks, even when I was out and about doing nothing out of the ordinary.

Normally when people are clothes shopping you go into the little cubicles and try the clothes on, but because I was mostly on the verge of a full-blown panic attack and suffering from anxiety, there was no way I could go into a little cubicle. Most (normal) people will not understand what you are going through when you are having a panic attack, because apart from shaking, everything else is invisible and I use the word (normal) very loosely. This was a few months after the curtain incident.

That night I stopped drinking and I was quite determined to stay that way. In no time at all I was climbing the walls quite a bit, but I was determined to stop. I lasted about two weeks before falling off the wagon and started drinking again. But in that two weeks, I had lost around two stones in a week as I could not hold food or even water down and I had the runs, so I was dehydrating quite badly.

I needed help urgently, but I didn't know where to go and of course I knew my family were the last people I could rely on. I had to do cold turkey on my own, at home. Not a good situation at all and looking back I was lucky to get through it. By rights I should have dried out in a clinic, but when you are a suffering alcoholic you have no one to signpost you in the right direction. So I had to do what I had to do and in the only way I knew how.

When I started drinking again, I decided to do it only at weekends, as in binge drinking. I found that my mind was a lot clearer, so much so I saw through my wife's lies and I fired her off, which amused my co-workers and bosses no end. They were now saying I should have got some money out of her while I could. Of course, this annoyed me, but I didn't let it show. Doing that would have made it a lot worse. The fact that I had finished with her cut me in two and it took months before I wanted anything to do with women. My trust in them had gone right out of the window, because of the way she had treated me and deceived me the way she had. So after a few months I started playing the field. I was in no way looking for a relationship, just sex, and I was not that fussy who I ended up in bed with. I was like a dog on heat, but in reality, it was a distraction from the emotional pain and the abuse I was suffering daily from total strangers in the street.

I also realised what my southern sister was all about.

I knew she was a backstabbing thief. I knew every time my back was turned and things went missing, nothing was ever safe where she was concerned. So I binned her too. I didn't want her anywhere near me anymore, but little did I know at the time that my mother was just as bad as her, if not worse and for that matter the rest of my family and their friends too, because of the way my drinking was. I was far too trusting of my family and their friends.

I can only see this by looking back, because at the time I was completely oblivious and believe me, ignorance is in no way bliss like a certain tabloid kept saying around that time.

I had to accept that my wife had only married me to stay in the country. This hit me like a lead hammer in the nuts and it took me more than twenty years to recover fully and start trusting someone else completely(I will explain that later).

I lasted another year at the sheet-metal work job before they sacked me for bad timekeeping. To be honest I thought I had done so well with the drink/drugs and it turns out I still lost my job anyway. I didn't stand a chance, as not many of my so-called friends (work colleagues) didn't have some kind of axe to grind where I was concerned. They were all two-faced in some way towards the end, but strangely they were all smiles to my face most of the time.

I attempted to take my ex-employer to a tribunal, but I ended up settling out of court. For some reason my ex-employer set the police on me two weeks before the tribunal date, as they were trying to blame me for some kind of arson attack on their workshop (if it really happened).

I felt at the time that if I didn't settle I would have

most certainly ended up in a criminal court through me kicking off with whoever would have turned up to the tribunal hearing from my ex-employer. I knew I was innocent where the arson attack was concerned, so I just got on with my life as best I could, although I was quite p-off about it all, especially after doing so well with the drink/drugs.

I thought, sod it, and took up my old drinking ways and it didn't take long before I was back with the DT panic attacks through the day. Throughout my eighteen years of drinking, I very rarely drank in the morning. I had given it a go once or twice, but to me I couldn't function that way. It was also strange as it might seem to a non-alcoholic, I could not do the all-day benders or all-night benders. That's what the drink does to you. It makes you an alcoholic. It's not the amount or when you drink or even what you drink. You can drink shandy and still be an alcoholic.

Jobwise, I couldn't find anything. For some unknown reason no one wanted to employ me, so, I ended up doing painting and decorating to help me feed my habits and to get by. I did this for family, friends, neighbours. I was also still babysitting for my sister's friend, co-worker.

In mid-1988 I had to go on an ET course for the DWP, as it was called in those days. We were based at Limehouse basin, under the arches of the overground train line. It was a bricklaying course. Trouble was I already knew most of what they were trying to train us because ET (Extra Tenner) was fairly new. A cameraman come and he asked one of the other guys if he would pose for a couple of pics pretending to lay a brick. The guy said if you pay me I will. The cameraman said sorry, but they didn't pay anyone, so the guy turned him down. Then he asked me and I said OK.

I was never told at the time exactly what the pics were

for, but apparently, they ended up in a lot of job centres around the London area, so I must admit I was a bit embarrassed about that and I got quite a bit of stick off the other guys on the course because of it. But it was nothing I couldn't handle; my automatic blinkers came into play as always.

In my love life, as they say, as one door shuts another opens. My daughter's mother's sister turned up out of the blue, one Sunday night with her boyfriend who was a bit of a knuckle dragger. He had long gone to seed quite some time before we met. My daughter's mother's brother and her daughter had also come to visit me. It must have been a family outing.

My nearest neighbour had warned me as I was coming through the gate that people were waiting for me at my door. She must have been worried for me, even she thought it was a bit dubious. When we all went in, my daughter's mother's sister asked me if she could brew up. She and her daughter went into the kitchen while her brother and her boyfriend were sat on the edge of the couch and kept giving me the evils. I thought that this looks like some kind of set-up and they were getting ready to jump me.

It also didn't help that I had rolled a spliff and I was halfway through it, so paranoia had well and truly set in as well, but sometimes a bit of paranoia is a good thing. Anyway, as luck would have it, I had my pickaxe handle in easy reach of where I was sitting. I put it in full view of them and soon after that they looked at each other and sat back without a word. My daughter's mother's sister came back into the living room. She had a puzzled look, which, at the time convinced me it was a set-up of some kind, but within half an hour they all left.

After that night, she kept coming round. I got the impression she wanted to rekindle what we had. Although sex had never happened between us, she kept trying for it, but because I'd had a daughter to her sister, I thought in no way would it be the right thing to do. Obviously I could have worn a Durex, but, she didn't like them.

We started going to the local pubs, but every time we went anywhere she always had to phone someone first. The penny never dropped at the time, because she kept saying, "I'm just checking on my daughter." I had no reason to think otherwise, so I believed her.

One Friday night we went to a pub across from Finsbury Park. After about an hour these two guys came rushing in and made a B-line straight for me. I raised my hand thinking I was going to get a slap or attacked in some way. But they just took a photo and left. Later on WTF when I went to the bar, the barmaid thanked me for not kicking off with the two blokes. The truth of it was that I had no idea why they took a photo of me. I believe it ended up in the magazine you used to get with the *News of the World*.

Things like this happened quite a few times. I met a woman from badminton sessions. We started going out, just as friends, mainly because of what I had gone through with my ex-wife. I didn't have any confidence in myself or trust myself to make a move on her or anyone for that matter unless it was on a plate. She must have thought I was gay or something and every time we went somewhere she also had to make phone calls. I thought at the time that it was strange, but I didn't concern myself too much over it. She had a young daughter and we all used to go to Britannia Leisure Centre in Homerton to go swimming every Saturday or Sunday.

A couple of times she had added to my suspicions

about her. The first time was when we went to the pictures together. She wanted us to go on the back row. For obvious reasons I declined because the cinema was jampacked and despite what some people might think of me, I cannot perform in front of them, not even drunk or drugged up. Not knowingly anyway.

On the second occasion, we had a day trip to Southend, it was a complete bizarre day all round. We had arranged to go for a swim in the sea. When we got there it wasn't the weather, but she kept banging on about me going in the water. It seemed quite a crowd had formed behind us on the prom and they appeared to be watching us, although at the time I thought nothing of it.

Eventually we decided to walk along the mile-long pier and we got the train on the pier back. For some reason some numpty was on the top of the train at one point and the police escorted him away. Then, when we were walking across the main road near the prom, another numpty fired at me with a starting pistol. I thought I had been shot, but it gave me the shock of my life. I heard later on the TV news he had been arrested. That was when I found out it was a starting pistol. Before that I put it down to him firing blanks. Shame his dad hadn't!

On one of our weekly visits to the leisure centre, I had just got changed into my swimwear and was heading for the pool, when this woman came over to me from the café area and started shouting "flashing again" at me. I stopped and motioning with my hand to the pool with people dressed similarly to me, I said, "Just like everyone else in here is love" and carried on to the pool. At no point did the woman introduce herself as a journalist, like any genuine journalist would have done, but I'm quite sure she was.

I got in the pool and was swimming up and down as

usual when suddenly these two young guys jumped right on top of me from the side of the pool. One nearly broke my collar bone. The lifeguard kicked them out within minutes of it happening and that was when I noticed a bloke with quite a large camera pointed in my direction. I didn't think it was a news crew. I even mentioned it to my friend, but she said nothing and we got on with our swimming and ignored it.

I didn't fully trust her though, because soon into our friendship she had asked to borrow a few hundred quid from me. When I said no because I didn't have that kind of money to hand, she went cold from then on. Obviously, she was seeing what she could get out of me or scam out of me. She wore a lot of bling as I remember, which I think is a dead giveaway, with users or gold diggers.

Although I didn't know at first, she was going out with a Greek guy who worked in a kebab shop just around the corner from where she lived. That made me trust her less and women in general even less when I found out.

Once when I went visiting her at her flat she made me a cup of tea, as normal or so I thought, but unbeknown to me at the time, it was not water she had made it from. She had urinated in a cup, then warmed it up in the microwave and put a teabag and milk in it, and this was in front of her daughter. So really good parenting skills, *not*, as I overheard her daughter asking her mum what she was up to. It didn't click until quite sometime later. She kept smiling at me as I was drinking the tea and saying I bet you would love to go where that tea has come from. I said, "Where, Ceylon?" She laughed. Tastewise, it was OK, in case any of you are wondering. This might give spouses ideas, so I will apologise now.

One day out, of the blue, she finished with me over

the phone and I must admit I was gutted at the time. I think I was more in shock than anything else because I thought we were getting closer, but I have come to believe, it was because she had seen the photo of me with my hand up in the *News of the World* magazine (I only know this by looking back). The photo was taken with my daughter's mother's sister. We were only friends out for a quiet drink, nothing more than that, but she must have thought differently. The photo I am referring to was when we were in the pub near Finsbury Park, but obviously she must have been a jealous kind of person to react in that fashion, so I think I had a lucky escape, to say the least, as bunny boiler comes to mind.

Life went on as normal and I was still seeing my daughter's mother's sister and she was still not happy with her boyfriend as he couldn't perform as much as she wanted him to. He kept getting pains in his chest every time they tried to have sex and she kept asking me for sex. But, as I said earlier, if I had not had a baby to her sister I would have, but even though I was a suffering alcoholic, I was not suffering that much that I had no morals left.

Once, she asked me to simulate having sex with her on her bed. She had this notion that the guy across the road from where she lived was watching her. He lived more or less on the same level as her (she lived on the fifth floor of a block of flats) and as a joke or a wind-up, not sure which, she wanted me to take my t-shirt off and make it look like I was having sex with her, with the curtains fully open. Of course, she was not under me and I was still wearing my jeans, but if he was watching he wouldn't have known this, because of the angle.. She was always coming out with strange things like this, so it was not at all unusual and I was stupid enough to take her on. I was so gullible at times.

Sometimes we would sleep in the same bed together, but as friends. I think we found it hard at times. After all, she was a very attractive woman, but in my mind we had to keep it as friends, so, no cuddling or kissing. But one night I woke up in the spooning position with her (usually she had her bed clothes on and I would be in my underwear). Now she was only in her knickers. She had my cock in between her legs and was riding me in the spooning position. I think she was quite turned on by it. So much so, she didn't know that I was awake at the time.

I had to resist temptation and just let her cum. I didn't cum, but I was very close to it. The trouble was the next day I couldn't find the words to say anything about it to her. It's not something you bring up in general conversation. I thought leave it to her up, but she never did, so I let it go. I must admit I was tempted at times and I should have been more patient when I first met her and not let my k- rule my head and go off with her sister like I did. I realise that was a really bad mistake on my part, but we all have regrets,because,if I was to compare both sisters, between her and her sister, the first sister I had met was a much better option in every way, but I firmly believe things happen for a reason.

Soon afterwards I felt that my daughter's mother's sister was out to cause me some kind of trouble. One day we both went to collect her daughter from school near Manor House pub. For some reason she sent me in to get her daughter, which I thought was unusual. I knew her daughter knew me and I saw no problem. But for some reason, her daughter said, as loudly as she possibly could, so all the teachers could hear her, "You're not my dad and I don't know you." The teachers heard this and naturally came running. Even though I knew I was guilty of nothing,

I thought it best to walk out. I told her mother what had happened and she went in for her daughter. I never got any kind of an explanation of any kind about it.

I cannot help thinking it was some kind of set-up, although, I didn't know why she would want to do this. I know now though, also her daughter knew me quite well as I had been to my daughter's mother's sister's flat hundreds of times before. It seems that money appears to turn people against each other.

She told me once that her boyfriend knew of a way to poison someone by putting some kind of maggot on a door handle. I knew her boyfriend didn't like me one bit, because the way I saw it at the time, he probably thought I was sniffing around his girlfriend and he was not man enough to sort me out in a man to man way. I think she wore the trousers and the truth was she was more sniffing around me in more ways than one.

Why I wasn't getting warning signs about these people I cannot say, but in my defence I will say that if you try and put a live frog in a pan of boiling water it will instantly jump out. But if you put the same frog in a cold pan of water and warm it up, it will die. The moral of my story is that when you are immersed in something, you do not see what is really happening around you, until it is far too late.

In mid-1988 I was asked to do an insurance job for an Italian chip shop owner, whose shop was across the road from where I lived. It was one of many calls when I was drunk, so I had got to know him and his Mrs and his son quite well. Because of the storms of 1987, quite a large tree had fallen down and had hit the back of the house, damaging the back wall. He wanted a cheap estimate, which I gave him rather naïvely. I didn't think I would have got the job. Obviously I must have been far too cheap. More fool me.

I have never thought of myself as a fast or slapdash kind of a worker. I don't cut corners and that is how I did the job on his house, but for some reason he and his wife were constantly on my case nearly every day. They kept coming to my flat banging at my front door, even on Sunday mornings. It seemed they wanted me on the job all the time and I soon got very fed up with them. In no way was I going to work seven days a week for next to nothing, so we very quickly fell out over money.

He ended up owing me £250. I had moved a studded wall to equal two rooms out and my labourer had finished off one of the walls with bits of leftover plasterboard. If I had plastered it he would have been none the wiser. Although it is not really the done thing it wouldn't have made that much difference, so he refused to pay me. I threatened to rip down the studded wall but instead I just walked off the job, something I have never done before or since.

I was not short of work, but it annoyed me that he had stitched me up like he had. I kept thinking that that was his intention all along. More than likely he thought I was a soft touch because of what had happened with my curtains. But how do you defend yourself from back stabbers when everyone is doing the back stabbing, unless you have at least one decent/genuine person around you? You cannot and I certainly was not blessed with any good or decent people around me at that time.

The guy I had working for me wanted me to go with him to a Filipino dance. He wanted me there just for moral support. Funny thing was, it was mainly West Indian women who were there. I wasn't looking for anything personally, but I spotted this very sexy lady. She was the spitting image of Donna Summer with long hair down her back. I managed to chat her up and we met a couple of times after that, but right from the start I felt I was being played. I had never been out with any lady as sexy as her, the reason behind that I suppose was my alcoholism.

I always seemed to be more attracted to slappers or two-legged dogs and I felt with this stunning lady I was punching way above my weight with her. I went with the flow. She had told me her name was one thing then I found out it was something different, so, we didn't last long after that. Without trust, there is nothing in any relationship.

I knew the workmate was a friend of my daughter's mother and her sister in North London and for the most part he helped me out only three days out of the six or seven days I worked on the house. Although I didn't realise it at the time he was feeding information about me back to my daughter's mother, so much so, that one Sunday night around 11pm, there was a knock at my front door. It turned out to be my daughter's mother's sister who I had never met before that night, and my ex.

My daughter's mother had come round for a chat, so she said, but it was less than an hour before we were in bed. I wanted her sister to join in, but my daughter's mother told me that if I had my sister as well it would just be a one-off. My daughter's mother would not want to see me again after that night and in some ways I needed to keep her sweet, as I wanted to keep in touch so in time I would maybe one day meet my daughter again (who I am glad to say is now back in my life).

I also realised that someone had been listening in at one of the air vents in my bedroom. They were outside my bedroom wall as I could hear them talking around the vent.

A few days later I went to the vent at night and to my horror I found I could see into my bedroom quite easily. But when my daughter's mother and her sister had come round I had switched the light off, but there were plenty of other times with other women when I had left the light on, so it was a bit of a shock. Whoever it was, could only listen on that occasion.

It goes to show just how perverted my neighbours really were and it makes me wonder just how long they could have been watching, maybe even before the gap in my curtains happened. Hopefully, they might have learned something while watching, but to be honest you have to feel sorry for people who do that kind of thing. They must be very sad.

One night I heard a neighbour's boyfriend beating someone with a baseball bat. He had caught the guy looking into one of their windows and it just happened to be the kid's bedroom. If I had not been in bed at the time, I would have helped him, but what I did in south London was by accident and I was drunk at the time. This guy did it intentionally, so deserved a good beating.

My daughter's mother and I kept on seeing each other for a few more months. Mostly, she came to mine or sometimes we would stay at her brother's flat, which, as it was only a one bedroomed flat, made it a bit overcrowded at times. On one occasion when we stayed there and made love, my daughter's mother told me to go and wash yourself. I normally did anyway, but, I thought, she might be giving me a BJ.

When I came back she got up and went into the living room. Shortly afterwards her brother came in fully dressed, sat on the bed and started feeling my testicles. I wasn't too impressed, to say the least, and I told him I wasn't like that.

Beside that, I had just had sex with his sister and to me, it did not feel right to do anything with her brother so soon. It didn't go down too well as her brother was a bit of a mummy's boy and he stuck his bottom lip out a bit. I wasn't that bothered in the slightest.

Then on another occasion, out of the blue, she turned around and started asking questions about my mother and my family. She told me to ask my mother about some guy whose name I had never heard of before. When I next saw my mother, I asked her about this guy.

She started to cry and was saying that she was sorry. I think I had unwittingly asked her about myself and because the newspapers or whoever were writing about me around that time had been calling me by another name (shows how cowardly they all were). My daughter's mother and her family and my mother and my family knew all about what the newspapers were calling me, but as usual said nothing to me.

I'm not quite sure about her motives. Perhaps my daughter's mother was using me to scare or take the p- out of my mother. I certainly didn't have a clue what was going on behind my back and people were using silly mind games like this to control me. I, in no way, would have done that to my mother intentionally, even though knowing what my mother had done to me was wrong. But, we have only one mother.

(Strangely, I still cannot tell if people are talking about me behind my back. Now I have more decent people around me and not the scum I had back then. Sadly, that included all my family, but I fired all of them off in 2015, so at least now I have a better chance of knowing about things going on behind my back).

The Greek greengrocer whose shop was across from

my flat had told me that the Italian guy (the chip shop owner) couldn't get anyone to work on his house on Graham Road. I just let it go until one night when I was walking back home from my mother's. In my drunken wisdom I decided to have a look to see if it was true what the grocer had been telling me. I didn't need to force entry, I more or less just walked in. It was a three-storey house and I looked all over but nothing had been touched since I walked off the job a few weeks earlier.

While I was in the basement I noticed a big pile of old paper in one of the rooms. I don't know why I did what I did, but I picked up a piece of paper the size of a small notepad, set it alight, threw it in the direction of the pile of paper and then walked out of the house. A neighbour's son spotted me, but I ignored him and just went home. If I'd had my wits about me I would have gone back in and checked to see if it had taken hold or not. If it had, it would have been easy to put it out, but I was that drunk and obviously did not think of the consequences of my actions.

Next day when I woke up and in the cold light of day I quickly realised what I had done. I was totally in shock and it took me a few days to summon up the courage to go to the house and take a look. But when I did it as discreetly as I could, I was shell shocked beyond belief. The whole roof was virtually burned off. I didn't know what to do. I didn't think that handing myself in to the police would have been a good idea, because I didn't fancy prison again and I knew it was going to be a long stretch when the police caught up with me.

Anyway within a couple of weeks there was that dreaded knock on the door at 7 am. It was three CID officers from Dalston. I put my hand up to it more or less straight away. There was no point in trying to deny it. I was bang to rights and because I knew from past experiences, it is never a wise move to mess the police about.

I knew from what other guys in nick had told me that they would have charged me with everything they could think of. That's why in the past I have always put my hand up to whatever I have done, no matter what it is and I have even given TICs (taken into consideration). My thinking was to come clean. That way there's less chance of getting a gate arrest etc., I must admit I am far too honest for my good at times. But that's the way I am. Why make life even harder for yourself?

There have been times when I was stupid enough to take notice of what my family and others had told me, but I learned the hard way from my mistakes and have kept it simple ever since then and just come clean. It's far, far easier.

The following day I appeared at Highbury Road Magistrates' Court and to say I was bricking it was an understatement. I felt ill I was that scared. I was in the waiting area just up from the cells when this young copper came out of the courtroom and said, "You OK to go in court." I laughed at him and said, "Why, do I have a choice?" He laughed and said "No." In court, I was bailed to go to Snaresbrook Crown Court. I had bail conditions set including a curfew plus I had to sign on at the police station every night at Dalston. At least I was still walking the streets a while longer, which was a bonus in some ways.

So when my daughter's mother found out I had been nicked again, she wasn't very happy at all. Within a few weeks or so we just finished. I cannot remember why, but I know she wasn't pleased about me getting in trouble with the police again and we both knew I was heading for a long prison sentence.

Just before Christmas of 1988, I wanted to go north to

Chorley to spend Christmas with my dad and sister, so I had to go back to Snaresbrook Crown Court to change my bail conditions, temporarily.

While waiting to go up, my solicitor brought to my attention something a local newspaper had said about me, They didn't use my real name, but a completely different one and my solicitor said we could sue them because they hadn't printed my real name. I wasn't that bothered either way. I didn't think anything about what they had written about me as all it said was 'builder in court over arson attack'. My solicitor asked me if I had done the crime to get in the newspapers. I denied it of course, because I hadn't and said, "I don't think that the story would have done my career as a builder any good, do you?" In no way did I link the article to me being in the tabloids. I hadn't got a clue about the tabloids hovering behind my back.

Roughly a month before my sentencing, I had to go to court for a committal hearing. My southern sister and another of her work colleagues came to support me, but something strange happened before we went in.

My barrister called me into a room to have a quick word about the case, but my sister barged past me and sat in the seat I was meant to be sat in, obviously wanting to take control of everything it would seem. My barrister ordered her out and even he was a bit puzzled about what she was up to. I thought she was still drunk from the night before or on something she should not have been. I know she dabbled with speed a lot of the time.

I knew I was looking at a lot of bird. Anyway, the dreaded day finally arrived in early January of 1989. I was told by my barrister the night before to expect around four years, which scared the s- out of me, to say the least, but, thankfully I only got two years.

Then I was taken from court to Brixton and as luck would have it, I got talking to another guy who had been to the same court. Once we got to Brixton and got through reception, we ended up on the psychiatric wing or what is more commonly known as fragile rock. I think it was A wing and, no offence to any black people, but it was at least 95% West Indian. It must be what weed does to your head.

I didn't get much sleep that night because we ended up padded up with a psychogenic who wouldn't let us turn the light off. He kept saying he would have nightmares when he was left in the dark. I told him straight that the light was going off and true to his word, as soon as it did, he started making all kinds of funny noises. By that time, I was that tired I fell asleep anyway. The next morning after breakfast we were allowed to shower and I saw the other patients on the wing and I thought O my god I am in deep s- here. It was spot the white man. I had visions of me fighting every day and I was, of course, a bit dubious about bending over in the communal showers. It had been a long time since I had showered with other guys and I have always said my a- is one way only. Nothing goes in, outwards only.

Thankfully, good news arrived soon after I had showered. I was getting moved to another prison. I had never been there, but, I thought it must be better than Brixton, which was a s- to say the least. When we got to the other prison, we had quite a long wait to get on the wing and I had a bit of aggro with a few black guys over a bag of sugar. Believe me, I have had fights over bread before now, (in Walton in 1977), so I knew not to back down, but it was nothing I couldn't sort out verbally.

While we were waiting to get on the wing, we were all shown Ronnie Briggs' property box. It was right on top of all the shelves. The screw told us all, "it is waiting for him for when he returns."

Eventually, I was put on A-wing, on A2 to be precise. I was right across from Mad Frankie Fraser, but I hadn't heard anything about him until then. I was padded up with a black African and he seemed a bit weird. Trying to have anything like a conversation with him was like pulling teeth, so I gave up and put it down to the black/white thing (and they say whites are racist). He wouldn't even tell me what he was in for, which I found a bit suspicious and he very rarely spoke most of the time I was with him. It was like being padded up with a cardboard cut-out of someone.

The first time I saw Frankie was when we were slopping out before being banged up for the night. He had a pp9 in a sock and was looking in my direction, but, as I look back, I'm not quite sure if it was for me or my pad mate he was looking at. A few weeks later I saw my pad-mate in the exercise yard with all the nonces. The next day, I had a cell search. They told me to drop my trousers and undies and squat. I asked why and was told some guys shoved drugs up their a- and by squatting, if there was anything up there, it would fall out.

We got chatting and they told me that jobs were going on the works party, so when I was being allocated work, they tried to put me in the kitchens, so I asked for the works party and I got it. Soon afterwards I was moved to A4, which meant, that because I was now on the works party I was out of my cell for most of the time and I had more than enough money to get by quite easily. There was quite a lot of drugs about in the nick, plenty pot, and that is all I wanted, Tennent's Super would have been brill though. I was writing to friends and relatives, but I didn't know at the time that my letters were being passed on to a low life tabloid newspaper who in turn was printing them.

While I was in there the screws went on strike. The police and deputy governors took over control and as you can imagine the police were as welcome as a fart in a space suit and it didn't take long before it started to kick off. Normally the screws sent two out of the four wings out at a time on exercise. The police and deputy governors sent all four wings out at the same time and as soon as they came round for exercise I knew it would kick off. I didn't want any kind of hassle so I stayed in my cell.

My cellmate went out though and when he came back he told me all about what had been happening and what was about to happen. They had a mini riot on our wing. I could only listen, but it sounded like a scene out of the *Zulu* film. They were chanting before charging each other, but as always they didn't get away with it. If they didn't get shipped out to camp hill, they were beaten up on the quiet and in some cases, beaten and shipped out. I remember there was blood, hair and teeth still on the bottom floor the next morning when we went down for breakfast. The Old Bill might have left it like that to put the rest of us off from kicking off again. Of course, this is were I put an "allegedly".

I have seen guys kick off loads of times on the wings in all the prisons I've been in and the screws take them down the block by using their faces to open the gates. Of course, the gates are unlocked first.

I could see outside the prison from my cell window and while the screws were on strike there were television news crews outside and unbeknown to me someone had hung a banner out of his window saying "guess who's next door?" (meaning me). I didn't ask why or questioned it in any way. Prison can be a very dangerous place if your face doesn't fit. I have found it pays to keep your head down and your mouth shut and just do your bird or sit on your p- pot and do your bird. All the same thing really.

One day, one of the telly crews wanted to talk to me. I couldn't hear exactly what they were saying, so I gave up and made a w-gesture and waved towards them and went back to reading my book. Of course, after that I was watching my back even more.

The picture below was taken by the news crew and was used as part of an intro to an alleged comedy show. Thankfully, a few guys in nick noticed. I was never asked if it could be used and I was not aware it had been taken until other inmates told me. People think that someone in prison cannot be trusted. I would say that they are more trustworthy than all the media and newspapers put together.

I was working mainly on the bricklaying gang and
the guy in charge of us was called Tony. He was quite a
character. He hadn't a tooth in his head and you could see
he loved the drink. To watch him using the two-way radio
was hilarious. He was a sound bloke though, and while the

screws were on strike, he managed to get me and another guy out of our cells to work. That meant we were the only ones out in the whole prison working or out of our cells. Generally, the whole prison was on lockdown, but because we were working on one of the nonces' wings, we noticed that they were all out of their cells as well, because we could hear them playing table tennis. Tony also told us they were all out too, which is usually the case. The screws do tend to wipe nonces' a- for them. Again, "allegedly".

I did get a bit of flak from some of the other guys for working while others were all banged up. When we got paid I had more money than the others, which isn't a good thing. It was good for me, but jealousy can get you a nice Mars bar, but not the eating variety. I also found out a newspaper had secretly taken photos of us from some tall flats just outside the prison walls and caught all three of us walking with a ladder. Sneaky or what?

After about five months or so, I was transferred to a prison in Surrey. It just so happened we were the first twelve in there and the first night it seemed the screws kept checking us every ten minutes, so there was no smoking weed for quite a while. One of the first things we were told was, "if you screw up here the next stop is the camp hill". No one wanted to go there. From what I have heard it is a right s- and a very violent place, although I had been in similar prisons before and survived. But, why make life hard for yourself if you do not need to? KI SS is always best I think,"Keep it simple Stupid".

I was in my early thirties at the time, so to the other inmates we were classed as old compared to most of the others, who were mainly in their early twenties. I got on with most people in there, although, after a while, as the prison was getting fuller and in any place you start to get the numpties. Trouble started. I was attacked a couple of times, the first time there was about eight of them who all piled into my cell. It was just before dinner, fists were flying in every direction, but there were that many of them they were hitting each other instead of me. I thought at first that they were just messing about, until one connected with my jaw. That is when I started fighting back and as soon as I did they all ran off like the little cowards that they were.

The second time I was attacked, there was no warning beforehand, no shouting, no verbal abuse. About four of them came up from behind and started hitting me around the head with pp9's in socks. I didn't go down, I knew that if I did, that would have been fatal for me. As luck would have it there was a riot button within arm's reach so I pressed that and the screws came running and my attackers scampered away like cowards. The screws asked if I needed to see a doctor, but apart from being a bit shocked and a bit bruised, I felt fine.

After that there was one other guy who was from Brighton, who kept saying to me that he had never seen anyone still standing after being hit around the head with a pp9. I think that might have put quite a few off attacking me further, which of course was a good thing for me.

I found out that my attackers were all from the Brighton area, but were only brave in a group, which is usually the case. I didn't know why I was being attacked or why I was getting verbally abused daily from most of the other inmates. I just put it down to the fact that I had a plum job (education orderly) and I thought people were jealous of me because of that. I started watching my back more and unknowingly started living on my nerves 99.9 % of the time, which is not a good thing for anyone.

There were a couple of Jamaican yardies on our wing

and they didn't live that far from me outside, (Lower Clapton Road area). One of them tried to get me to smuggle drugs when I got out. Before that he had been on my case every day, giving me all kinds of abuse and hassle, so I went along with his little scheme, just to have a quiet life. I had no plans on doing anything for him when I was released. It was far too dangerous. What he wanted me to do was pick up a package of some kind somewhere in Africa and smuggle it to America. He said I would get paid well for doing it, but the way I saw it at the time it didn't matter how much money they were offering. If you're dead, you can't spend it and to me, that was highly likely.

Throughout my sentence, in my letters to my family and friends, I had been promising to keep off the drink, but really I was never in any danger of drinking at all while inside. Weed had taken its place, plus the canteen never sold Tennent's Super and I certainly felt a lot better by not drinking. I was writing to one of my southern sister's friends and my ex-girlfriend's sister who I found out much later on, were both passing my letters on to a low life tabloid newspaper.

While in prison, I started getting pains in my neck and upper back which gave the other inmates and some of the screws something more to take the p-. To stop my head from shaking and to help ease the pain I would hold my neck with my hand. (Sometimes I still do the same now. I know now that this was the start of my dystonia). I suppose I could have gone on protection. After all, I felt very vulnerable most of the time. The prison doctor prescribed what is called aspirin water. In most prisons they dole this stuff out as a cure-all, but it worked and that is all that mattered to me. I thought if I went on rule 43 it was like admitting that I was a nonce and that followed you wherever you went, even though I knew I was neither a nonce nor a grass. But mud sticks.

My time was nearly up. I had two weeks to go and one Friday just after tea two screws came to my cell saying the governor wanted a word with me. When I got to the office the governor told me that there had been a mix up with my release dates and my date had been changed, but didn't know when. It was because of non-payment of maintenance that time had been added on.

I had let the court know that I was in the nick and that I couldn't pay, and they had added time on when I was in the other prison. I had no idea what the game was, because they should have already taken all that into account when they gave me my parole date. They offered me home leave to quieten me down, but I knew if I had taken it I wouldn't have returned. I kept asking the screws every day about my release date, but they wouldn't tell me.

Roughly two weeks later, the board of visitors was there as we were lining up for tea. I had chatted with the board of visitors' guy in the past so we knew each other by name. He asked me how I was and I told him what had been happening with my release date. The SO tried to shut me up and grabbed me by the arm to move me on. I refused and the board of visitors' guy stopped him. I told him everything there and then and he looked at the SO and said, "Is this right?" The SO didn't know what to say or do. He gave me such a black look. I didn't give a s- if I spent the rest of my bird in the block, I was way past caring what could have happened. I just wanted to know my release date and within a few days I got it, but I knew the SO and some of the screws were now gunning for me. I had effectively put a target on my back.

While inside I have since realised my family and

friends were all passing my letters on to a low life tabloid which published them. The reason I know this (in hindsight, that is), is that one day out of the blue, I received a photograph from two black girls. They wanted me to write to them with a view to meeting them when I got out. There was no address because there was no letter with it and to be honest, I wasn't interested as they were both on the plump side and I have hardly ever been with big ladies. Just not my thing.

A couple of weeks later, a lad from the other wing asked me, if I had got the letters. I told him about the photo from the two black girls and he said that there were a lot more letters that I should have had. Because I had no proof, just hearsay, I had to forget about it and move on.

Some of the lads were trying to wind me up about me getting out. I knew it was friendly banter, but to shoot them down I said I wasn't banking on getting out until I walked through those gates. Then I knew I was getting out. They knew I was right and left me alone, apart from one guy, who wanted to have a go at me when I just had a week before my release. I had upset him with something I had said to him the night before. I thought there's no way I am risking not getting out on my new release date, I thought that even if I go out with black eyes and missing teeth I am going home on that date and I told the guy this. I said to him, "Beat me, I will not fight back because I am going through those gates next week." He understood and walked away and didn't bother me again.

When I finally got out within half a day I was back on the booze and I was still smoking pot which is the most I've ever done. I'm far too scared to do anything else and at the time I was far too ill with panic attacks and stress caused by all I had gone through while in prison. I seemed to be very angry all the time, shouting for no reason. I think I was totally stressed out and in constant pain in my upper back and neck, which all made it worse. I couldn't hold or keep my head straight and my head was constantly shaking and going into spasm. Drinking as I did didn't help, but when I was drunk it eased it for some unknown reason.

It seemed to amuse my family and their friends and even my own friends no end that I was suffering as I was and they added to my pain as much as they could, mainly by name calling, saying things like spastic, etc. and constant put downs and ridicule. It made me feel lower than a snake's belly at times. I know now that was their intention and they seemed to want to put more and more pressure on me and force me on a downward spiral and into a more depressed state and of course even more introverted than I was normally and more likely to keep to myself more. It all worked.

It was their way of controlling me. I have found out about the true meaning and not everyone who smiles at you is your friend. Sadly, in my case this included all my family, their friends and all my friends.

Within a month of getting out I went with most of my family to Blackpool for a long weekend to see the Lights. There was my mother, my southern sister, her friend (one of my sister's and mother's co-workers), my southern sister's son and daughter. As usual the p- taking still carried on. I didn't realise at the time that it was their way of controlling me. They simply didn't want me to be in anyway better than them, but in reality, my little finger had more decency than them all put together. In my mind when you sell your body, you can't get much lower than that.

The mickey-taking even carried on in front of my dad, who sat there and did nothing to stop them. My northern sister and her hubby and their family were more or less the same, firmly on the fence getting splinters in their behinds.

The hotel where we were staying had a small bar and because of the weather being pretty wild, we all decided to stay in and have a drinking session. Most of the other residents had the same idea. My mum and dad were sat at the other side of the room.

Suddenly my mother started verbally abusing me in front of everyone, including two old ladies. They looked at each other and one said, "I thought I knew him (me) from somewhere." I didn't say anything or even look at them mainly because I was so annoyed with my mother. I knew my dad knew nothing about what my mother and my southern sister and my sister's work colleague did for a living, i.e., they were sex workers, so I turned round to my mother and in front of everyone, I said, "Do you really want to wash your dirty clothes in public?" She shut up very quickly. I think she knew I would let everyone know what their jobs were, although looking back I doubt if I would have been believed. For most of my life I've been the black sheep of the family, but as I found out in early 1993, all my family have the morals of alley cats. Ripping off your own family in my book is a total no, no. Thankfully, we were only there for a long weekend.

We went to a pub on the north pier on a night out. I think it was called The Merry England at the time and there were two parts to it. There was the adult section, where the bar was) and a part where kids were allowed in. Because we had kids with us, we were all sat in the kids' bit. There was a stage in the adult bit and there was a so-called comedian dressed in a grass skirt. He was trying to get people up on stage to strip off completely naked, for a bottle of champagne. At one point, he was trying to get me up, but

I blanked him totally. Some of the audience tried to take the p- out of me, but I ignored them.

I nearly got involved in a fight when I next went to the bar. Someone took exception to me not getting up on stage, but I stood my ground and he backed down fairly quickly. I was fairly fresh out of prison so it didn't take much effort to sort him out. I didn't think it was fitting to strip in front of kids and my dad reminded me there were kids around at the time, although I had no intention of taking my clothes off for anyone.

When it was time to go back to London, all the southern part of my family, plus the cling-on, got the train back to Euston. It took about four hours and most of it was spent trying to persuade me to move back to Chorley. At first my mother was having a go at my southern sister's friend, saying it was "her fault for carrying it on". I hadn't got a clue what she was talking about at the time, (I now know that my southern sister's friend had been passing my letters on to a low life tabloid newspaper when I was in prison). After about three hours I gave in. What won me over was that they said that my dad would love me to move back up there for good, so I caved in and agreed. My motives were that I needed a fresh start. London had been nothing but heartache and constant trouble for me throughout my time there.

My thoughts on moving back north where I could sort myself out with my drinking and get my dystonia sorted too (although I didn't know it was dystonia until 2006). I was in constant pain 24/7 and it was soul destroying every day. It wasn't just the pain I was in, it was how most people were treating me because of it. What I thought about at the time was my dystonia, (but, it could have been that I was in the newspapers too. Only they know their motives). I was suffering constant verbal abuse and always felt threatened physically when I was out and about. Even though all my family saw this, none of them lifted a finger to help.. They did their best to make it even worse for me, by adding to it. At the time I couldn't understand why they were doing this to me and to be honest even now I don't fully understand why. I suspect though that it could have been that they didn't want their skeletons coming out of the cupboard, but what goes around comes around, as the saying goes.

Moving took a bit of organising and a lot of phone calls to my brother-in-law. It wasn't just a matter of packing a suitcase. He had found a haulier who wanted a backload from London. I didn't have a lot to take. All my cookware, utensils, plates, etc. had been thrown out or nicked while I was in prison. Someone even took my out of date passport. My mother and sister would have sold my false teeth given half a chance. They had all lost all their morals decades before. I hadn't noticed.

During one phone call, quite out of the blue my brother-in-law said to me, "Why don't you just stay in London and face them?" I had no idea who "them" was. My mother was sat in the kitchen with me, so I asked her what he was on about. "Who's them?" She snatched the phone off me and went ballistic with him. I tried to earwig, but my mother ordered me out of the kitchen. She was shouting that much I could still hear bits of what she was saying in the other room. But it was so vague I couldn't fully work out exactly what they were on about.

Before I moved back north, I kept visiting my ex-girlfriend's sister. Once, I went round and just her boyfriend was there. She had gone to the supermarket with someone, so her boyfriend had told me. He hardly said a word to me while I was waiting, but I knew he didn't like me at all. The feeling was mutual. When my ex-girlfriend's sister came back, she had this bloke with her who looked a bit like a farmer by the way he was dressed. There was no introduction and to be honest I wasn't that bothered who he was.

He suddenly started to call me a dirty bastard. I hadn't got a clue why. I told him to shut it otherwise I would shut it for him. My ex-girlfriend's sister stepped in and said she didn't want any trouble at her place and seeing that I was on parole, I didn't need any either, so I let it go.

Then she started trying to make me stay in London, by saying I was "running away" (although she never explained what I was meant to be running away from and I did ask), but it was totally not the case. I was completely fed up with London and even now thirty or so years on, I still hate it.

She even offered to go out with me (as in a relationship) if I stayed in London and she said this in front of her boyfriend. To be honest, if a girlfriend of mine had said that in front of me, I would have walked out on her, there and then. But money makes some people take a lot of s- and I still have no idea who the guy was. I think he could have been a journalist of some kind, but obviously a journalist with no common sense or manners it would seem. He never said a word to me after I had put him in his place. All he needed to do was ask in a proper manner and say who he was and I would have told him whatever he needed to know, but after money had crossed my palm ,of course.

About a week before I was due to move back north, I came home at my usual time and as I opened my front door there was an overpowering stench of s-. There was no sign of a break-in. I looked around and found quite a lot of what

I thought was human excreta on my bathroom mat and in the bath itself. Nothing was missing as far as I could see.

It was the final nail in the coffin for me. I suspect it was someone from my family who was behind it, mainly because there were no signs of a break-in. I suppose in their way of thinking it would have been the final push from them to make sure I moved out of London and I know from experience just how sick they all were and are.

I thought by going back north, my stress and alcoholism and my dystonia would have been sorted: better doctors and better people. Anyway the day finally dawned. The haulier arrived about 7.30am with his three-ton lorry. There was plenty of room for what little I had left. As we were loading my mother popped round to take the door keys off me (the arrangement was she would hand the keys into my landlord, as soon as possible. I found out six months or so later that she hadn't done so, as I received a bailiff's letter, I think knowing how my mother was at the time, she more than likely rented it out to someone or even more likely used it as a brothel, because around that time she was working as a madame in a brothel in Croydon. So anything was possible).

My nearest neighbour came out to say bye. She was one of the best neighbours I've had, before and since, and she was the only reason I was sorry to be leaving London. As a leaving gift for some of my other not so nice neighbours that I didn't like, I left a pottery clown on my window sill. It was like giving them the middle finger. My biggest grievance was against my next door but one neighbour. I hated them. They were total wrong 'uns.

I blame them partly for letting people through their house, so that the peeping toms and the press had more viewing points. I think they would have been charging people so they could fund their drug habit.

Months after the curtain incident people were trying their best to spy on me. Someone even wrote on my front door that I or they enjoyed bum sex. I'm not quite sure what their message really meant.

Because of the traffic it seemed to take forever to get to my dad's house. I knocked on his door with my suitcase in my hand and to say he wasn't pleased to see me would have been a total understatement. I saw his face drop as soon as he saw the van outside with my furniture on it.

It would seem the rest of my family didn't have the decency to warn him or give him a chance to refuse if he had wanted to, which I'm quite sure he would have done. As time went by, my sister and her husband and all their friends had the same kind of welcome for me. If I have a problem with someone, whatever it is, I tell them to their face, then move on. When I was brought up in Chorley one thing I always admired about Lancashire folk was their openness and no b- approach to things.

As I look back now, I suppose there was no money to be made from telling me their real feelings and about the press. There was more money to be made by not telling me anything and treating me like s-, instead of being honest with me. Or was it maybe they all had a guilty conscious in some way and were frightened I would drop them all in it? But why tell lies? Liars never win and the truth always finds its own way out in the end no matter what you do to avoid it.

While staying at my dad's house, I went to the local pub nearly every night in all weathers, mainly because my dad didn't like me drinking at home or for that matter smoking in his house. On one of my many visits to the local, the landlady once said to me (although I thought she was joking at the time), "Stop washing your cock in the sink."

I thought it was a strange comment to make and I didn't have a clue what she was talking about. Months earlier my nephew (he was about six at the time) had once commented about people washing their willies in the sink. He had mistaken the urinals for sinks so I thought that was what she was referring to. I just laughed it off and forgot all about it...

What I now know she was referring to was that my dad didn't have proper bathing facilities, so one Friday night after I'd been to the pub I needed to top and tail. I felt very dirty and clammy and my skin felt like it was crawling. I was desperate for a wash, so I washed in the sink. I'm sure that I'm not the first or the last to do this, but someone with a camera caught me in the act. As I remember, there was a bright light shining from outside the kitchen window as I was bathing. I thought that it could have been lightning, but strangely I never heard any thunder.

Whoever it was had to climb over my dad's gate and in doing so damaged the top part of it. My dad, for some reason best known to himself, accused me of damaging it, but for the life of me, I'd had no idea exactly what he was talking about as I could not remember damaging anything.

I now know what really happened. Whoever it was with the camera damaged the gate by climbing over it. Why my dad couldn't have said in an honest, upfront way how the gate was really damaged is beyond me.

If I do wrong I put my hand up to it straight away. I always have and always will. I have always taken full responsibility for all my wrongdoings.

Even one Christmas Day, my dad had heard that a family in Whittle-le-Woods had had all their kids' presents nicked from under the tree by a burglar and for some unknown reason he was trying to blame me for it, as if I was the only burglar in the area. I have done a lot of bad things in my life, but I would never stoop that low. It is one of many things I would never do, but I've noticed people deflect from their wrongdoing by accusing you of stuff. It helps them live with their own guilt more, I suppose.

When I first moved back north I gave my dad a carriage clock that had been gifted me by Sun Life Insurance, but, for reasons best known to himself, he never once put it on show. I think he thought it was stolen goods, but I think I was probably being pre-judged on hearsay or my history of wrongdoing decades previously, or just out and out lies from most of my family. As I know my southern sister constantly dripped poison about me in my dad's ear and so did my northern sister.

Even when I bought my dad something religious in Malta in 2015 and I was 25 years out of any kind of trouble with the police, once again he didn't have the decency to put it on show. That is how he has been with me for most of my life. I put it down to small-town mentality and my northern sister pecking at his head with anything negative she could dream up to throw at me. I really have had some sad, bigoted people around me in the past.

I must admit that after a few weeks back in Chorley I hated it, mainly because of how ill I felt most of the time. There was no support from anyone. It was also how slow it was compared to London and the fact I didn't really have any friends or anyone halfway decent around me.

I got so depressed that one night I rang my mother after I had been to the pub (bad idea). I suppose I just wanted a moan or to vent my feelings. I hinted about moving back to London. She got very angry and was quite adamant she didn't want me back living there. She wouldn't say why and I got quite angry with her so much so that my dad told me off the following night for abusing her. When I asked other members of the family, including my dad, why I couldn't move back to London, I was met with a total wall of silence. It was like having the three wise monkeys round me most of the time. Looking back, I'm glad I didn't move.

I firmly believe things happen for a reason in life. My family in London had tricked me into moving back north, but when I think about it I could never see a good future for myself in London. I was totally surrounded by scum in every way, family included.

Maybe if I had stayed in London I might have found out about the tabloids a bit quicker. I think that is why my family in London tricked me into moving back north as they did. Maybe the tabloids were getting too close for their comfort and they and their friends and even my friends certainly didn't want that to happen, it would seem.

I must admit I had to tell lies to get a flat off a housing association and it's not something I ever enjoy doing. My mother gave me a letter to give to them and I was forbidden from opening it. I found it hard not to and I must have been a mug not to.. I had to tell them that I was sleeping in a car on the flat iron market in Chorley. I was desperate.

Because of all the messing about, I had trouble with my benefits, so much so, I had to go to Barry House in Preston. My sister from Chorley gave me a lift there and back, but I had to give her £10 for petrol and that was £10 I didn't have, so she showed her true colours even then.

Mind you, one skeleton she will not want outing is that she had three attempts at getting her present surname. She first went out with her now husband's cousin, who was married at the time, then when she was seeing her now husband she was sleeping with his brother behind his back and out of the three of them she married the one with a bit of money. Talk about keeping it in the family. I do believe there is some doubt over her son's dad (allegedly) so the questions are: is he her husband's or her husband's brother? The jury's out on that.

For a couple of months when I first moved north, I babysat my nephew every Friday night. Once, I had to walk to my sister's house from my dad's house, as my bike was out of action and I encountered some problems on the way there. I had to run from a gang of youths who wanted to attack me for no apparent reason or that is what it seemed like at the time. It frightened me as I think it would do anyone. I'm no s- , but I know my limitations and eight against one was a little unfair, I thought. So just in case they were following me I ran the last half mile to my sister's house.

When I got there they were still showering and generally getting ready to go out. I was sat in the dining room with my sister. I was fast reaching the end of my tether with everything that was happening around me and everything that had happened since late 1985, so I asked my sister what the hell was going on. (I assumed that in the past she had been brutally honest about everything and never held back if she had something to say).

So I thought maybe she would tell me what I desperately needed to know, but I had no joy there either. I asked her why I was being attacked and abused in the streets and why had all the abuse, physical and verbal, followed me north from London. She said she didn't know anything about it, then she got my brother-in-law to have a word with me and he said the same. That was one of many times I asked for help and got nothing back from all my family, so there was definitely no cross talking or misunderstanding. They knew I didn't know anything.

I genuinely thought that when I moved north I had left it back in London. In no way did anything that was said or done towards me at any time before I found out in 1993, signpost me in the direction of the newspapers, either in London or in Chorley.

I admit that if I hadn't been drinking as much as I was I would have realised much sooner what vile people I had around me and I would have put distance between us. As ill as I was with stress, dystonia and alcoholism, I still noticed the abuse and the physical attacks. How could I not? I simply had no idea why I was suffering all this abuse and in no way did I know how to resolve it.

When you are in the thick of it, struggling in every way to survive and no one wants to help you, you just cannot see a way out of it, unless you fully understand what is happening around you. It is very much like drowning with no one offering you a lifebelt. In my case, instead of a lifebelt I was being thrown weighted-down sacks to help me drown quicker.

I think two things got me through, the main one being my stubbornness not to give in or let the bullies win and all the abuse I had lived through as a child and as an adult.

All the people who got violent with me didn't at any time say to me what it was for. The only thing that might have been possible was maybe to read their fists as I was being beaten by them, but most would have only had hate or love on their fists, assuming they could spell. Anything else they would have had trouble spelling, but by me not reading the newspapers, I was unaware of anything to do with the tabloids. How much effort would it have taken for someone, anyone, to have put a newspaper article in front of me and just say to me read that, or even leave a newspaper where I might just pick it up and read it? The nearest I ever got to this was when I was working at the sheet-metal workplace. Someone had cut out the headline about someone flashing and left it on my workbench. Later on, while I was chatting to one of the guys in the welding bay I found the newspaper it had been cut out of. I tried reading it, one of the bosses came in as I had just started, so I had to go back to my bench. When I returned to read it ten minutes later it had conveniently disappeared and I had only read maybe a couple of sentences at the most. Any genuine person would have left the whole page, so it was no wonder it took me seven years to spot myself and why I was none the wiser.

One night when I was having a drink in the local pub the owner's son was kicking off with me, verbally, because one of my southern sister's friends and work colleagues had phoned the pub earlier on in the day and asked them to ask me to ring her back. I didn't see any harm in it, but the landlord's son was trying to tell me that she was using me or taking the p- out of me in some way. If only I had listened to him. Because of my alcoholism and dystonia I sometimes found it difficult to do basic things. I was far too trusting.

I'm 100% sure my family and their friends and my friends knew or could see that I needed help. None was ever given or has ever been offered in any way. Quite the reverse.

So I'm quite sure if anyone else had been in the same situation, they wouldn't have done any better than me.(I'm not a Turnip head or a Richard Cranium as the tabloid in question had labelled me). I know it was a deflection from the real truth by the gutter press, but it was only my upbringing that helped me get through all the abuse I suffered from 1985 till 1993. My bad childhood had toughened me up without even knowing it had toughened me up. But before anyone thinks it, I don't see myself as a hard man. There is always someone harder, no matter who you are.

Life seemed to carry on as normal, the verbal and physical abuse still continued. I did my best to ignore it as much as I could, because it was mainly knuckle draggers who were doing it. I even had a bottle thrown at me when I was cycling into Chorley one day. Luckily, it never came anywhere near me, but it smashed in front of me and I got a puncture. I ended up having to walk at least a mile, before I could get it fixed at my brother-in-law's workshop.

His brother was there at the time and I told them what had happened and his brother said he had done it. When I asked him why he would do something like that, he just walked away laughing. My brother-in-law said nothing as well and it wasn't the first or the last time my brother-in-law's brother gave me verbal abuse. It was nearly all the time we were in each other's company for months on end. He was saying things like, "no smoke without fire", to which I mainly answered, "depends on who's fanning the flames". On other occasions he would say "nowt down for you lad", like my number was up or that I was due to get a good hiding from someone. Another one was "we are raping you with your clothes on". It was as if they were playing piggy in the middle with any information or just simply playing stupid mind games. But it was help or information that would have helped me out of the abuse.

He never ever explained himself and nor did anyone else. Even when my brother-in-law's brother used me as a bail address in mid-1997, because he'd been nicked for kiddy fiddling a 12-year-old lad, I didn't think he was guilty. If I had, I would never have vouched for him. My good deed was never repaid and I have never been told what was said in the newspapers.

On one occasion when my brother-in-law's brother came home from the pub when he was staying at mine, he was a bit drunk and in tears because of what he was facing. He was crying and kept saying, "why me? Why me?" I told him straight. "Why not you, are you someone special? At least you know what you've been accused of. I didn't or don't. He thought about that for about 10 seconds and said," I can't tell you anything."

Perhaps I should have tried the ouija board to find out. It just goes to show how false they all were around me and as the saying goes 'you are only as good as the people around you', is very true.

The biggest laugh was when I found out about the newspaper. My brother-in-law's brother kept saying, "that will never happen to me. I have genuine people around me." He ended up doing time for kiddy fiddling, so you could say I have seen karma in action and it was quite satisfying to watch, although I didn't take any joy from seeing him go down for something he didn't do. As they say, "what goes around comes around'.

Right from day one, when I moved back to Chorley, he was constantly abusing me. He was always accusing me of selling my a- when I lived in London, which I never did. He had a good business and a good name around Chorley as a businessman, but I truly cannot understand why he and the rest of that part of my northern family were siding with working girls like my mother and sister in London, unless maybe they didn't know they were working girls. Either way, if you are a decent person, you wouldn't treat other people in that way.

I would never tell lies about someone for any reason. Truth is always the best option and far easier. No comebacks that way and if the tables were turned (and they will be, God willing, when I publish this book) and I had been in the same situation as my brother-in-law, I would have stuck to the truth throughout. I would never have got roped into something that could turn out bad for myself. It's not worth it.

I'm sure that it will not do his business any good, as I'm sure not many people would trust someone who rips off their in-laws or for that matter someone who rips off anyone.

I must say that is not the reason for me writing this book. It's not revenge. I am simply telling people what really happened. I'm just getting even, not mad, although the tabloids withheld my right to reply and even my right to know of any allegations that were being made against me, which to me is a basic human right.

Health wise, I started suffering quite badly with panic attacks if I was in a stuffy shop or a crowded place. At the time I put it down to the extreme stress that I was having to endure and had endured while in prison in 1989 and since 1985. What didn't help was that none of my family or friends ever helped me.

Once, when I was helping my brother-in-law move workshops, I went with one of his lads to the baker's. It was packed, to say the least, and I started sweating. My heart started pounding. I was visibly shaking so much that I had to leave the shop as quickly as I could. The attack was that bad I couldn't open the door to get out. When we got back to the workshop, his lad told my brother-in-law what had happened and he told me off. "Don't ever do that again," he said as if it was my fault for suffering the way I was. (Some folk are so chronically stupid). He was hardly the expert witness he thought he was in 1993.

My health was getting worse. My doctors and consultants didn't seem to want to help or maybe they couldn't help. They were treating my dystonia as arthritis. I was in intense pain 24/7 (even now I am still in pain, but, at least I know what is wrong with me. In their defence, not many doctors know anything about dystonia).

By now I was drinking Kestrel Super, as it was cheaper and 0.5 stronger than Tennent's. I still only drank half a dozen cans per night, but that was more than enough. My daily units were 42 units per night on average. I think I just drank to forget all the abuse and the abuse I had suffered growing up and it also helped me to sleep. The trouble was I couldn't afford to drink and eat properly, so I bought cheaper food. I stopped buying clothes and shoes, but I paid my bills as much as possible. I was walking around like a tramp with long hair and holes in my shoes.

One day when I was walking back from Leyland police station after being caught and arrested once again trying to break in somewhere in 1991, a group of young lads were calling me a tramp. I was a tramp, but being told I was one didn't help me at all. It made me feel even more depressed and it seemed the whole world had turned against me for no apparent reason that I could work out. If I'd known why it might just have straightened me out, but not knowing was just pushing me deeper and deeper into depression.

The tabloid in question kept banging on about how ignorance was bliss in 1993. Not that I ever read this. I found out many months later, but it's quite obvious they were talking rubbish as per usual, because, believe me, it is a long way from bliss.

Around that time my daughter's mother and I were writing quite raunchy letters to each other. I didn't see any harm in it at all, as we were ex-lovers and I would have done or said anything, to stay in contact with her, as this was my way of maybe one day meeting my daughter again and to me, I had to do my best to keep my daughter's mother sweet.

Out of the blue, my son started writing to me, which was quite a shock. Previously, he had never ever written. I had never had a Christmas card from him. I sent him Christmas cards and birthday cards with money in most of the time. I never got any thanks. I blamed his mum for that. I knew she was a vile, toxic person and would have filled his head with all kinds of rubbish about me.

I should have known that there was something not quite right about my son asking me to write to his mum. Like a fool I did. In fact, I was writing to her and my daughter's mother and my daughter's mother's sister. Thankfully, apart from my daughter's mother's letters, the other letters were maybe once a week. I should have realised three women wanting to know me was unbelievable, when in the past they would not have crossed the road for me.

While I was in police custody at Leyland in late 1991, I was questioned for around three hours non-stop with the tape switched off. The two CID blokes kept asking me over and over again to admit something. They kept saying, "We know you're guilty of other things. Come on, admit them." At one point they wanted me to join a gang who lived around by me, in Clayton Brook and grass them up and they would pay me for doing so. I told them in no way would I ever do that, which annoyed them.

I think this was the nearest I ever got to being interviewed by the police about the curtain incident of 1985 and this was October 1991.

I was forever borrowing money off my brother-in-law and very rarely off my dad. He moaned far too much about it. I borrowed it mainly to get drunk. I was now at the stage in my drinking that I was having blackouts and even worse more panic attacks. I didn't smoke weed or take drugs of any kind, apart from strong pain relief and anti-inflammatory tablets which were prescribed and I never took more than what I was prescribed at any time, although anyone who had never walked in my shoes would assume that I was abusing my medication.

I was also totally on my uppers. No one seemed to want to know me or have anything to do with me. I put this down to my drinking and the fact I had dystonia. More than likely, I looked a right mess. A few times I would tag along with people on my way home who were also on the same government course as me (at King Street, Chorley) but I could sense they didn't want to be seen anywhere near me. Most people are image-conscious. One even told me to get away from him though not in so many words. When I asked him why, he wouldn't explain and got quite violent towards me. So much for genuine people. Even now I get funny stares from people when my neck goes into spasm(dystonic storm as it's more commonly known), but very few know for certain what is actually happening and most intellectually challenged people tend to take the mick out of what they cannot understand. Thankfully, most people are genuine enough and just carry on regardless.

While on another FT course, which this time was based at the bottom of Stump Lane in Chorley, at the old leather works, we were meant to be training, but actually working on people's houses. We were still just getting the extra tenner. I got on with most of the other guys on the course quite well and I had been to school with one of the guy's elder brothers, but I never told him that I had once beaten up his brother for bullying my cousin when I was in primary school (*what goes around comes around* is very true).

At our base there were quite a few courses there for men and women, including a woman from Upper Adlington, who, I must admit I took a shine to. She was a bit too snobby for me. I think that was what attracted me to her. I made no secret of how I felt about her and most people knew that I was interested in her, but I knew deep down I had no chance with her. She probably thought of me as something she had stepped in on her shoe. At least that was my impression.

On one occasion one of my work colleagues asked me if I had been making nuisance or abusive calls late at night. I told him the truth. I didn't have her number so how could I phone her. Not that I would have done that anyway. That shot him down big style, but it probably didn't stop him or others talking behind my back.

Around that time we were working on a pub's gable end at the bottom of Brook Street and it was very, very close to where I had pushed off the coping stone killing the train guy when I was quite young. At one point one of my work colleagues told me to stand under where the coping stone was, which I did. He couldn't move it because it was cemented firmly in place and was far too heavy for any one man to move. . I stood under the bridge expecting it to come crashing down on me and end my life. You could say I was suicidal at the time.

I was nervous like anyone would have been, but, my self-esteem was minus 100 at the time. Ending my life seemed a good option. It would have been a blessed release from my troubles and the daily pain I was in. I loathed myself, but it was not to be. I got fed up of waiting after about five minutes although it felt a lot longer and just went back to work. No one said anything about what had just happened, including me.

Soon after that, I was put on a placement working in Holmeslack in Preston on a printer's extension. The builder had the same name as a famous Hollywood legend. When I was taken to be introduced to him by the woman in charge of the courses, the builder said to her, "Do you know who that is? (me)." The woman replied, "We just ignore that." I ignored it too.

Once again, I had no idea what they were talking about. I thought it was a strange remark to make and I wondered what he meant by it. I knew no one would tell me, so I had to let it go over my head because I knew if my family would not tell me anything, I had no chance of a total stranger telling me anything and I had long given up hope.

At first the builder and I got on quite well, but I soon felt I was having the meikle taken out of me because I was working over my hours and when we were working in Southport, I had to get to Croston, easily five miles from where I lived to where the builder lived and he would take me the rest of the way to Southport. Once I missed him by half an hour. His wife said that he wanted me to cycle to Southport. I refused. He was taking the mickey even asking me to do that.

On my last day, we were working on his house when he virtually accused me of interfering with his young girls. I lost it with him and told him in no uncertain terms that in no way would I ever do such a thing. He also mentioned about a newspaper offering him free advertising. To be blunt, I hadn't got a clue what he was on about and I was glad I didn't have to work for him anymore.

This meant that I had to go back on the original course, which, in reality, wasn't a course. It seemed to me very few people ever get trained on these courses which they are designed for (I think it is so the DWP/ Government can turn round and say so many thousands are off the dole this month, when, in reality, they are still on it, because they are still getting paid from the DWP. The only difference is they are on a course).

As usual, I consoled myself with my virtual friend Mr Kestrel Super to help me get through or so I thought at the time. Occasionally, I would do some work for people to get my drink money, mainly for family or friends of the family, so, I never got the going rate. They took the meikle big style on many occasions, but, when you're desperate as I definitely was, you will do anything within reason. I did my best to avoid getting into trouble with the police, so the fact I turned my hand to a lot of things to earn my drink money is at least something positive I have achieved through alcoholism.

While I was writing letters to my ex, I made some comments about people including my doctor in Bamber Bridge and my local hospital. I can only say sorry for my stupid remarks. I was in intense pain throughout and I felt that I was not getting the right kind of help.

I was being treated for arthritis, when I should have been treated for dystonia, and one consultant told me the pain on the right-hand side of my neck and upper back was due to me breaking my collar bone when I was twelve in the early 1970s. You don't need to be a doctor to work that out and I knew this guy hadn't got a clue what he was talking about.

When I told him I had broken my left-hand side collar bone when I was twelve, not my right-hand one, it deflated him. He knew his comment was wrong and said no more after that and I lost all faith in the doctors and consultants until fairly recently.

That's why I felt that I had to lash out like I did and that is all I was doing at the time, but in no way did I know my letters were being passed on to anyone else, so in no way was it deliberate. But it took me from 1989 until 2006 to find out I had dystonia and how to get proper treatment, simply because the doctors knew/know very little about dystonia and that they had never properly listened to me. Sadly, the same goes for alcoholism. There's far too much ignorance in the medical profession on things that matter and it is this that is killing people and costing the NHS more money. In quite a lot of cases it seems to me that it is the blind leading the blind.

One thing that doctors have in common is that not many actually listen to the patient. If you're lucky they will read your notes, then go on to tell what you're feeling, when in reality the patient is the expert on their own health.

If you don't know you should not treat people for other things. In truth, they have made my pancreas worse. They were treating me for arthritis of the spine and the drugs I was given were very strong pain relief and anti-inflammatory and other treatments such as traction and manipulation. Not one of them worked because they had not sussed out properly what I was suffering from, obviously, the doctors/consultants were not listening to (me) the patient, and they were more talking at me. Thank God for nurses who often correct the doctor's mistakes.

When I was about to receive my first session of traction, my brother-in-law made a point of telling me a scary story about a friend of his (should have guessed he was lying, he has no friends) who had had traction and the hospital had dislocated his hip bone so badly he was unable to walk properly. (It was one of his many little mind games to stop me doing anything that would have helped sort myself out and maybe get better). It was a clear sign of a guilty conscience.

When I was finally diagnosed with dystonia in 2006, I was put on a drug I should never have been on (olanzapine). At the time I was quite ill in hospital with chronic pancreatitis, because of gall stones. One of the side effects of olanzapine is pancreatitis, so for about three or four years I was in and out of hospital. My pancreas is now in a chronic condition and probably because of this, I am now suffering from type 2 diabetes, which is controlled by insulin.

So the doctor who put me on these pills has seriously shortened my life quite considerably and made my quality of life even more unbearable. All he needed to do before prescribing the medication was to check the side effects of the medication. Mind you, I should not have been so trusting and checked it out.

I also made some comments in my letters about two people connected with my northern family. One of the comments was that I very much fancied my friend's wife. I'm quite sure that it would have angered her husband no end, but he didn't let on in any way that he knew what I had said and just for the record, nothing ever happened between us. My brother-in-law, as per usual, was probably stoking trouble like the old woman he is and was.

The next person was my brother's-in-law brother. I called him a t- in one of my many letters to my ex and fair enough he did offer me out because of it. But I must add he never explained why he wanted to fight me. That was the nearest I ever got to being told about the tabloids by any of them and he is very much like his brother, as in, they both get off on mind games. They are sad and toxic people.

I did say I was going to be brutally honest, because I've nothing left to hide. For a while I had had some quite strange people knocking at my door. One asked me if I wanted to buy my flat. I said of course I would love to, but how am I going to do it when I am on the dole and skint? Without another word he turned and walked away.

Another guy kept coming to my door asking me if I wanted a lifetime supply of dog food. On each occasion I told him I had no dog, so I had no need for dog food. He then offered me the money alternative. I asked what was the catch as you never really get a stranger coming to your door offering you a lot of money. Again, he walked off without a word.

When I went to school it was common sense not to b-people if you have something to say. You front up and say it. These guys couldn't have had much intelligence and I genuinely suspect they were journalists and the newspaper they attempt to write for has a reading age of five to seven and it seems they lack the common sense they were born with, if indeed they had any in the first place,as not everyone reads newspapers. I find it's always best to treat people as individuals. That is what I always try to do and I never assume things. Assuming things makes an ass out of you and me.

My neighbours kept coming out with strange comments and doing strange things. For instance, one Saturday afternoon I was doing some washing up. No problem there you might think, but my kitchen window overlooked a grassy communal area. I noticed my rather rough Scottish neighbours from across the way, who were hanging around their grandmother's front door. I was not even looking at them, I was more daydreaming if anything, but for some unknown reason they all started throwing stones at my kitchen window. I moved away from the window as fast as I could before any of the stones reached their target. Luckily for me, none did and their grandmother stopped them fairly quickly, but I thought it best not to go out and ask what was that all about, because I would have been asking for trouble and I was seriously outnumbered.

One night I came round the corner to my flat on my pushbike. It was a nice sunny Saturday evening and some of my neighbours were sat out drinking. One of them asked if I wanted to join them, which was most unexpected. I said, "No, you're all right, but thanks for the offer." One of them turned around and said, "You (me) bought it and thanks, again." I had no idea what they were talking about as I had not bought anyone anything, so I just forgot all about it until now that is.

One morning when I was leaving my flat to go to work in late 1992 or early 1993, my next door neighbour seemed to be waiting for me. Both hubby and wife were saying they were going to get me kicked out of my flat, as my name wasn't on the tenancy agreement.

It would seem that they thought that I had given the wrong name. It still worried me quite a bit and it didn't help that I was also being a noisy neighbour as well.

I was so worried about getting kicked out that I phoned my landlord and it turned out that they knew nothing about it. I think my neighbour thought that what the tabloid was calling me was my real name. Some people are so daft and gullible. I suppose they believe *Coronation*

Street is real.

Even my brother-in-law took the p- about me potentially being homeless. It was his way of trying to control me, with his childish mind games.

One Sunday afternoon, I had six angry neighbours at my door. Someone had taken a couple of paving slabs from the path leading to the main road from the communal area and dumped them on my very small bit of a garden and they were accusing me of nicking them. I said I didn't have any need for them, so why would I steal them? One of them said, "Well, if he doesn't want them, I will take them." I think the penny dropped. We all knew it was him who had taken them from the path and was trying to blame me. I didn't get any kind apology from any of them.

One night, about six months after finding out about the tabloids, the same neighbour who stole the paving slabs and his son were shouting abuse at me from their living room window. He sounded p- and he was calling me names from his window, but I soon put a stop to it. Months earlier I had bought a mini recorder to try and catch my family out with their lies. He spotted the red light that shows it was recording and he stopped straight away. His behaviour changed towards me after that, for the better.

For some reason I got into the habit of playing loud music until around midnight and sometimes I would sit at my open bedroom window and have a couple of fags before going to bed. It was my way of chilling out and sometimes I would get a bit leery. I was *blind* drunk and most of the time I was in a blackout situation, as strange as this might sound. I know only another alcoholic will fully understand what I'm talking about. I knew that I was doing wrong, but I couldn't control myself when I was drunk. Drunk or sober, I still did it and I can only say sorry for my behaviour which lasted for about six months.

Then in mid-July of 1992, totally out of the blue, my ex suddenly started writing again. I was a bit shocked at first, but I went with the flow so to speak, not thinking anything about it or if anything would come of it.

Shortly after starting writing to her, while I was working for my brother in law, my northern sister came in as usual. My brother-in-law said, "We're not buying your letters." I hadn't a clue what he was referring to, so I asked him to explain. They looked at each other and laughed and walked away. It wasn't unusual to hear half a tale from them and by this time I had long given up on finding anything out in the way of truth about what was effectively happening behind my back.

My life was fast spiralling out of control, although my drinking was not getting any worse or for that matter any better. The effect it was having on me was getting worse. I was getting more and more depressed and my life was totally out of control and definitely in chaos. My brother-in-law and his brother and even one of the guys from a neighbouring company, all started giving me all kinds of grief on a daily basis. Once, they stuck something on my back and were constantly belittling and ridiculing me in any way they could.

On the day they put the sticker on my back, I went ballistic and demanded it was taken off that instant. When I asked to read what it said, it was quickly destroyed. I thought at the time what cowards they all were. It was one of many things they did, it was pure mind games to confuse me or deflect me from finding out as much as possible (which it did) and maybe it was their way of forcing me over the edge into attempting suicide, which at times, I was very close to. I think it was only because I was drinking as much as I was that cushioned me from all the abuse I was suffering daily. I suppose I was self-medicating with alcohol.

Surprisingly, my brother-in-law bought me a brand new bike. He wouldn't tell me why. He simply said, "I need you to be more reliable, so now you have no excuse." At the time that seemed plausible, But my mother told me one Sunday months later it was because my second stepdad seemed to be getting interested in us, in a bad way, once again. He never came anywhere near any of us, so it was more lies to mess with my already befuddled head.

The abuse seemed to be getting worse and my drinking was also affecting me more and more mentally. I hadn't altered the amount I was drinking nightly, but I felt I was losing my sanity at times and no matter who I turned to for help, I wouldn't get any.

One night I came home after a very s- day at work and I knelt at the side of my bed praying. I was contemplating suicide very seriously. I was crying uncontrollably and begging my higher power (God) to help in whatever way He could.

He answered my prayers a few months later. At first, it certainly wasn't the way I would have liked to have Him answer my prayers, but in the end, it worked out. It's is like they say in AA, "be careful what you pray for, you might just get it" and I got through it. Only God knows how.

I went visiting my family in London. It seemed by now that I had even lost my own identity. My name was now w-, w- this, w- that. It's not that I cannot laugh at myself, but when you are ill and suffering as I definitely was, no one was forthcoming with any kind of help or advice

At the time it felt like I was being pushed to breaking

point or as if they wanted me to commit suicide and to be honest at times I wasn't far from doing that. It was just my sheer stubbornness and cowardice that didn't allow me to. In some ways as I look back now all the abuse I had suffered at school and at home with my second stepdad as a teenager and while in nick, had made me stronger without even knowing it had. I feel sure if it had not been for my bad upbringing I would have committed suicide.

I have never found abuse of any kind funny. I can't even watch violence or bullying on telly. To me, it is a form of bullying. I was fast reaching the end of my tether most days because of the name calling. On one occasion while I was in London visiting my southern sister I went ballistic with my niece and her friends because they kept calling me w-. My southern sister calmed me down, but I was adamant that I wanted to know what the hell was going on around me and behind my back. Why was everyone calling me w-? Why was I constantly being attacked in the street for no apparent reason?

Eventually she told me, waiting until I was completely stoned and p- out of my head before she said anything. I was still no wiser. Even if I had been stone cold sober I doubt I would have understood what she was trying to tell me and I also noticed that she had a big carving knife to hand. I think that was intended for me, so it was a good job I calmed down. All she said was that I had to be very careful what I said. Dangerous people were watching me although she wouldn't clarify who they were. If anything, I was more confused, but even more on my guard against everyone, apart from my family.

The next night I was moved from my sister's to my mother's flat. Within minutes of me entering, she said, "If you kick off here you're out on the street." I thought that was totally out of order to say to your own flesh and blood, but I felt that I was getting close to finding out the truth and they were scared of what might happen.

One of my mother's girls called round later that night with her boyfriend. I knew him vaguely. He had been in Wandsworth when I was. He was there for breaking his parole conditions and had done life for stabbing his girlfriend to death. All three of them suddenly started giving me verbal abuse. They waited until I had had a spliff and for it to take full effect, so by the time they started on me I was totally off my head on pot and booze and so in no way could I understand fully what was being said, or so they thought. It seems my family took a leaf out of my second stepdad's book; getting me out my head to cover themselves.

I knew that he was threatening me to keep my gob shut if I knew what was good for me. I didn't respond at all and at one point he was right in my face, threatening me.

He was spitting as he was shouting and it crossed my mind that I was going to get knifed here, so, I didn't not react at all and although up until then I had thought we were friends I had never really trusted him. My mother sat there with her work colleague and kept laughing at me. I must admit I hated my mother even more then. I was disgusted in what she had now become. I was so glad I was going home the next day. What kind of mother does that to her own flesh and blood or for that matter what kind of family does that?

When I saw my dad the following Sunday, I mentioned what had happened, but I put it my way, as in, I didn't like the way they (my mum/sister, etc.) had treated me like some kind of punter (a prostitute's customer). My dad didn't know this about them and I don't think the penny fully dropped with what I had said to him. I still don't think he knows even now, more than 23 years later.

Around the time my dad said to me that my mother had told him to tell me to stop sending my ex letters, I, of course, asked why. He said because your mum said so, so I said I didn't want to because eventually I wanted to see my daughter again and I would do anything to make that happen. Normally, this would have been a cue to sit me down and tell me what the problem was, as to, why they didn't want me writing letters to my ex. But, I was not dealing with genuine, honest people I am sad to say.

My northern sister and her husband were talking about me at home behind my back. One day my nephew came running up to me while I was working on a bench outside the workshop. He was about seven at the time and he said, "My mum and dad are going to get a hit-man for you."(At that age kids have no discretion filter, so they just repeat what they've heard their parents say). I don't think he fully realised or understood what he was saying. I laughed and said, "Make sure they pick a good one."

My sister and her hubby were getting their kids to call me all kinds of names and belittling me in every way they could. Even my brother-in-law's brother and cousin took part in getting the kids to do the same.

The cousin told a low life tabloid that I wanted to take on Frank Bruno in the ring, which in no way was true, as around that time physically I could not have fought my way out of a paper bag, (this was roughly six months or so after I had seen myself in the newspaper). It seemed around that time that people, in general, were trying to put words in my mouth, even without me opening my mouth in most cases. Of course, most of this was behind my back. The tabloid in question was not genuine enough to ask me anything. They had gone back under their allotted stones.

My alcoholism was at the stage where I had no confidence in myself. I couldn't defend myself verbally or even physically. One night when I went to the off-licence near my home, I was attacked by some young teenagers. At first, they threatened me and then one of them sucker punched me in the gob once from behind. It just added to the ridicule I was going through at the time. I even had a bit of trouble at a local supermarket on my way home with some knuckle draggers. The manager told us all to take it outside and I was quite willing to do that, but they ran off.

I think by this time I had reached the point where I no longer felt I wanted to take any more c- off anyone and so I started fighting back as best as I could. I thought, win or lose, I would do that. I didn't give a monkey's anymore about whether I ended up back in the nick. I was past caring.

My letters finally made my ex want to meet me again. I knew sex was on the agenda, although I wasn't certain about that, but to be quite honest I was quite looking forward to our meeting. I went by coach on a Thursday afternoon. My mother was expecting me, although she wasn't there when I arrived at her flat. One of my many uncles, stepdads was. He was with his daughter, my little sister, and was filming her behind my mother's small bar in the corner of her living room. It resembled a scene from *Coronation Street*, well sort of. I thought it a bit weird at the time, but I let it go. It was London after all. My mother came home an hour or so later with her Vodafone brick in her hand. To look at her, anyone would have thought she was a businesswoman of some kind. In reality, she was a madam in charge of a brothel. Anyway, I had a few Tennent's as usual and went to bed early.

Next day I caught the 48 bus to London Bridge. We

were meeting at her brother's flat and to be honest, to say it was unhygienic would have been an understatement. You wouldn't need to wipe your feet going in, more wiping your feet going out. Her brother, mum and sister were there and a big fully grown male Alsatian.

After a brew and a bit of a chit chat they wanted me to get on the bed with my ex and her sister. There wasn't a curtain anywhere in the whole flat and the flat was overlooked by Tube trains going in and out of London Bridge station and there was one parked up waiting for something. I thought in no way am I getting my kit off and the fact her mum and brother were there as well was a bit offputting to say the least. The Alsatian kept sniffing and growling at this single mattress in the corner. I didn't know why at the time. I found out later that there was a woman hiding behind it, more than likely with a journalist with a camera.

They all soon realised I was not going to perform with an audience of any kind and I thought if I had done anything there would have been a good chance her brother would have taken advantage.

At one point my ex-girlfriend's sister wanted me to look out of the kitchen window. I think this was so the journalist who was hiding behind the mattress could sneak out, but the journalist needed the toilet, so my ex-girlfriend's sister pushed me back in the kitchen. I could only hear what was happening and it's only in hindsight that I have realised what was going on.

A few hours later my ex, her sister and I all went to my ex-girlfriend's flat. On the way I bought four Tennent's Super. I was quite horny at the thought of having sex with both of them. I thought it would be a threesome, but, apparently, they both wanted anal. My ex-girlfriend's sister started with the cowgirl position, but she was so wooden and doing it far too slowly. It wasn't doing much for me, so I rolled us over so I was on top. My penis came out of her a- , so I put it in her vagina. She seemed to like that better. I washed afterwards. My ex was next and she also wanted anal.

I knew from past experiences that she adored it, then when we had finished, we all went into the living room. My ex went for a bath. At one point I could hear her talking to someone in the bathroom. I asked her sister who she was talking to and she said probably herself and we laughed about it. I thought that could be highly likely.

I noticed while I was there that there was red brick dust under the mirror and on top of the gas fire in the living room. I asked my ex if she had been having work done. Quite stroppily, she said, "What you on about?" That should have been a warning sign for me, that something wasn't right. I let it go. I wasn't that bothered about it, but when things don't gel it sticks in my mind, until I know what has happened as I do now.

As I look back now, what my ex and her sister did, i.e., having sex with me for money (the money coming from the tabloids) is what working girls do. I am certain it wasn't because she loved me or was still attracted to me in anyway. It was purely for money, so she was nothing more than a working girl and the tabloid in question were her pimps.

My ex-girlfriend's sister sat on my knee and started kissing and fondling me. I suppose it was to keep me occupied so it slipped my mind for a while. Later my ex came back in the living room in just her knickers and a t-shirt and in no time at all we all three ended up on the floor. We gave it up as a bad job and shortly afterwards I was asked to leave.

I knew there was a cab office just around the corner near the fire station. I asked for a cab and got quite a rude answer from one of the drivers. He said, "We don't like gays here." I had no idea why he was saying this. I thought at the time that he had missed or failed the customer services' classes, so I replied that I had just shagged two women so how could I be gay? There was no answer so I got my cab and that is all I was concerned about.

It was a silent journey back to my mother's flat. I wasn't in the mood for chit chat anyway. I was trying to work out the day's events. Something wasn't right. I felt sure someone was behind the single mattress at her brother's flat and why was there a BBC vehicle outside my ex-girlfriend's block of flats? My ex had told me it must have been something to do with the school that backed on to her flats, but with hindsight, I seriously doubt it.

I got back to my mother's place. I wasn't expected, and my little sister refused to give up her bed again, so I was on the couch. It wasn't the first time that I had slept there, so I wasn't that bothered. I had a couple of cans of Tennent's Super and went to sleep.

Next day, I went to my southern sister's flat, one of my many stepdads, uncles, whatever you want to call him was also there. After they'd given me a strong spliff I was off my head for at least an hour and although I knew that they were taking the p- out of me, I couldn't be bothered to defend myself in anyway so just left them to it.

Later on at around tea time, I left to see my ex-girlfriend. We'd arranged to meet at her brother's again. It always puzzled me why there were four adults in the flat most days and not one of them knew how to clean the place. They were more concerned with fagging it, having cups of tea and pulling people apart with their gossip. There is more work in a sick note than any one of them put together.

After about an hour at my ex-girlfriend's brother's we went for a walk, nowhere in particular. We stopped for about 10 minutes near a junction of Tower Bridge. She kept kissing me and she hugged me. To be honest, it was so tight a hug it hurt, but it was a pleasant kind of hurt. It was a hurt I didn't mind as I had not been hugged in quite a while from anyone, for years in fact. I couldn't remember the last time I had been hugged in that way and she was also trying to persuade me to move back to London, but I wasn't keen on uprooting all over again, not on an uncertainty like it would have been.

I wanted to go back to hers for another sex session, but she said her fellow would be there. (It never really dawned on me to ask where her boyfriend was when I was with her sister and her the night before. He must have surely known. I think there was only me who didn't know what was really happening (i.e., getting filmed, etc.). At first I said I didn't mind as I wanted a word with him anyway for what he had done to our daughter.

I wanted to bounce his head off the ceiling or maybe the walls or floor, anything harder than his head, as he had done to my daughter. She didn't think it was a good idea for us to go back to hers and looking back, she was right. The police should have nicked him for abusing our daughter, instead of taking all her kids off her as they done. They should both have been nicked, because by my daughter's mother turning a blind eye to what her boyfriend was up to with our daughter and more than likely her other children too, I'm quite sure if he did that to my daughter what could he have been up to with my ex-girlfriend's other kids? (To me, turning a blind eye is as bad as actually doing the crime, so my ex was just as guilty as her nonce of a boyfriend).

We strolled around the docks around the very expensive flats and at one point were heading towards the Thames through some waste ground. I stopped because I had an uneasy feeling about going any further. I suddenly had a sickening feeling that she could have had someone waiting to fit me with concrete boots. I knew her from past experiences and her family knew these kind of people, so I just made an excuse not to go any further that way.

We parted company shortly after that and I got the bus back from London Bridge. When I got back to my mother's flat my mother was still up. I chatted with her about moving back to London, just to see her reaction and as expected she was dead against it. To be honest I was not that bothered about it either. I hated London anyway, even just visiting London to me was quite unbearable and I wasn't that interested in carrying on with my ex, because it was only ever sex with her. She was never the one I would take back to my parents. My only interest was meeting my daughter again at the end of the day.

Next day, I got the coach back north. It was about half full and when we got on the motorway for some reason a small plane flew very close to us, within a few feet in fact. It only happened the once and it just flew off after that. I thought at the time, that it was some k-head showing off to his bint, so, I continued reading the newspaper. I only ever read newspapers when I was travelling somewhere mainly because I got very bored looking through the window watching the world go by.

I got talking to a middle-aged woman and after a while, I got fed up of reading it so put it down for a bit. The woman asked me if she could read it and I lent it to her. I was thinking I would get it back, but I never did. I did however overhear the woman telling a younger woman behind her "that's him", and she was pointing to something in the paper, then pointing at me. Nothing else was said, it was just whispering after that.

We stopped at Birmingham coach station and this oldish guy was stopping people getting off our coach. He was foolish enough to try and stop me and I simply told him if he didn't get out my way I would make him move, so he moved. As soon as I got off all the other people he had stopped earlier got off too, so he must have felt a right plonker. I'm not a bully of any kind, but I don't suffer fools gladly.

When I got back north, life was much the same. People were no different with me, my brother-in-law and their friends were still p-taking. My ex sent me a photograph of her, but I didn't realise at first that it was taken through a two-way mirror. She was obviously playing a mind game by sending it, then for some reason, I started reading in between the lines of what the p- takers (mainly my brother-in-law) around me were saying. I think he was thinking he was a lot cleverer than me, as he was telling me things, but in a mind game-playing kind of way. For example, after I had already noticed myself in the newspaper, there was an article in the tabloid saying I was going to be made homeless, but he didn't know that I had already been in touch with my landlord, so I knew he and the tabloid were talking rubbish.

In saying that I doubt very much that it was my fault that I didn't know I was in this low life tabloid because they never had the common sense to approach me before printing anything about me. Surely, I'm not the only one who doesn't read the newspapers.

What if someone for whatever reason cannot read?

Who do they rely on to let them know? It is quite obvious that you cannot rely on a tabloid journalist to be genuine or honest enough or is that just my experience?

So by my reading beyond what people were saying to me and paying more attention to my brother-in-law's mind games, was how I found out. I doubt very much that my brother-in-law intended letting me know anything at all, because a few weeks or so later after I had spotted myself in the tabloid, he was trying to convince me that I was being paranoid about what I had seen. I think he thought that he was the only person talking to me. It turned out that seeing myself in the tabloid was the missing piece of the puzzle and that was all I needed to start sorting it all out.

He also tried to convince me to cover up for them and tell lies to the tabloid and before I spotted myself in there my brother-in-law questioned why I was suddenly buying newspapers and he was not too happy about it. But what could he do? He would have had to give me a proper reason why I should not read the newspapers and he knew he couldn't do that. Liars always get found out in the end.

So I thought I would start reading the newspapers. I started to read two low life tabloids because I knew my brother-in-law read one of them. I felt at first that I was being a little paranoid, well more hoping I was, but within a few days I found my face staring back at me in one of the papers.

I was in no way mentally prepared for anything like that. It was such a total shock to the system that I couldn't read what else the newspaper was saying about me. Just the photo alone was more than enough trauma. I had no doubt it was me, I didn't know whether to laugh or cry. I know that my first reaction was, what the f-.

Months before my brother-in-law had positioned a

mirror on top of an electric plug socket in the office. I suppose it was to watch anyone behind him in the office without actually making it known he was watching them. But I had sussed him out quite quickly months ago, so he saw the look on my face when I found myself in the tabloid and he ran out of the office shutting the door so I couldn't get out. I think he thought I was going to kick off big style. I think it was more than likely that my mother and my two sisters would have said quite a few things to scare off people from telling me anything or to make people fear me in some way and not come anywhere near me. If you were OK with me, I would be OK with you. Despite being a suffering alcoholic, my favourite saying is "I am a good friend, but a bastard of an enemy".

Everything started to fall into place. All the strange things people had said and done over the past seven years now suddenly made sense to me. I couldn't get my head round how underhand everyone had been throughout those seven years. I admit I am no angel, but ripping off a member of your own family has never been something I have ever done or even contemplated doing. Only very low life scum do that and my feelings for my family and their friends and my own friends, went from unconditional love to hating them all. I could not bear to even look at any of them.

At one point I felt I could have very easily killed them all, one by one, but I knew if I did anything like that, it would mean a long spell in a nick and they simply were not worth it. My anger towards them was nothing to do with the potential money I could have earned or that I had missed out on. That was totally irrelevant. I had never had it so how could I miss it? It was the fact they had watched me suffer all the abuse, physical and verbal, which in turn had made me very ill with dystonia. It even pushed me to the point of suicide quite a few times and even now I cannot fathom out why they did what they did. Yes, they ripped me off, but I'm the kind of person who would have shared their good fortune with people around them, so, in turn, they ripped themselves off as well. If that is not crazy nothing else is. To me, blood has always been thicker than water.

As much as I wanted to tell the press everything I knew, the fact was that I didn't know what had been said by the newspapers in those past seven years from late 1985 to early 1993 and the not knowing scared the hell out of me. Fear of the unknown had well and truly set in. They could have said I was the best thing since sliced bread, but from how I had been treated by everyone in those seven years, I very much doubted that.

I have since seen how the newspapers treat people and it seems like it is fairly common to be treated badly. Is it just jealousy or are they just trying to get some kind of reaction from people, who then go running to the newspapers? The bottom line is money. By me not knowing, it made me an easy target for these low life people and being the tabloid was of a similar status, I was easy pickings.

I can't understand why, when the tabloid in question was in the business of communicating news all over the world, for some unknown reason they had forgotten to tell me or ask me for my side of the story. Once again it shows what a low life tabloid it was and is. I can honestly say I have only ever once knowingly had the press at my door. It seems they were like the majority of people, in that, they thought because I was in the newspaper I must know I was in the newspaper, but I only have one pair of ears and eyes and one mouth and I have never had the luxury of having a decent family or friends around me. Or, could it have been that this tabloid knew that I didn't know and they were playing some sick mind game? Only they know.

I know that the tabloid was constantly changing my name over those seven years. I suppose it was to try to keep me off the scent or maybe they were in the dark about me not knowing. Not sure on that one, but to be honest, to ridicule someone who is mentally ill as I most certainly was with alcoholism, is a cowardly thing to do.

Because (from the early 1980s when I was twenty-two till the late 1990s when I was in my mid-thirties), I was a suffering alcoholic for eighteen years in total and to me, to abuse or ridicule someone the way the tabloid, my family, my friends did, was in my book a very sick and cowardly thing to do and that is being polite. Even now in 2020, not one of them has had the decency to be honest with me over this issue.

I think throughout those seven years and even before that, because of the amount I was drinking I must have been under some kind of illusion that my family would have told me or maybe a tabloid journalist would have been professional and genuine enough to have informed me, but I was gobsmacked at even being in the newspapers as I was.

In fact, it was only *Granada Reports* in roughly March 1993 who have ever called me by my real name. They have this item on there every night where they ask the viewers for their views on the subjects in the news and they were asking whether I knew that I was being filmed at my ex-girlfriend's place having sex with my ex and her sister. That hit me hard. My ex was not the best looking of ladies. I use the word lady very loosely with regard to her and her sister. So, I was a bit embarrassed, but in no way did I ever consider going to a solicitor about what *Granada Reports* had said about me.

To be honest, as I look back now, to film someone without their knowledge is like raping them and is very cowardly and it is something a nonce would do. I liken it to what perverts do on the Tube when they are secretly filming some unsuspecting woman. Upskirting I think they call it.

Because of my alcoholism, dystonia, panic attacks, I was in no fit state, mentally, to face the press, media in general. Rather foolishly, I asked my brother-in-law to face them for me instead.

This must have been a godsend to all my family and their friends because they could blacken my name even further than they already had. So in no way was I thinking straight by asking him to step in as I did and at the same time I was trying not to speak to anyone about anything, including my brother-in-law. It got to the point where I couldn't trust what came out of my mouth at times and because I didn't have a clue what had been said by anyone in the tabloid, I thought it best to say as little as I could to everyone. It seemed that whatever I said was being spun into something else.

When I saw my dad at weekends he would keep telling me that he had kept reminding my northern sister that I was not her proper brother. I was only her half brother and she should not be helping me at all, but my sister and her husband were more helping/defending themselves and my mother as none of them wanted the truth to come out about any of them. But, truth wills out no matter what you do or say to stop it, as they say, and believe me this book is 100% truth, as bizarre as some of it may be, Why tell lies when you have nothing left to hide?

Around that time I got an invitation to go on *Upfront*,

but I was in no fit state to face anything of that nature. I did watch it and I would just like to ask what was it with the blow-up doll?

Obviously, the family never thought about what I had been through before saying what they said, but even so it was very unprofessional of them. For seven years and for most of my life I had experienced violence and verbal abuse. At the time in March 1993 I was a suffering alcoholic and I also suffered with dystonia and panic attacks since 1989 all because of the abuse and violence towards me and this presenter expected me to go on a stage or in front of a camera. It would have been far easier to climb Mount Everest walking on my hands. It just goes to show how ignorant, bigoted and self-centred some people really are.

I still never feel safe anywhere. I'm always anxious just going into most shops or anywhere where there may be a crowd. When I first found out I was in the newspapers, I was suffering very badly with panic attacks (a blind man on a flying horse could have seen how ill I was) and after I found myself in the tabloid I tended to notice more the judgmental stares people gave me (even now in 2020 I still get this), but now I put it down to my dystonia. When my neck goes into spasm, people tend to stare or point and even at times start laughing at me and taking the mick, which puts me on edge and can bring on a panic attack.

So to sit in front of an audience of any kind was a definite no no in my mind, then and even now. But, as I have said before, I am never in the right no matter what I do with some folk. I never sit on my pity pot over anything for too long. If people don't like me for whatever reason they may have dreamed up that day, then it is their problem not mine.

I went through seven years of absolute hell, so much

so, I was very close to a nervous breakdown most days and at times very suicidal. I know my sister and brother-in-law attended the show, but they never even offered me a lift or any kind of advice as to what I was going to be asked like most genuine people would have done. I know now if I had been willing to lie for them all, I would have had help in every way possible, but why should I lie for them? They never batted an eyelid when I was being attacked or abused in the street.

All I kept thinking about was the lies my family and so-called friends had told me for those seven years and I suppose I was grieving for all of them, as I had unwittingly put them all on pedestals. My family were everything to me before I had seen myself in the tabloid. They could do no wrong in my eyes. Even though my mother and sister were prostitutes I still loved them unconditionally. If I had been sober and never had a drink problem, I know I would never have believed any of what *any* of them had said to me.

My love for my family and my family's friends and even my own friends quickly turned to hate, because in my heart of hearts, I hated them all for what they had put me through in those seven years, from late 1985 until early 1993 and I must admit some days when my dystonia is playing up and very painful, I still resent them all. As you can imagine at the time I was in a deep depression and at the time I felt very isolated, very vulnerable and alone. Sometimes I would nearly have a panic attack just going near the front door to go out, but I wasn't suicidal at this point, although I was close to it quite often. I knew I had to keep putting one foot in front of the other to get through it. I couldn't let this filth I had round me win.

Just as I was coming to terms with what I had just found out about being in the newspapers, much worse was about to happen. Quite a few times it was said to me that if I put the drink down I would be fine. Only another alcoholic will know just how stupid that statement really is. I needed drink like I needed air to breathe or so my head was telling me at the time. Also, it didn't help that there were more questions than answers running through my head. Everyone it seemed had closed ranks on me.

There was no such thing as a two-way conversation. They were all feeding off me like leeches, but, in reality, they had been doing that for seven years previously and looking back even throughout my life they had never been there for me ever.

It was like finding that first part of a giant jigsaw puzzle when I saw that photo of me in the newspaper and as time went on, everything seemed to fall into place, piece by piece, but it was a very painful process to go through.

I felt my family and their friends were urinating up my back most of the time and telling me it was raining, big style. I totally clammed up and if I was asked anything I just grunted. Stupid I know, but it was the only thing I could think of doing at the time to protect myself from further abuse. It was my way of looking at it at the time and even now.

I still think it was the right thing to do at the time. I was the one who had gone through hell for seven years, so to me, I had to be the one telling my story like I am now. Why should someone else benefit from my suffering, be they family or friends?

One thing that I found unbelievable was being told that Michael Jackson had asked me to stay at his ranch. This was according to my brother-in-law, but if you can't trust your family, who can you trust? He kept banging on about it, but I didn't believe a word he or anyone else around me, said. The fact that I didn't have a passport added to that mistrust of what he was saying and at the time it seemed just too bizarre to be true. Even now, if I think something is too good to be true, it generally is.

My brother-in-law also told me that one of the Kray brothers had said not to trust anyone south of the Thames. It was good advice, but, I was so stressed out with everything that was happening and being said around me that I said, "What the f- would he know?" If they were still alive I would apologise sincerely to them, face to face, for that remark. If I have done wrong I put my hand up, but I'm sorry to their family. They should never have been kept in prison for as long as they were.

I was still being the neighbour from hell with my music blurring away at night, every night, but never after midnight and I was getting near the edge of suicide. At the time loud music and booze were the only things stopping me from ending my life. It was acting as a cushion. I hadn't attempted suicide before, but much worse was about to happen.

The Attack

One night I was playing my music far too loudly as usual and making a first-class nightmare neighbour of myself, but apart from one of my neighbours, no one had said anything about it, because they were more than likely talking to me through the tabloid. The tabloids were coming to my door, but I didn't know they were journalists at the time, as they never introduced themselves as journalists. To me they were strangers who were not getting to the point of why they had come to my door. I'm guessing they came all the way from Manchester or wherever and mostly went to my neighbours before me and never even attempted to approach my door for my side of the story.

So why did the journalists come all that way and just ask silly questions and keep going to my neighbours? Is it not common sense and decency to go to the person themselves who they were writing about?

I believe journalists have to go to university to do their job. I knew this at the time and I was a suffering alcoholic, so I seriously doubt the ability of the tabloid journalist in a big way. But we are talking about people who are always right even when they are wrong and from what someone has told me the reading level needed to read the tabloid in question is five to seven. Says it all really.

One night while I was playing my loud music, there was a knock on the door. It was quite late about 11 to 11.30 pm. I was naked as I was close to going to bed. I didn't intend to open it fully, simply because I was naked. Stupid I know, but I was p- at the time. I shouted through the door to ask who it was. My neighbour's boyfriend answered and said he just wanted a quick word about something. I opened the door to pop my face round, then suddenly it was forcefully opened. Fists and feet were raining down on me from everywhere. I was dragged bodily upstairs while still being beaten. Then I was forcibly bent over the edge of my bed and, to muffle my screams, someone put my quilt over my head and upper body. One of the attackers lay on top of me while I was being repeatedly raped by around fifteen men. In no time at all I passed out.

Because of the guy on top of me I couldn't breathe and even though I was screaming for them to stop, perhaps it was a godsend that I did fall unconscious, less to remember I suppose. But what I do remember is being suffocated unconscious and that will haunt me until my dying day. It's never far from my thoughts, especially when I'm in a crowded place.

I found out a week or so later that one day an old Cockney guy who kept coming into my brother-in-law's workshop for different things was in the office chatting to him. He drank in the same pub where the rapists drank and he knew the ringleader. He had quite a loud voice, so it wasn't that hard to hear what was being said. At one point my brother-in-law shouted at me to stop earwigging and get on with my work, which I pretended to do, but still kept listening. That is how I learned how many guys attacked me that night and the ringleader's name.

The next morning after the rape, I woke up in the same position I had been left me in, with the quilt still over my head and bent over the edge of the bed. I swallowed like most people do when they first wake up and unintentionally swallowed a mouthful of sperm. I was violently sick for about 10 minutes and I was also in a daze because of what had happened the night before. Even though I had blackouts because of my alcoholism, I knew what had happened the night before, but I couldn't work out what to do next for the best, so I went to work as normal and tried to carry on as though nothing had happened, but I was in bits inside.

When I got to work it seemed my brother-in-law and his brother already knew what had happened to me the night before, so the tabloid must have known too. He told me to look at myself in the mirror and I was shocked at what a mess my face was in. My brother-in-law's brother was trying to persuade me to go to the police or to the press. He even told me off when I went to the toilet as I poohed the evidence away. As time went on, I got more and more depressed about everything that had happened. I felt totally helpless and depressed about everything and I started to attempt suicide on at least half a dozen to a dozen times, mainly strong painkillers and booze. I didn't want to involve anyone else, so jumping in front of a lorry or train was never an option.

One night while I was going home from work one of the neighbouring firm's lorries nearly accidentally ran me over. It was a long wheel based lorry and I had assumed it was going straight because I didn't see any indicator light telling me otherwise. When we both set off at the same time, I intended to use the lorry as a shield to get across the road, but when he started turning I knew then, that wasn't the case and I only just managed to get out the way. My bike was badly damaged, but fair play to the firm and the driver. The driver gave me a lift home that night and his firm fixed my bike the next day. They couldn't have been more genuine.

The next day the driver came into our workshop and asked how I was and said to my brother-in-law, "I very nearly killed him(me)last night", to which my brother-in-law said, "You should have done". The driver couldn't believe what he was hearing and asked my brother-in-law if he was serious. He said yes and laughed. The driver just walked out in disgust and rightfully so.

It was comments like that, that constantly played around in my head. In my mind I'd done nothing wrong to anyone of them to warrant all the abuse and violence I was getting daily and had suffered since 1985. My only crime was accidentally leaving a gap in my front room curtains when I lived in London.

On one occasion, things started to get more and more on top of me. I didn't want to live anymore. The pills weren't working, and even strong painkillers didn't help. I kept waking up in the morning. I wasn't one who rang the ambulance before taking the pills. I didn't even have a phone at the time. I never had any regular visitors, so I wouldn't have been found for at least a few days or maybe until the bluebottles could be seen at my windows or maybe the smell would have got too much for my neighbours. Either way, they were not half-hearted attempts.

So one night I decided to try to hang myself. The strong painkillers were not doing the trick, so hanging myself seemed a better option. I went to an electricity pylon just up the road from where I lived, which was near an Indian restaurant. There was barbed wire all the way around the base of the pylon at around ten to twelve foot high.

I had some wire cutters and my intention was to wrap the wire around my neck and jump. I knew it would have been quite messy to say the least and I certainly wouldn't have been able to change my mind like I had done in Croston. But that wasn't my concern at the time. It would have been quick, but looking back, I wouldn't have liked to have been the person who found me. Again, I wasn't concerned with that either.

It turns out I was that p- I couldn't climb the pylon to get to the wire and ended up giving up on it and going home even more frustrated and depressed than I had started out. So when I got home I took as many strong painkillers as I could stomach and once again, I still woke up. It seemed I couldn't even do that right.

Years later when I discussed this with someone, they said maybe the reason I survived was more than likely because I took the painkillers regularly ,so maybe I had become immune to the effects it might have had. Not sure if that is true, but it does seem plausible.

Because I was attempting suicide nearly every night I seemed to be in a zombie-like mental state during the day. I was just going through the motions. I kept putting one foot in front of the other each day and eventually I started to get myself in some way sorted even though I was on auto-pilot most of the time. Everything seemed in black and white around me. I was still getting a lot of abuse from everyone around me, left right and centre or just plain p-taking at times.

The tabloid was implying in the *Badlands* cartoon (according to my brother-in-law, it was meant to be about me) that "I needed a kick up the arse to get myself sorted". But because I had been raped (according to my brother-in-law) the tabloid in question was taking the p- saying, "we meant a kick, not a dick up the arse". My brother-in-law would keep reminding me of this daily for months, which is something a rape victim doesn't want or need to hear.

My brother-in-law was/is a sick person to even think like that, let alone say it and it seemed that he got off on abusing me and he said some very vile things at times. Once, he kept saying to me, "if you had known they (the rapists) were coming you would have baked them a cake, would you not?" and even made remarks about wanting to f-my son. I had to totally ignore everything he said.

I knew he wanted me to react and if I had bitten and lost it with him, it could have easily been me doing fifteen or more years for him. But none of my family was worth doing bird for and still aren't, but I didn't give a toss about anything. In my eyes at the time, I didn't have one decent person around me and I still feel the same now in 2020.

All my abusers are long gone, under their stones no doubt, but I had to show them all I was in no way bothered. So instead of getting angry I pretended that nothing had happened and that I still liked them. I smiled until it hurt, but deep down I wanted them all dead. Sometimes it did get a bit much for me. My brother-in- law once told me we were getting an alarm fitted at home and without thinking I automatically said, "Does it fight fire?" Instantly, I could see the penny had dropped about what I had said, even though it was an idle threat. I would never have gone through with it. None of them was worth a minute behind the metal door and the only thing that has stopped me doing anything bad against them is that the finger would have been pointed at me. Even when I've done nothing wrong, they've accused me of things, but I put that down to their own guilty conscience. I suppose it might have been their way of dealing with their own guilt.

One night after my usual quota of cans, I decided to go to the local police station. I had no proof of the rape, but, I had honesty and truth on my side. A couple of lads were already there waiting to get dealt with and they were both within earshot of me. The copper motioned me over. I did my best to be as discreet as I could, but the lads heard that I had been raped, and started laughing. I rounded on them and the copper told me off before taking me to another room for a statement. It took around three hours to tell them everything and they took some of my clothing to test. Apart from the ghetto blaster, I never got any of them back.

It wasn't until a couple of weeks later when two CID officers called round one tea time. They told me if I wanted to carry on with my complaint I would be at risk of being ripped apart even further by the press and media. I felt I had no one on my side, so I told them not to proceed any further with it. I know that the police asked my neighbours questions and went round the local pub quizzing people. All in all, it p- me off big style.

My thinking then was that it seemed the press was on the side of the rapists. Of course I say allegedly here, (I have to say that as three to six months later, while I was writing to the tabloid in question and constantly blaming them for me being raped, as in, because of their non-existent journalistic skills and them not actually knocking on my door for some kind of response at any time or just simply making me aware they were on my case, as a genuine newspaper would have done, I felt at the time, that if they had been decent and honest upfront with me it would not have led up to me being raped, but, now in 2020, it seems to me it was more my family's faults, but I'm still 50/50 on that one, so once again I will say, allegedly and I will let you the reader decide. The tabloid in question threatened me with court action if I didn't stop writing to them. Perhaps I was hitting a nerve or something.

As each day went by, I was getting angrier and angrier about everything that had happened to me. It all seemed so unfair. I have always hated nonces/rapists, mainly because of my second stepdad being one and what he got up to with my family. One night I decided to get revenge on the ringleader of the rape gang. I knew he drank at the local Flying Bottle so I rang him up at the pub, I took the p- out of him to just wind him up a bit, then offered him out. He probably thought it would be a straight fist fight, but I knew he would have his mates behind him or have some kind of weapons. In no way did that bother me. I would have hurt as many as I could before going down fighting and they would have had to kill me to stop me.

So days before I bought a meat cleaver and I fully intended taking his head off with it, literally, but, as I cycling around the corner and saw him standing there waiting, (well I assumed it was him at the time as I had never seen his face or anything else for that matter). I say this because he didn't look like a hard man at all. He looked normal, in fact a bit of an idiot to be honest, even a bit of a mummy's boy. But rapists are idiots.

As I cycled past the pub and saw him waiting for me, I think I must have had a moment's clarity, as I realised if I had harmed him in any way, I would lose even more than I had lost already and filth like that are just not worth doing two minutes in a cell. More than likely, I would have been doing life for killing him and to be blunt about it, he just was not worth p- on, let alone doing bird for.

I also felt the same about all my family and all their friends and even my own friends and still do, although most of my resentments have gone now (in 2020). I don't let anyone live in my head rent-free for long anymore, but I firmly believe in karma. It would have been far too easy to grab hold of each and every one of them, in turn, and hurt them, as they had hurt me, but I knew I would have been the loser in the end, as I would have been doing bird for a long time. I have learned since that it p- people off more if you are nice back to them and get on with your life regardless of what they have done to you; and even better yourself (like up to now). I have always done my best to do.

On the positive side though, this was the night that I decided to do something properly about my drinking, although I didn't know what. It was a start, admitting to myself that I had a drinking problem and my life was very, very unmanageable because of it, which I now know is half the battle against alcoholism or any addiction.

Looking back at my family, they did everything they could to stop me finding out, even to the point of making sure I was permanently topped up with a drink. That doesn't mean I was permanently off my face. What topped up means(in case you don't know) is that I would not have passed a breathalyser test, but to look and listen to me I was sober as a judge (if there is such a thing), so, my ears and eyes worked perfectly fine throughout my eighteen-year alcoholic drinking, as they had done seven years previously.

Hence the eavesdropping, plus even after seeing myself in the newspaper one day my brother in law tried to convince me that I was being paranoid about the newspapers and saying "no one will ever believe a drunk like you" which I must admit as put a lot of doubt in my head quite often over the years till now, but, to put it bluntly, I am now nearly 23 + years sober and I don't do drugs at all. I don't even smoke normal fags.

Of course, I am expecting a lot of flak if this book gets published but, I am more than prepared for that. All I need to do is stick to the truth. Why lie when there is no need to? But if some people don't believe me because of me being a suffering alcoholic in my past, these people I know for sure will have a guilty conscience and will have the same mindset as Jimmy Savile. He thought that because the people he was abusing were mentally ill they wouldn't be believed.

To back up what I am saying in this book, I would take a lie detector test or swear on a Bible, because I know absolutely that the police have never openly questioned me about it at any point. I have lost count of the times they have stopped me in the street to search me, i.e. in London and Leeds and even Lancashire, but because I have been in trouble in the past people (including the police) very lazily think I've done wrong in the past, so everything I do is wrong.

Believe me in no way have I ever wanted to be well known for being someone who was caught masturbating, even though most people do it and really there is nothing to be ashamed of by doing it. But my family and their friends did their best to make me feel ashamed of what had happened with my curtains and I was deeply ashamed and I mostly blamed myself for it happening, but now as I look back, if anyone else was faced with the same thing, I am certain no one could do any better, no one knows what is happening behind their backs.

As I look back now I realise, in no way was it deliberate like some have tried to make out, the only thing I did wrong is trust people I should have been able to trust. They did their utmost to control me and stop me from finding out. To be honest, I don't fully blame the drink or drugs for what happened to me, I blame the scum I had as friends and family. If you haven't got decent people around you, you have nothing and to be honest since 2015 I no longer have any of them around me. If you cannot trust your family and friends it is better to be on your own, as I have found out to my advantage now and to be blunt about the curtain incident, I was in my living room, not sat on a park bench with my c- out, so what is the problem? Why did the press even want to get involved like they did? Perhaps they were short of things to print or maybe they wanted to take the heat off a politician who was up to no good as usual. Who knows?

Although I am fully aware that there are people who dress up as women to achieve fame, I am not having a go at Lily Savage. Paul O'Grady looks quite sexy dressed up, but more the likes of Dame Edna. Imagine waking up to that. What a nightmare and some people degrade themselves even further. I must admit I have always wanted to be rich, but who wouldn't want that. I have never wanted to be well known for being caught like I was.

I even contacted the tabloid in question a few weeks after I saw myself in the newspaper in 1993 and I spoke to a journalist, who at first took the p- out of me, then we had a bit of a chat. He gave me the free phone number for the tabloid's news desk and said he would come to see me that day. I waited in for him with the telly off, so there was very little chance of missing him. It was a nice day so I had the windows open a little.

I know he visited one my neighbours as I overheard one of them refusing to talk to someone unless he spoke to first. I still didn't get the knock at the door, so they are good at giving it out, but not very good at putting their hands up when they have done wrong..

After 30 years of being straight I lost a three-hour a day office cleaning job, because I didn't tick a box. To be honest, I wasn't that bothered about the job, but I thought how petty-minded and bigoted some people are. I've even been turned down for a care assistant job because of my record. There is nothing sexual or violent on my record and I can prove this with my DBS.

So, I have had to put up with the fact I will never be

allowed to forget my past, because of ignorant bigots. In my experience, I have come across more wrongdoers who have never been nicked or even seen the inside of a police cell or station and I have found that they are usually the ones who give it the 'holier than thou stuff', so, think on, as the saying goes *"people in glasshouses should never throw stones"*. They still will because that is how stupid these folk are.

The strange thing is, apparently there were questions in parliament in late 1985, early 1986 about the curtain incident. The police were in some way interested and the press were hovering around like flies around s-, but no one involved me. In my defence, I was a suffering alcoholic, but my ears, eyes and my mouth all worked quite well, but only within a range of my eyes and ears.

All that happened or what people witnessed was a suffering alcoholic acting up. What about the press/the police/the MP and my so-called family and friends? What is their excuse for not being upfront and honest with me? How can you judge someone without their involvement? Thank God the courts don't go off hearsay. Well, for now, they don't.

My recovery

After having an eighteen-year drink problem, it was not in any way a lifestyle choice to become sober. I didn't send away for it from a mail-order catalogue and if the truth be known, my alcoholism chose me. Addiction, so I am told, is a great leveller. It doesn't matter who you are, what class, race or sexuality. If, like me, you have an addictive personality it will happen, it is just a matter of time before it does. I have been told many times, according to all the non-alcoholic people around me, that it is so easy just to stop drinking. Of course, these people have never had an addiction, so they have never walked in my shoes.

I was told many times this same thing by the people I had around me when I hit my rock bottom. "Just put the drink down and you'll be fine", but it is nowhere near as easy as people try to make you think it is, the only way I can describe it is, try thinking about giving fags up and times it by more than a hundred at least. Most times I needed alcohol like I needed air to breathe, although that is what my head was telling me at the time. I wanted to put it down nearly every day, but deep down I didn't want to put it down at all. I knew my drinking was killing me and if I didn't do something about it I would end up dead.

I knew one day I could very easily p- someone off enough for them to kill me or have an accident while p- and die or become ill and die. All these were certainties and apart from the dying bit, they have all happened. I have used all my nine lives up for certain. My Guardian Angel has had to retire, due to exhaustion. I can laugh about it now, but none of it was funny at the time.

When I finally decided that I had to do something about my drinking, the first thing I felt I should do before anything else was to get checked out for AIDS/HIV as I was fairly sure that the gang who gang-raped me were not the kind of people who wore a Durex on the night of my rape by them and I would have probably been a break from their usual conquests, sheep and slappers. It took a few weeks to summon up the courage to go to the SDT clinic at my local hospital.

When I finally found the courage to go, the first thing I had to do was talk to a counsellor who, I don't think really wanted to talk to me at all at first. I have found since falling ill with dystonia and all my other illnesses I can add to the long list, people in general treat you totally different when you fall ill or have a problem of some kind. I think they think it is your own fault or you are not intelligent enough to stay well enough, but they are the intellectually challenged ones. Usually they take one look at you and pre-judge you and just write you off, but as the saying goes, *'they are more to be pitied than scorned'*.

I say this because before we went into the room to chat, the counsellor said to a nurse to come back in ten minutes, which I thought was very callous of her, but once we got talking I started to open up about most of what had happened to me. When the nurse came in the counsellor sent her straight out again with a flea in her ear, but she was only doing what she had been told to do by the counsellor earlier. I have found at least half of the people in the caring profession are only doing it for the money. They lack the main requirement of empathy(I know this because since 2006 I have been in and out of hospital with chronic pancreatitis and I wouldn't leave my dog with some of the consultants and that's being polite).

It took about a week for the test results to come through. It seemed like a lifetime, Thankfully they were negative, which in a couple of ways, I was quite surprised about. The first and more important reason was that I had been raped by fifteen guys and secondly some of my ex-girlfriends were very dubious, to say the least. It was only by luck that my son or daughter did not come out of the womb wagging their tails. Those were the kind of women my ex-girlfriends were. Of course, I am not guilt-free on that either, but mine was just an attempt, nothing more than that and I was a long way off being sober or congruent at the time.

Even though the test was negative, I was still in a deep depression, the only way I can describe it is that it was like going down a very dark tunnel with the occasional chinks of light. One of these chinks of light are stuck in my mind and it is quite funny thinking about it now.

One day I was in a petrol station just around the corner from where I lived on Clayton Brook, Lancashire. There were quite a few people around including a guy I knew from work, who came into our workplace quite often for different things and he worked for a well known ice cream firm in my local area.

We had the usual banter between us, then when I was on my way to the counter to get served, these two youngish lads were basically calling me not fit to burn, but I just ignored them and carried on to the counter. Then as I was going out, the two lads were talking to the guy I had been talking to earlier and were so up his a- (not literally), even saying to one another (after their conversation with him), "Do you know who that is? He is the owner of the ice cream firm." It helped me quite a lot, as I thought well if that is what they think of him, what they think of me doesn't really matter because they knew nothing about him or me for that matter, as I knew he was just a driver.

Nothing more than that. It was just little things like that I think that pulled me through those very dark times

Because I had been to one to one counselling for my drinking when I lived in London, I thought I would give it another go. I had decided to go to one to one counselling in Preston, but my first time was not that good an experience. I had just gone to enquire and maybe make an appointment, nothing more than that, but the manager was quite off with me, to say the least, and basically said that if there was any trouble I would be kicked out of the premises".

I had only been sat down a few minutes and before he said that I had not shown the slightest signs of trouble or that I was going to cause any kind of trouble, so perhaps he had read some of the rubbish the tabloid had written about me and worst still believed it. Nowt like being pre-judged on hearsay, but after about 20 minutes I did get to see someone and I kept going to one to one therapy there for a few more months.

As luck would have it, the therapist finished for some reason and they gave me the option of seeing someone in Chorley or someone else in Preston. I decided on seeing someone in Chorley, as I thought at the time that that would be a better option. It was more or less on my way home from work and as it turned out, the woman I saw was loads better than the one I saw in Preston, far more helpful and more empathetic, and I grew fairly quickly into being able to trust her 100%, which believe me helps a great deal in a therapeutic setting. After what my family had put me through I had big trust issues.

The counsellor I was seeing helped me to stop drinking, not only by talking about my problems with drinking, but giving me advice about other stuff that was bothering me. I must admit I was not helping myself at first.

I could talk for England at times, but never about what was really bothering me. As I got to trust her I opened up more and more and she even helped me come to terms with me being raped. She told me it was all about power and control. meaning that for the time they are attacking you or doing whatever it is they are doing, you're under their spell.

Looking back now, the only thing that still haunts me to this day they had left me for dead until I was unconscious, then carried on doing what they did. Looking back, I'm in some ways glad that I did not follow through with my plan to behead the ringleader.

He was not worth doing a second behind the metal door, but I am gobsmacked that I could not go through with taking them to court like I should have been able to, but from what I have heard since, it is quite common not to get any support from the police and I suppose being as I had been in trouble with the them I had even less chance of getting any support from them. It seems there are more judges outside the court than in; some people put a uniform on and think they are God. They simply don't have the brain cells to cope with the responsibility of wearing a uniform.

I just pray to God that no one else has suffered the same fate from the rapist who raped me and the reason I felt I could not take them to court was simply that I was told by the police that the tabloid newspaper in question would have torn me (a rape victim) apart, that is according to the CID at the local police station. So I ask you, the reader, is that fair? But we all know what the gutter press is capable of, unless you're a sheep and buy it.

My counsellor signposted me on night classes, as in, self-help courses, one was the power of positive thinking. This was the main one and really helped me get sober and

I still try to live my life in that way now. I must say I have learned a lot from the course and I certainly needed all I was being taught. The main part of stopping an addiction is changing the way you think. Drinking was never far from my thoughts every second of every day. It was a daily struggle to get enough money to drink at night, but I stole only once to get a drink and I was truly in the depths of alcoholism. Even then, I would never have stolen from my own family or their friends or even my friends. That in my book is a definite no-no, even as ill as I was, I have never stooped that low.

As I look back now I know for sure that all the staff at the Chorley one-to-one alcohol centre played a very big part in getting me sober. When I first went to the Preston branch, I never had any confidence in them. All they kept saying was you cannot just stop dead like I wanted to. You have to cut down slowly, slowly or you risk epilepsy by stopping dead, which is true and if you try to stop too quickly, it can also kill you. It gave me an excuse to carry on my drinking, when deep down I wanted to stop, desperately stop. It is like telling a person who is drowning to stay in the water a while longer or instead of throwing them a lifebelt, you throw them a weighted down sack.

Also what did not help was that my first counsellor in Preston just happened to have gone out with one of my mother's boyfriends sons when she lived in London, I must say I lost trust in her from that point on, which was maybe the first or second time I had seen her. I felt sure anything I would have said to her would have trickled back to my family in some way back in London. It might not have been the case, but at the time with everything that was happening around me and what had happened with the press, my family and all their friends and my friends, that is how I saw it at the time.

I trusted no one, not even myself at times. By rights I should have gone into rehab for my alcoholism, but because it was quite bad, I didn't want to be labelled a nut job by the tabloids even though in reality, I was. I went to one to one counselling in total for about two years, but at the Preston branch for about six months.

It turned out to be a wise decision on my part, as the next woman I saw was a lot better. After a few months of seeing her once a week she sent me to a psychiatrist for me to be put on medication to help stop my drinking. It was nicknamed antabuse and what it did/does is make you feel like s- if you drink.

Eventually, I was determined to start the antabuse, but within a couple of days I picked up a drink again and what I was told would happen, did... I felt like I was dying, but still kept drinking, that is how mad alcoholism is, it tells you that you are OK and that everyone who is telling you to put it down, is wrong, but alcohol, if given the chance, will trick you into the grave and I am not b-. I have lost friends and relatives to it, as in, my sister and my mother. It doesn't matter who you are, it will get you, if like me you have an addictive personality.

When I saw the psychiatrist she mentioned going to AA. I had been to meetings before when I was in Wandsworth prison, so I knew a little bit about it and it just so happened that I knew someone who went to my local meeting in Clayton Brook, not far from where I lived.

One of the things that held me back was how angry I felt inside all the time. I felt that I needed a safe way to vent it all, so I bought a punchbag from my catalogue and I would come home from work and punch or kick hell out of it until I was physically drained. Some nights I would be crying uncontrollably while knocking seven bells out of the punchbag. But I knew it was better the punchbag than someone's face, far, far safer and less likely me ending up back in prison.

There was one occasion at college when someone kept trying to bully me and he got what was coming to him because of it. For weeks he was on my case, poking me in the back when he was behind me queuing for our brew at breaktime and belittling me all the time in class. I warned him a few times, but he took no notice until one night when we were all getting ready to go home. I went to the toilet and he followed minutes later and started with his nonsense and slapped me round the back of the head.

I can't say what happened next, because I totally lost it. The red mist descended, it would seem, and when I came to my senses I was stamping on his ribs and opening the door on his head. As soon as I realised what I was doing I stopped immediately and walked away. Even now I remember very little about it.

Later, as I was unlocking my bike as he was being helped out by two women, he threatened me with retribution, but I never saw him again.

When I plucked up the courage to go to my first AA meeting I told my friend that I would stay for half an hour, to see if I liked it or not. No one had any problems with that, so I was quite relaxed about being there. I ended up staying the full meeting, the whole hour and a half. I wasn't one of the lucky few who put the drink down straight away from my first meeting. It took me three years roughly and in that three years I was b- other AA members into thinking I had done it, but I was only kidding myself there. The other members were not tricked.

Even a blind man on a flying horse could see I was

still drinking, although I had never once turned up to a meeting p-, but I stuck at it and cycled around Lancashire in all weathers to different meetings. I put the same effort into stopping drinking as I did in getting my drink when I was a suffering alcoholic and eventually I got the message one sunny Monday morning (March 24, 1997) roughly three years after going to my first meeting.

I woke up and said to myself today's the day. I went straight to the medicine cabinet and took my first antabuse, but this time I was 100% I was going to do it. When night came, I sat in front of the telly and started to watch my usual programmes, *Coronation Street, Emmerdale* and *EastEnders* and it wasn't long into my programmes when I realised they are all centred round pubs, which was something I certainly didn't want to be watching. In no time at all I was climbing the walls, but I just kept remembering what AA members had drummed into me "just do it for a minute at a time or an hour at a time, eventually it will be days, then months, then years".

Its been the hardest and the most worthwhile thing I've ever done and in no way do I regret it. I doubt that if medical science came out with a drug that would help me drink in a normal way, it would not remotely interest me. I love not drinking and not taking drugs apart from my medication of course. I would love to stop them too. That will never happen, they keep me alive and well, so it's not really an option.

I started to set myself goals, the first one was passing the driving test. I could drive, but I had so many bad habits that I would never have passed. I decided to keep it to myself as much as I could, the only people I told were my brother and his now-wife, my sister and a few members of AA (just to clarify, my brother and sister are from a different father than the rest of my family. The only thing my family have in common is our mother).

I have no problem with this side of my family. I love them both, as though they were full-blood relatives. The other members of my family don't like them because of what their father did to my younger sister and in no way do I blame my brother or sister for anything their dad did. I'm sure if they could have stopped him doing what he did, they would have, but they were both far too young to even know what was going on around them, so to me they are blameless. But for some unknown reason the other members of my family blame them. To me, that shows how mentally ill they all were and are.

I decided not to tell my brother-in-law or any of the rest of my family. They would have ridiculed me to the point where I would not have had the confidence to even open the door of the car. It took me three attempts at my theory test and two at the practical before I passed. It was then that I told them all. At first my brother-in-law didn't believe me and he wanted proof that I had passed. He was more than a bit p- off when I showed him my pass certificate, also my mother was more than a bit miffed I think because I was bettering myself and not drinking.

It made me realise that whatever I did to better myself seemed to p- them all off, so I knew if I was p- them off, I was doing right by me and that is all that mattered at the time. All my family hated the fact that I had managed to stay sober for as long as I had. They were all dead set against me putting the drink down, as they had lost their control over me, plus, given the chance, I was more than able to tell the truth now to the newspapers.

My mother and I phoned each other every Sunday afternoon and she was constantly trying to plant some kind of negative seeds. She told me to be very careful about what I said to anyone, because I could end up doing more time in prison. I gave this a lot of thought for quite a long time, as you would expect. I felt I had done more than enough time inside and a second more in prison, and for the life of me I couldn't think of anything that I might have done to end up back inside.

So just for peace of mind I thought the best thing to do would be to write to a police station in north London near to where I once lived. I thought if anything was still pending they would more than likely know about it, so after a few letters to them, I found out nothing was pending, but they did say that there was no central police computer so I contacted Scotland Yard and found out that nothing was pending there either.

So now I knew for certain that my mother was telling me lies. It made me hate her even more.

I think she might have thought that I wouldn't have the guts to write to Scotland Yard or to the north London police. I've never been one to run away from my responsibilities, and if there had been anything pending I would have handed myself in within days. I wouldn't have wanted to be looking over my shoulder every five minutes. I simply couldn't live like that.

About six months later, at one of my regular AA meetings, I was worried about something to do with my brother-in-law, who wanted me to sign something to do with his bank. With all my family had done to me in the past, I in no way trusted my him enough to sign anything for any of them, so I asked a guy in AA who I knew he would know about these kinds of things. I braced myself for having the p- taken out of me, which was something I had grown accustomed to due to how my family and their friends had all been treating me for as long as I could remember.

He was nice and explained everything in a proper manner. At first I couldn't believe my ears. but because of that conversation my trust started to grow with people in the AA. I have found without trust we have nothing, but, even to date (2020) I still have trust issues with most people. I'm constantly on my guard about what I say and do.

It took me about three years in the AA before I managed to put the drink down. In that time I was trying to cut down, but one night I could control it another night I couldn't...

I have said as much as I can say about AA. I'm not sure if I have said too much now, but we'll see. Sorry I cannot name names, but it isn't called anonymous for nothing. I'm truly grateful to all of them everywhere and of course to Dr Bob. I'm still a member and still attend meetings nearly thirty three years on.

In all this time I was also trying to find out what the newspapers had been saying about me from 1985 till 1993, as no one was very forthcoming and even now in 2020 they are not helpful in any way. They likely have something to hide.

The only place where I might just find out something or view backdated issues of this newspaper was in the newspaper library in Colindale, London, but, all I found was pages missing or empty spaces on pages and even full pages missing.

Someone else was complaining that things were missing from the same tabloid I was viewing, so I wasn't alone in my dilemma. It seems the newspaper in question can give it out, but not take it. Total cowards and hypocrites it would seem.

The tabloid I am referring seemed to have hidden behind my friends, family and anyone else I ever spoke to.

I still had the freephone number that one of the journalists had given me, and one night I made the silly mistake of phoning them while drunk and I offered them my story for £100, 000 not thinking that they would take me seriously. To my dismay, they turned up the next night, but once again I had no idea who they were. They didn't even tell me their names or where they were from. They assumed I knew them and got quite annoyed when I asked them who they were and what they wanted.

As time went by I was constantly confronting people who I thought might know about what the newspapers had been saying, but they denied any knowledge of it. Even a few weeks after seeing myself in the tabloid, my brother-in-law tried to tell me that I was being paranoid about it. He did his best to convince me, but all he achieved was to confirm my feelings about every member of my family and how I despised them all.

As time went on, it got to the point where I just had to give up on trying to find out anything out, because I was just chasing my tail all the time and it was not paying the bills and the fact that every time I thought about the tabloid it triggered thoughts of the rape, which I found very traumatic most of the time, so I had to throw myself into work or just deflect my thoughts in any way I could, just not to think about it.

So that is why I have no prior knowledge about what the tabloids have said, although I did hear on the radio a discussion about me. I was at work at the time and when I came back from making a brew, my brother-in-law had changed channels. It seemed at times they were doing everything not to let me find out anything.

On another occasion a DJ was slagging me off and more or less offering me out over the radio. It was quite a brave thing to do and I had not got a clue what he looked like. He worked for Rock FM, but not for long it would seem. A few weeks later he ended up getting sacked, so he did bring it on himself.

Around the time I was going to night classes. I wanted to get out of my flat and meet people, but not to be in a drinking situation to do it. The classes were mainly self-help and I also went to drama classes, which helped me to regain some self-confidence. As an actor I was wooden. At least I tried.

While in the drama class I was asked to put more emotion into what we were trying to perform. The teacher said to think of something bad that had happened in my past. I noticed that a woman in her sixties had the same problem, so I had a word with her and we agreed we didn't want to go back into our pasts for any reason. Like me, she had been abused as a child.

We had a bit of a chat and it got me thinking more about my past. I suppose I thought I had drowned it all with all my drinking the way I had, but now I had to deal with all of this soberly. This in effect gave me all kinds of nightmares. In fact, it still does , but the biggest problem was I had no one I could trust enough to talk through my problems.

In mid-1998, my emotions were on a roller coaster. Most days I would have all kinds of flashbacks, but I knew the only way to get myself through it all was to stay sober, even at times through gritted teeth, but as time went on, life got easier.

I constantly had my family pecking at my head most days with negativity, saying do not say this, do not say that.

They didn't want anything coming out about what they had been up to in the past and even in the present. One day I was begging for answers from my brother-in-law about the newspapers and I kept asking why everyone had done this to me. His answer was "because we could".

Well, I am writing this book because I can and I am not getting mad. I am getting even and there is no b- here, just pure truth and the good part of this is I have no need to lie in any way like you all did to me behind my back. This is the truth, hope you can handle it.

I'm not sure if this is true, but the newspaper in question had offered a reward to anyone who got my story, no matter how they got it. To me, that is like putting a target on someone's back. The problem is the people who read this tabloid have the reading age of between five and seven so anything could have happened, but thankfully nothing ever did.

In 1994, I got into the habit of going on the phone chatlines and I ended up meeting a lady from Prudhoe, near Newcastle. She was suffering from MS and was confined to a wheelchair. She was in her mid-twenties and had a son who lived mainly with his dad, because of her illness. Meeting her was a wake-up call for me. Until then I was always on the pity pot and constantly feeling sorry for myself, but I more or less fell for her within weeks of meeting her. The travelling took around four to five hours from leaving mine to getting to her's. But she was worth it.

On the downside, one of my sister's buddies rang me one Sunday afternoon, which she was never in the habit of doing. I suspect my mother or sister might have put her up to it. She was taking the p- out of me because my new girlfriend was in a wheelchair. I saw no difference; people cannot help who they fall in love with. When my sister's workmate said that I would go with anything, I replied, "At least I haven't shagged you, have I?" That totally shot her down and even my brother-in-law's brother tried the same put-down. I totally ignored him because I knew by then what their motives were, so I knew not to respond in any way.

I felt quite uneasy at times every Friday evening and sometimes in the week when travelling to see my girlfriend, especially when on foot. I felt very conscious of my dystonia(although I didn't know it was dystonia at the time) and of course the stares I got from people and even the out and out p-taking from some people made me feel quite vulnerable.

On one occasion when I was on the train from Carlisle to Prudhoe two young guys were taking the p- out of me and because my neck was going into spasm and making my head turn to the right, which was in their direction, it may have made it look like I was going to kick off with them. That was never my intention. When the conductor was checking tickets they said something to him and within minutes I was told to get off at Hexham, which was the next stop and was halfway roughly to my destination. When I was on the platform the two guys were pointing and laughing as the train was setting off. Some people are just vile and to be honest, the guard must have been as thick as pig muck. To be honest, I would wish dystonia on these kinds of people because they are more deserving of it than I am.

Then on another occasion in 1985, I was travelling on a Fishwick's green bus to Preston train station from my place, because I was stressed out. My head was shaking and going into spasm quite badly. (This still happens. I have no control over it and I still don't know what the triggers are).

I happened to notice that the driver kept watching me in his driver's mirror, which made me more nervous and made my symptoms worse, even though I was not up to anything.

When I finally got off at Preston, I looked back at the bus as I was crossing the road to the train station and noticed that the driver had got up out of the driver's seat and was checking where I had been sitting.

I think he thought I had been masturbating. Apparently some people do things like this. I think it is called risky masturbating, but I can assure everyone reading this, it was my dystonia and nothing else. Even though I am well known for masturbating, it was done in my living room in the privacy of my home and not in a public place. Of course, I was totally unaware I was being watched in late 1985. Being watched actually turns me off, no matter what I'm doing. I'm just not into that at all.

Even in a work situation I hate it when someone is stood over me watching me doing something. I always seem to get nervous and f- up in some way.

Since I fell ill with dystonia in mid-1989 I have come to realise just how close we all are to having bad health. With the remarks that people have made towards me around that time and since (I know my sister and her husband and his brother were making daily comments, about me being ill with dystonia). My brother-in-law's brother was blaming my dystonia on going with black women in the past. Of course I ignored him, mainly because if the doctors didn't know what had caused it or for that matter actually know what it was, how could he possibly know? Then there was the name calling from my sister's kids, as in, spastic and retard. Words like that and worse, when you're ill, cut deep like a knife, even small comments are still etched on my mind. But as I was a newly sober person and getting stronger day by the day, I never really took any notice of them on the whole. I realised it was all mind games by their parents and it was their way of trying to control me, but like cowards they hid behind their kids. My brother-in-law once said to me, "We don't trust people who don't drink, "so I replied, "Ain't life a bitch?" and walked away. Another time he commented about my dystonia. He turned round out of the blue and said, "It is all over now. They don't want to know any more (meaning the tabloids) so you can stop shaking your head." I looked at him in disbelief and said, "If only I could." He soon realised, what a stupid comment he had just made, but I know from experience that a lot of people make such comments, so I have learned to ignore them and class them as stupid people, which a lot are. Even so- called educated people can make stupid remarks at times.

It took me around eighteen months before I felt sure about going into a drinking situation, but, even to date I always have a way out. In 2013 I went on a free boat trip in Turkey. I didn't realise it was a booze cruise until it was too late, but I should have known. It was a total nightmare for me, the only escape would have been to swim back. In general, it is mainly advisable to have an escape route or plan, especially if you have just put the drink down like I had.

One day when I was travelling back from London to Preston on the train, I was minding my own business, when this middle-aged couple entered my coach. I was sat on my own. The seats across were reserved and out of politeness I told them so. Instead of thanking me like most genuine people would have done, the guy very nastily told me, "We didn't want to sit f-anywhere near you anyway." He said it loudly enough for quite a few other people to hear him, and they started to take the p- out of me.

Surprisingly, a woman turned round and told the whole coach load of people to shut up and leave me alone, which they all did. I couldn't spot the woman, who I would like to thank. It's good to know that there were decent, genuine people around at that time. I didn't deserve any of the abuse I was receiving. When some people see a weakness in others they zoom in on it. They are mainly cowards and bullies with low self-esteem making themselves feel bigger about themselves. By rights, they should be more pitied than scorned.

While at my doctor's I met a fairly well dressed woman patient who was quite attractive for her age (50), but had quite a vile attitude. I sussed this out quite quickly while we were in conversation waiting to see the same doctor. Weeks later I was doing some photocopying in a newsagent's in Bamber Bridge. I was about halfway through it when the same lady (not sure if lady is the right word to use) came in. She noticed me and said something to the shop manager who came over and more or less ordered me out of the shop. I asked him why but he couldn't give me a reason. He let me finish what I was doing and all the time the woman was watching. I think she was trying to attract my attention in her own way by causing me trouble, but it didn't work. It put me off her more than make me interested in her.

When I first put the alcohol down I had a lot of problems knowing how to do everyday basic things, such as how to be civil with people who are not civil with me. I knew I couldn't use my family as an example of normality, before and even during being an alcoholic. I just did my best to treat people as equals or as I would like to be treated. My favourite saying is, "I am a good friend to all, but I am also a bastard of an enemy." I'm still like that now, so, even though I was confused at first, most of the time I still wasn't far off the mark with how I should be with people.

When I was visiting my ex-girlfriend's sister in London, as a thank you for letting me stay at hers, we went for a drink one afternoon at the Manor House pub. We were just chatting and not bothering anyone else when my ex-girlfriend's sister noticed that one of her daughter's teachers was also having a drink so she went over for a chat. While she was away I went to the loo. On the way there, this obviously gay lad said hello to me. He was coming on to me a bit strong, but at the time I wasn't interested, so I blanked him. When I came back my ex-girlfriend's sister had returned to the table and within ten minutes of me sitting down, all the people in the pub started verbally abusing me. They kept shouting and going "uuuurrrrgggghhh" (which was the noise I had made when I first found out about the tabloids and I didn't want to be misquoted so instead of saying no comment, I made that noise). Shortly after one of the teachers called my ex-girlfriend's sister over and I heard the teacher say to her, 'Why are you with him?'

From what I know now it seems that quite a few people believe everything the tabloids say. Some treat it as the gospel truth, even so-called intelligent people like teachers and even some MPs it would seem, which to be honest is quite scary. It's no wonder the country is in the s-it's in when people are so stupid as to form an opinion on someone or something without even knowing the full story or while using an unreliable newspaper as a reference. The only thing I would rely on as being true in this tabloid is the date or page number, nothing more than that. The stupid thing is people think they know me because of this loo roll (newspaper), but the tabloid only wrote about me and never asked for a response.

Then, my brother-in-law's brother started up again with a different way of slagging me off. Once again it was about my girlfriend from Prudhoe. He kept saying 'well at least she cannot run away from you.' I came to the conclusion my family and all the hangers-on didn't want me to be happy in any shape or form and they certainly didn't want me bettering myself. Even when I got my first mobile, they all took the p- out of me, but by that time I knew their little game plan, so it didn't work, but it helped me suss them out, that by me p- them off I was doing right by myself, so from then on, that was my game plan. I made sure I p- them off as best I could, as much as I could.

Even my brother-in-law's cousin got the p- taken out of him when he got testicular cancer and had to have one of his testicles removed. Listening to them at times was like being back at infants' school. I realised age is just a number and they more than likely had not fully matured mentally. When I was a suffering alcoholic, I might have laughed at some of what they said, but that was when I was mentally ill with alcoholism.

I never took them on. I knew by then what their game was. My relationship with my girlfriend from Prudhoe lasted about two years and we only broke up because she fell very ill with her MS. It got so bad that she had to stay in hospital for a few months and I couldn't cope with seeing her ill. It broke my heart to finish with her, but I had to be selfish for my own good and look after myself. In no way did I want to pick up a drink again and to me that was what I was risking. That was the way I saw my alcoholism then and still do. The one thing that scares me more than anything is picking up a drink again. I might have another drink in me, but can I guarantee I have another recovery in me? In no way do I want to look down that road. I might as well commit suicide and I also have far too much to lose now as well. I wouldn't last very long as I suffer with chronic pancreatitis and I would be dead in less than six months if I went back drinking.

In 1997 my mother died suddenly of cancer. From going into Homerton Hospital to dying was a matter of a couple of weeks and I must admit even though I grieved for my whole family in 1993, I still cried like a baby when I found out she had died and I even cried at her bedside when she was dying and also at her funeral. I missed our phone calls on a Sunday afternoons for at least a few weeks. But what my sister in London did while my mother was dying was disgraceful. She ordered £400 of stuff on my mother's Littlewoods account, obviously to sell on for her drugs and drink and one of her male friends was phoning his mother in Jamaica every day on my mother's phone. How do I know this,?

I went to probate to sort out all my mother's affairs after her death and even my dad demanded the £25 that was in her bank account. I found out just how true the saying goes, (where there is a will, there are relatives) but my mother never left a will, hence me going to probate. I wish I'd never bothered. I got no thanks from anyone, all I got was stress that I didn't need, but it did make me realise just how affected I was when I was wearing my drinking goggles. Alcohol made my eyesight very blurred, as to how I never saw how dysfunctional my family was I will never know and to me witnessing what my sister did to our dying mother helped me realise just how low she would go to get money. What she and others did to me was nothing in comparison, but to do that to her dying mother and not bat an eyelid, made me realise that she would not have even broken into a sweat with what she did to me.

When I informed my dad about what my sister had been up to, he shrugged it off like it was nothing but recently (2015) I wanted to take my half sister from another dad to my uncle's funeral and I refused to take my other half sister from Chorley and my dad to the funeral. I felt at the time that they were treating me as some kind of taxi service. They turned round and wanted nothing more to do with me. It was no great loss. I was a lot happier without those vile users in my life.

I later found out my dad had no part in banishing me, it was all my northern sister's doing. She wanted my dad's money when he died, but I would prefer my dad being around than his money. I've never been a person where money is king. As long as I've enough to pay my bills and put food on the table, that is my only concern. As bad as I have been in my youth, I've never wanted to rip off my family. It's just not my thing.

At times, my southern sister was really bad with ripping off people. On one occasion when my mother was in Jamaica and I was watching her flat and looking after her dog while she was away, I was greeted one night after work by one of my sister's male friends, who wanted his gold rings, etc. back from me. I didn't have them. My sister had told him I had lent them. Why I would have done that I don't know. What really had happened was she had pawned all his gold. I'm not sure what he did about it. I know if it had been me I would have binned her big style.

I am fairly certain that my southern sister was the ringleader in systematically ripping me off and keeping the newspapers away from me. I doubt my dad knew anything about what jobs my mother and sister and their friends were doing, but from what I now know my sister in London was scamming my dad, who only had a pension to live on and he was fool enough to fall for her tricks and lies. That is what prostitutes do though, they have no depths to their dishonesty.

I honestly thought with everything my sister and I had been through as kids through my second stepdad, I would have been spared being ripped off by any of my family. My mindset is that blood is thicker than water although I'm grateful to my daughter's mother, simply because if it hadn't been for her greed, I would never have found out about the tabloids/family and I would have more than likely carried on drinking and more than likely ended up dead from alcoholism or alcohol-related accident or incident. I'm quite sure that was far from her intention at the time.

Some might say and more than likely have said, that my life is boring. Believe me, compared to when I was in the depths of alcoholism (hell), it is a long way off boring and it is far better than it ever was when I was a suffering alcoholic. The thing is alcohol is a legal drug, but, in a lot of ways it is much worse than heroin. I honestly don't miss it and wish I had never picked it up in the first place. You live and learn, as they say, even though it was a very painful lesson to learn. Being an alcoholic has in a lot of ways sorted me out and made me a better person, but I would say that.

So I am very grateful to my daughter's mother who by her greed pushed me to my rock bottom and believe it or not, I am even grateful to the fifteen guys who raped me and left me for dead and made me see just how vulnerable I had become and in turn made my rock bottom bad enough to do something about my alcoholism (although I cannot say I will be shaking any hands soon, I am grateful for where I am now and that is the main thing).

The night before my mother's funeral, I slept in the same room as three crates of lager. When I lived in London I sometimes stayed at my mother's at the weekends. Nothing alcoholic was ever safe when I was about, so to sleep in the same room as three crates of lager and not even be tempted that night before my mother's funeral, I knew then I had got the AA message and I had turned that corner.

My Dystonia

My dystonia started when I was in prison while serving a two-year sentence for an arson attack on a house that I had been renovating. I don't know for sure what was the cause, but I was constantly verbally abused and was attacked physically at least half a dozen times. It was no different from when I was on the outside, the only difference was it was more confined and I had no escape.

From what I know now all my family and friends were using me as much as they could as a meal ticket or as an ATM and watching me suffer as a result of their lies. They never did anything to help me in any way, because if I had been aware of what was happening behind my back, I would have acted accordingly and closed the ATM permanently. But that is easier said than done.

The 24/7 pain that dystonia causes me is unbearable. It gets so bad at times that I get very angry mainly through frustration and because of the constant pain and muscle spasms. Pain relief helps, but the ignorance and bigotry which I still endure even today and have endured since falling ill in 1989 with dystonia, makes it even more unbearable. Even now, it's a toss-up between the two which is worse.

At least with the pain I can take medication. Some days, the bigotry and ignorance I must admit does get to me when I am in a lot of pain and my head goes into tremor or spasm. It gets quite bad and more noticeable for people to see. I ignore the bigots as much as I can.

When I first started suffering from dystonia, I tended to shut myself away until night time. For some reason I felt less vulnerable at night, plus when I was p- (which at the time, was mostly every night) the alcohol was like a painkiller or a muscle relaxant. But when daytime arrived, the pain was still there and I also suffered from panic attacks so badly at times I thought I was going to collapse. Apparently, it is impossible to collapse because your blood pressure is high through your panic attack or so I have been told. Dystonia is a chronic illness and as yet there is no known cure for it as far as I am aware.

I have had to learn to cope and accept all my illnesses. I should be classed as disabled, but the way I see it, my illnesses have not only taken my quality of life away, they have even taken my dignity, if I let them that is. But I do honestly think that if my family, the press and my friends had been more honest and genuine with me from 1985 till 1993, I would not be suffering from dystonia and more than likely would never have suffered from panic attacks and wouldn't have been raped and left for dead. So yes, you could say there is a big resentment there and yes, I blame them all for my being ill, but that's my opinion. I will let you, the reader, decide who is to blame.

When I was working, one thing I noticed quite a lot of the time was that quite a few bosses or fellow work colleagues took one look at me with my dystonia and more than likely said to themselves, *what a useless waste of skin and air he is* because of my dystonia or so I have thought many times judging by some bosses and work colleagues' reactions when we first meet. So I have had to work that extra bit harder to prove my worth, which I did quite easily most of the time, but because of doing long hours on nights when I was working in a large dairy in Liverpool, it has now badly affected my health and because of my dystonia, I now have diabetes.

This came about because of a consultant who decided to put me on tablets which I should never have been on in the first place. When I fell ill in mid-2006 with chronic pancreatitis due to gall stones, I suspected it was due to a bad diet because of the long hours I was working. I was off work in total for nine and a half months. Most of the time I was virtually bedridden at home. At one point I was so ill I had to have five pints of blood and a lot of care from the nurses, doctors and consultants at my local hospital. I owe my life to them all.

A consultant from another local hospital came to see me while I was very ill with pancreatitis and decided to put me on olanzapine which is for people with mental health issues and is an antipsychotic medication. Apart from alcoholism I have never had any mental health issues (by the way, dystonia is not a mental illness, it is a neurological disorder) although I'm very sure some would disagree. The consultant still gave me a drug which had the side effects of pancreatitis. Surely, he never checked or perhaps didn't give a monkey's. Mind you, I didn't check either. Wrongfully, I took it for granted that the consultant knew what he was doing. I check now, but my trust in doctors and consultants has totally gone. Understandably so, I think.

I tried to sue the consultant who put me on those pills on a no win, no fee basis, with a law firm in Preston, but halfway through discovered that I had seen a psychiatrist on a couple of occasions. I wanted to come off the drink and the psychiatrist needed to check if I was suicidal before putting me on antabuse (at least the psychiatrist looked into the medication). The solicitors said they would carry on if I funded the rest of the case myself, but I think this was a loophole to get money out of me. Or, in layman's terms, bigotry and ignorance or just an out and out scam. No win, no fee, my bum.

Because of my illnesses, I had to stop working in early 2013, mainly because nearly every six weeks I was ending up on a drip in hospital for three weeks at a time. My pancreas is now in a chronic condition. I miss working, but I don't miss the three-week stays in hospital, being on nil by mouth, tubes up my nose and walking round attached to a drip. Of course that was when I felt fit and able enough to get out of bed. The last time was quite a horrendous experience. I felt well enough to be discharged, but they kept saying I was nowhere near well enough. The daytime staff were quite vile in the way they treated the patients. I reached the point where I would have walked home naked I was that desperate to get out. Thankfully, the night staff made up for their colleagues. It was just a shame they were not all the same. I have to admit I now dread getting ill and having to go back to that hospital, because I've been told by one of my diabetic nurses, that next time I go into hospital I might not get out.

So I do my best to keep fit and healthy and because I can't work that is why I decided to write this book. I used work as a deflection from the abuse I went through and to stop me thinking about what my family did to me with the tabloids, which in turn, triggered thoughts of how close to dying I was when I was raped and how depressed I got. They were interconnected. That's why it has taken so long to start opening up about it all.

Because of the Jimmy Savile saga, which I am not going to comment on, I decided I'd best get my side of the story done and dusted before I pop my clogs. I must admit it hasn't been easy writing this at times. In fact, its been a total nightmare. I've been constantly reliving every moment over and over again without my alcohol and drug cushion, which is how I got through it the first time around.

Once I managed to put alcohol down I set myself goals, but because of my dystonia, my chronic pancreatitis and my type 2 diabetes, I am now very limited in what I can do, so I volunteer with maybe a view to finding a suitable job that I can still do. The way I see it I might not be able to do physical jobs as I could before, but my brain still functions quite well.

I have done quite a bit of volunteering as a way of giving back what help I have received from different people in the past. I'm not one for sitting on my backside day in and day out watching telly and so far I have raised awareness by walking in the parade at Manchester Gay Pride and collecting money for the Samaritans and even answered the phones for around a year. Then, one day I had an active suicide and it affected me quite badly, so I had to give it up.

Because of all the abuse I have suffered as a child with my stepdads and some members of my family, the problems I have had due to tabloid journalists who did not have any common sense or decency, the eighteen years of abusing drink and all that involved and the suicide attempts, everything that has happened has affected my mental health in such a way that it does not take much to take me back to the dark days of my life.

I am very aware of my triggers as regards my mental health. One thing I have noticed and seems to be quite common, is the fact that when you need help of any kind the only person who can help you is yourself. I was the one who at the depths of my alcoholism was the one who did all the legwork to get sober. AA helped to keep me sane enough to stay sober and by me attending their meetings it gave me a suit of armour against the bad things that can, and often do, happen in life.

My path to sobriety has not been easy, nothing worthwhile ever is. From my drinking days to now, I am a totally different person. The northern part of my family I would class as sheep or just bystanders who didn't have the guts or decency to let me know anything and to me, watching another person suffer as I obviously was, and doing nothing, is as bad as abusing the person yourself.

I have no idea why but my brother-in-law really pushed me to my limits with his lies and s- stirring but I have gained more than I have lost. I am more than 23 years sober now. That to me is better than any big lottery win. If I had kept on drinking I would have most certainly died in my early forties.

While writing this, I am now 63, so I have lived longer, got a much better life and met the most genuine person ever (my wife). I have had to kiss a lot of toads to get to my princess (I say toads, because they are uglier than frogs and believe me there have been some really ugly ex-girlfriends along the way. Maybe from the outside they might have been quite good looking, but they had totally s- personalities and there were one or two mentally- ill ones).

Thankfully, I got there. If you stick at it that is what sobriety can give you. It's very hard at first, but very worthwhile. and I would like to thank my daughter's mother. Her greed helped to bring me to rock bottom. Then there's the tabloid who again helped me to see just how vile the people I had around me really were and lastly the 15 rapists who left me for dead. In all their own ways they showed me just how vulnerable I really was and what vile people I really had around me. It's like they say, *what doesn't kill you makes you stronger* and I'm a lot stronger and more resilient now than I have ever been in my whole life. My courage muscle has a six pack for sure.

It goes without saying that the money I maybe could have made if I had known from the start in 1985, I don't miss because I have never had it to miss. By rights, it was the tabloids who got scammed/ripped off, not me, but I have lost my health through all the lies that have been told. That, of course, is a big loss to me and of course my biggest regret. Without your health you really have nothing and this is where I have my biggest resentment.

Every time some bigot slags me off because of my dystonia, I mostly just ignore them. They know nothing about me or my illnesses or what I have been through to be as ill as I am now. I often think to myself, how I wish pain was something visible or just for an hour or two I could pass it on to the bigots and I'm quite sure their laughter would turn to tears in minutes. But I have to endure it 24/7 and smile as I put up with it. If I could pass it on, people just might understand more about my suffering. The thing is I have endured out and out abuse through people's lies.

I now realise it could have been far worse when I was gang raped, suffocated and left unconscious. As far as I'm aware the rapists did nothing to make sure I was still alive. I didn't wake up in the recovery position. I woke up in the same position they had raped me. Maybe if I had died that night, it would have been a godsend to all the people who had told lies about me.

I truly have no idea where the strength came from to get through all that I have been through and I am quite sure I have p- off quite a few people by getting through it. Sorry, but life doesn't work like that. People should keep in mind that what you give out you will eventually receive and I'll be sure to make karma come to their doorsteps.

My Daughter's Return Into My life

My daughter came back into my life for roughly five years. I set all kinds of goals for myself, one of them was to get in touch and meet her again. I was told all kinds of stories about her, one was that she had moved to America. These came from my daughter's mother's family and their friends so it was hardly reliable information.

As I was living in the north at the time occasionally I would visit my family in London, so I decided that the next time I went I would try and trace my daughter. For some reason my southern sister was dead against me doing it, as she thought I would bring the social services to her door. I had no idea why she thought that. She was smoking weed like a normal fag and drinking strong lagers from getting up to going to bed, so I think paranoia had well and truly set in.

I had been sober for a year roughly, so it was mid-1998 when I went to the local social services and asked about tracing my daughter. They sent me to Tower Bridge social services who in turn sent me to the Elephant and Castle social services.

I had already written a letter to pass on and at first, the social workers were very dubious as they thought I was connected to my daughter's mother. I assured them I wasn't and told them I just wanted them to pass the letter on. In my mind, I had done as much as I could. The ball was in my daughter's court from then on.

Then out of the blue roughly a year later, I had a phone call telling me she had received my letter. To be honest, I didn't take it too seriously, as people were still around me playing mind games, so I had to accept it could be a mind game of some kind and as upsetting as I found it, I had to forget about it as there was nothing I could do. It was totally out of my control. Then in 2009 I received a letter from my daughter with a photo of herself. She's a very pretty woman and to be honest I thought far too pretty to be my daughter. They do say two uglies make a bonny baby, so I put it down to that. I felt like I had won the lottery. I couldn't stop smiling. I was so happy, but a small part of me was waiting for the sting in the tail. It was something I had become accustomed to because of everything that I had gone through in the past.

It turned out my daughter had been fostered by a couple who both worked for the NHS in London and both had well-paid jobs. They had retired early and moved over to Dublin. I felt that my daughter had fallen on her feet with this couple and she ended up going to university and getting all kinds of degrees.

If she had been left with her blood mother or even me, her life would have been the opposite. I would have done everything I could, of course, to help her in every way, but I was skint most of the time and also a suffering alcoholic and I am quite sure her mum would have been hounding me every five minutes, so I reckon it was better for my daughter to have been fostered.

I decided the best way of going about things was to take a back seat. She knew I was there for her as much as I could be, but she needed to keep in mind her foster parents had brought her up and had done a really good job by all accounts. They and my daughter were born again Christians and at first my daughter tried to convert my girlfriend (now wife) and me, but, neither one of us was going to change. My thoughts were my daughter either accepts us as we are or not at all.

I thought my daughter had accepted this and for around five years we visited each other, we would go there for a few days a few times a year and my daughter came to see us and meet all my family. All seemed well.

Then strange things started to happen. My girlfriend and I were getting married and by a strange coincidence my daughter was getting married the day before us, so neither of us could go to the other's weddings. I didn't think anything of it at the time. I just thought that is life and I didn't dwell on it for too long.

Then six months later she gave birth to a son. I kept asking, whether we could see my grandchild. She kept coming up with different excuses so there was nothing I could do but live with it.

Then I found out that she had visited London a few months before getting married and although she denied meeting her birth mum, it seemed to me that all the signs were there that she had. I didn't resent my birth mum, after all, she had done me a big favour by making me aware of the tabloids and in turn, brought me to rock bottom and in reality saved my life in the process.

I did notice that when my daughter and I were chatting on Facebook, that it seemed that I was talking to someone completely different. She seemed more aggressive in the way she spoke to me, and didn't sound like the born again Christian she had been in the past. I put it down to the fact she had broken up with her husband roughly eighteen months after they were married because he had become too controlling and it had put a strain on her.

Then one night out of the blue my daughter started to accuse me of doing something to her half-sisters when I was going out with her mother in the early 1980s. She didn't say what I was meant to have done to them, but I know for certain even though I was a suffering alcoholic at the time and drinking like I was, I was not suffering blackouts and can or could remember everything I had done the night before.

So I knew for sure that nothing had been done by me to her sisters, but I know her mum's boyfriend had done things to my daughter. I was told this. I never actually witnessed it, but I know her mum had all her kids taken from her around that time and the sick thing is my daughter's mother still kept going out with her boyfriend, who, to me, was nothing more than a nonce.

I think the truth of it is that my daughter knew or knows that I am writing this book and she will have mentioned it to her birth mother. I'm quite sure my daughter's mother would not want anything coming out about her, but I've not said anything that isn't true. What I have said about her is not out of resentment. After all, she effectively saved my life.

As I don't know what allegations have been made by the tabloids against me, I'm having to second guess what may have been said to try and address it.

Even though I now realise my daughter was being used by her mother to get at me, I found that I had to draw a line under my daughter and our relationship and to be honest from when she first got in touch to having that conversation I have had serious doubts. But I ignored it and put it down to my paranoia which has served me well in the past, as in, when I found myself in a tabloid in 1993.

The fact that my daughter did this to me sent me into a deep depression and I contemplated suicide or even picking up another drink, which would have had the same result, because of my pancreatitis.

The thing that got me through it all was my love for

my wife. I knew if I ended my life it would have hurt her a lot and that was the very last thing I would ever want to do. I could just imagine my daughter's mother and her eldest daughter and God knows who else sat in their dirty flat in south London revelling in the fact she had kicked me in the nuts once again, hypothetically, of course. Some people are not happy unless they are f- with someone else's emotions and head.

It took a few weeks to get through the depression of it all and start to accept what had happened. On reflection, I have been through far worse than that, as in being raped and left for dead. No matter what life throws my way now, nothing will be as bad as that.

The sad thing is that as much as I loved my daughter and my son for that matter, they were/are connected to their vile/toxic mothers, who, for whatever reason, only wish me harm. It has backfired on my daughter's mother, as in 1993 she unwittingly helped me. So, positive can come from negative it seems.

So the fact I cannot change my past means I will never have my children in my life. I realise that alcoholism has cost me a lot; it took away my kids and at times my liberty, and very nearly my life on a few occasions. But there is a positive too, as, in by needing money to get the drink, I had to turn my hand to a lot of things, lawfully where possible. So now I am quite capable of doing most jobs and I have hardly ever sat on the pity pot for long. Why dwell on things you have no control over?

My favourite prayer/mantra and how I try to live by now is:

God grant me the serenity
To accept the things I cannot change
The courage to change the things I can
And the wisdom to know the difference
So help me God.